A. Baker Who Coached Football

Angels on my Shoulder

ARTHUR W. BAKER

AND

JACK B. EVETT

ISBN: 1985377764
ISBN-13: 978-1985377769

DEDICATION

For both authors:

To our wives, children, and grandchildren. They are duly noted in the last chapter (Chapter 15).

For Arthur W. Baker:

To Coach Harvey Kirkland of Newberry College, probably the most influential person in my life, besides my family. Not only did he teach me a lot of what I ever knew about coaching football, he also taught me how to be a Christian, how to live my life, and how to treat others.

CONTENTS

PREFACE

Did you notice the period after the word "A" in the title? Actually, the "A" is not a word; it is an initial. It is the first initial of Arthur W. Baker, who did, in fact, coach football. Perhaps a comma should follow the word "Baker." That would change the meaning and the reading of the title slightly. Take your choice.

I first met Coach Baker in 1959 when he came to Eau Claire High School in Columbia, South Carolina, as head football coach. I was entering my senior year at Eau Claire High. I was not a football player—at least not much of one. My dad felt every boy should play football, even if it meant just warming the bench. I had virtually no athletic ability, but to please dad I did a bunch of bench-warming. I did play in a few junior varsity games and one memorable varsity game. I don't remember how I got to suit up for a varsity game, but I did. I think it was at Camden High. I made runs, caught passes, and scored touchdowns. The announcer called my number all night. There was just one problem, however. Another player had "my number" on the back of his jersey. I never left the bench! But I hope dad was proud anyway. I decided not to try to play football during my senior year. I know dad was disappointed but, as always, he supported me in whatever I did.

Although I did not play football, I was fortunate to get to know Coach Baker, and somehow I wound up being his game videographer during my senior year. I attended all the games, climbed up on top of the press box with my (or rather Coach Baker's) movie camera, and filmed the games. It was high-tech stuff! I had a camera, a tripod, and some blank rolls of film. I had no experience doing this kind of thing, but Coach told me to just "follow the ball" with my camera. Every so often, the film would run out, and I would have to load a new roll of film. This required a time lapse while I removed the spent film and inserted a new one, during which time I missed filming a play or two. Coach never complained about my work, and as I think about it now, I don't remember him saying I did a great job. But

I really enjoyed doing it and felt I was helping the team far more than if I had tried to play.

Perhaps more importantly, I got to know Coach Baker at my church, College Place Methodist Church in Columbia. He and his wife, Edith, were youth counselors there. In this capacity they had a big influence on my spiritual growth at the time.

Both Coach and I left Columbia in 1965. After five years of undergraduate and graduate study at the University of South Carolina, I moved to Texas A&M University for additional graduate study. After two years and completion of my Ph.D. program, I moved to The University of North Carolina at Charlotte where I was a civil engineering professor for 32 years, retiring in 1999. Coach left Columbia in 1965 to become the freshman football coach at Clemson University. As is chronicled in this book, he coached football at six colleges/universities—Clemson, Texas Tech, Furman, The Citadel, East Carolina (twice), and Florida State—over the next 23 years. During these years, he and I more or less lost contact with each other. However, in 1988 our paths crossed again when he became associate director of athletics at my alma mater, the University of South Carolina. Having returned to Columbia, he rejoined College Place Methodist Church. Although I was living in Charlotte, North Carolina, I attended the church from time to time, as my parents and other relatives worshipped there.

Coach retired from USC in 1995. At some point thereafter, he began compiling extensive notes about his life and coaching career. During my career at UNC Charlotte, I had done a lot of writing, which included textbooks and as yet unpublished fiction and nonfiction. As we met from time to time over the next few years mostly at church, we talked about collaborating on his book but never got serious—until September 11, 2015. The occasion was my 55-year Eau Claire High School reunion held in Lexington, South Carolina. We talked at length about pursuing the venture.

On October 6, 2015 I visited him and his wife at their home in Blythewood, South Carolina. He somewhat overwhelmed me with 172 pages of handwritten notes (back and front of each page) he had compiled over the years. We spent three hours "talking," with him doing most of the talking, about his life. I did not write a single word on the yellow legal pad I had taken with me. I just turned on my tape recorder when we began and turned it off when we finished. For the next year or so, utilizing heavily the mail route and telephone lines between Blythewood (Columbia) and Harrisburg (Charlotte), we worked together to produce this book.

This has been a "labor of Love" for me personally. Coach Baker is one of the nicest men I have ever known, and he has had a big influence on my life. He is a Christian man and a true gentleman. And, he was a great coach. The opportunity to work with him on this project has been one of the highlights of my life. I hope you, the reader, will enjoy reading this book and getting to know him as I do.

Jack B. Evett
Harrisburg, NC
October 2016

P.S. Hereinafter, the pronoun "I" refers to Coach Baker.

ARTHUR W. BAKER and JACK B. EVETT

INTRODUCTION

I became a head football coach at the age of 17. My team went undefeated for the year. From this experience, I concluded three things: (1) I must be a pretty good coach, (2) however, coaching is not nearly important as having good players, and (3) coaching football was my life calling. The last of these certainly proved to be prophetic.

Following college and two years in the army, I was the head football coach at three high schools, assistant football coach at four universities, and head football coach at three colleges/universities. I ended my career as associate athletic director at a university. After formally retiring, I had the opportunity to remain in the football arena for ten more years as a consultant—five years with Coach Brad Scott and five years with Coach Lou Holtz. All in all, it was a great run.

This book chronicles my career and discusses as well my pre-career and post-career periods, i.e., childhood and retirement. I am grateful for the long and blessed life I have enjoyed, and I am happy to share it with you. I hope you enjoy it.

As we look back through our lives, we are reminded of those people and events that we feel were angels in our lives, who helped us in one way or another. As a rather poor and unsophisticated little boy, I needed, and thankfully got, many angels throughout my life who helped me become at least a gentleman and a good citizen and at most a good football coach. These angels appear throughout the book; it should be easy for you to recognize them. In the last chapter (15), I list them by name and discuss their help and influence.

Finally, I hope that in a few cases, when others "write their books," I might be included as an angel who helped and influenced them in their lives. After all, we are all in this life together.

Arthur W. Baker
Columbia, SC
October 2016

1 IN THE BEGINNING......

I was born on November 30, 1929. My parents were George Albertus Baker, Jr. and Sarah Holiday Baker. My paternal grandparents were George A. Baker and Marion Davis Baker. A month after my father was born, his mother (my grandmother, Marion Davis Baker) died as a result of childbirth. His father (my grandfather, George A. Baker) already had a number of children, so his parents, Arthur Wellington Baker and Martha Bradford Baker, decided to raise him. (I was named Arthur Wellington Baker after my great grandfather.) At that time my great grandfather and grandmother's three daughters (Bess, Ruth, and Kate) lived with them. They all welcomed him into the family and treated him royally. He played competitive football (his teammates called him "Rooster") and he enjoyed hunting and fishing.

My father's education was interrupted when he met a beautiful young lady, Sarah Adell Holiday. They fell madly in love and married on December 24, 1928. He was 17; she was 16. I was born in a small house near Sumter, South Carolina, on Highway 15 toward Bishopville on November 30, 1929. Nineteen months later, my brother, George Albertus Baker, III was born. My father, who was unskilled and untrained for any particular kind of work, began working for the State Highway Department. As this was during the "Great Depression," things were very tough economically; there was hardly enough food to go around.

Living with my Great Grandparents

Fortunately, for me at least, to relieve my parents of part of the burden of feeding a family, my great grandparents (Arthur Wellington Baker and Martha Bradford Baker, "Ma Ma") took me in to live with them most of the time together with Aunt Katie and husband Jim, and my cousin, Mary

1

Baker. Thus began a striking change in my life. We all lived together in a nice house on the Manning road. They ate huge meals and there was always an abundance of food. They had a cow (providing plenty of milk), raised hogs (providing their own liver pudding, hog-head cheese, cured and smoked hams, bacon, and sausage [I remember cleaning intestines to make sausage casings]), and raised chickens (providing, eggs, fryers for fried chicken, and hens for baked chicken). For nonmeat food, they grew strawberries, grapes, peaches, plums, pears, apples, sugar cane, corn, and field peas. In addition to plentiful meats and fruits/vegetables, Aunt Katie and Aunt Ruth baked breads, cakes, cookies, and pies of all kinds. And, Aunt Katie and Ma Ma were always canning fruits/vegetables and making jellies and preserves. Further, in addition to growing foods, Aunt Katie grew beautiful roses and camellias in several gardens.

I really loved the strawberry patch. I would sit on the ground awhile and pick and eat them immediately. Can't get fresher than that! I also liked the grape vines. The best grapes were usually found up high in the pecan tree where the vines had grown away from the arbor. I was usually the only one who could climb the tree to get these juicy morsels. Don't all boys like to climb trees?

With all the food available, meals were like feasts. Breakfast routinely featured fried eggs, grits, bacon, sausage, ham, gravy, oatmeal, biscuits (from scratch), home-churned butter, and home-made jellies, preserves and cane syrup. I learned from my grandfather how to mix oatmeal with milk or a mixture of milk and cream. Aunt Katie would have baked sweet potatoes and would slice them, fry the slices in butter, and sprinkle sugar on them. Granddaddy loved these slices in his oatmeal and milk. I too learned to love the mixture and even today I eat it every time I can.

Breakfasts were eaten on a dining table located in the large kitchen. Suppers, however, being the big meal of the day, were eaten in a nice, big dining room next to the kitchen. Like breakfast, they were feasts. Sunday dinners were special. Often present in addition to family were the preacher from Broad Street Methodist Church and Dr. Andrews, the family doctor. And, I was always glad to see my mother, father, and "Bubba," as we called my brother George.

During my lifetime, I have eaten food in many venues all over, prepared by great cooks and chefs, but Ma Ma and Aunt Katie could cook food better than any of them.

During this time, I learned two "skills"—making syrup and making butter. To make syrup, Granddaddy had a circular grinder with "arms" that stretched outward. A mule hitched to one of the arms would walk around in a circle, turning the grinder while my grandfather and a helper fed stalks of sugar cane into the grinder. The grinder ground the canes, and the juice from the canes ran down a spout and poured into a big vat or jug. The juice was put into a pot and cooked over a fire until it became syrup. After mixing in several other ingredients, the syrup was poured into Mason jars to store for future use. To make butter, milk was stored in pottery jugs and kept as cool as possible for a while. During this time the cream would rise to the top and could be used for many things in baking. The remaining milk was removed and churned into butter. The churn was a clay jug with a wooden top with a hole in it. The "churner" was a long stick that extended through the hole down into the milk. The stick had paddles at the bottom. The stick was manually moved up and down until the cream turned into a fairly solid mass. This mass was removed, the milk squeezed out, and the remainder pressed into a metal mold. The mold was usually quite artistic; hence, the resulting butter resembled a sculpture. The squeezed-out milk was retained, and as it began to sour it was turned into "buttermilk" (similar to present-day yogurt).

We also had some interesting kitchen equipment. Aunt Katie, Ma Ma, and the others cooked on a large, wood-burning stove. There was almost always a steaming kettle of water on the stove, and a water tank off to the side where water was heated for use in baths and such. My favorite part of the stove was the "warmers"—two compartments suspended above the stove two to three feet with doors on them. During the day, they always contained leftover breakfast meats, biscuits, and sweet potatoes. I could always get a snack there. And then there was the refrigerator (i.e., the "icebox"). It had a compartment for a block of ice, which kept the rest of the box cool. Uncle Jim usually brought a block of ice as needed from the "icehouse." Finally, there was the "safe." It was a rather ordinary cabinet, but it was unique in that it had a type of screen over it to protect the freshly baked bread and sweets inside from the omnipresent flies. I could always, with permission, get a cookie, which usually was plain "tea cake" with sugar sprinkled on top.

Other "interesting equipment" were the telephone and the outhouse. The telephone was a wooden box mounted on a wall with a small crank that had to be turned by hand to summon the operator, who placed the call. We had a "party line," meaning several neighbors shared the same line. When the phone rang, you had to recognize which ring was yours. Also, anyone could listen in on another party's conversation, so you had to be careful what you said! The outhouse was a small wooden structure with a seat inside containing two cut out, circular holes. When you had "to go," you sat over one of the holes in the seat and "conducted business." The result fell into (and accumulated in) a deep hole beneath the seat. From time to time, the accumulated contents in the hole would be cleaned out or at least lime would be added to kill the odor. In lieu of toilet paper, you used corn cobs, sheets from the Sears Roebuck Catalog, or newspapers. The outhouses were located 50 to 100 feet away from the house so the odor wouldn't be too bad at the house. They certainly were not heated, so using them during cold and/or stormy weather was problematical. We had "chamber pots" with lids that could be used at night and emptied the next morning. They were kept under the beds.

We did not have running water or "indoor plumbing." Water was obtained from a well—50 to 100 feet deep—with a hand-pump usually located on the back porch or sometimes in the kitchen. Often you had to prime the pump with a gallon or two of water. Later, we got electric pumps. During those early years, mama would fill a 50-gallon, round, tin tub with water, and she would gather us around the stove on Friday nights for our weekly baths, whether we needed them or not. Eventually, we got indoor plumbing, hot water, and a bathroom.

Sometimes, some of us—my mother, dad, grandmother, and/or granddaddy—would drive me and my brother George over to Columbia about 45 miles to the west. To get there, we had to cross the Wateree River. That sounds innocent enough, but in this area the "river" was actually a swamp some eight to ten miles wide. It contained tall pines, oaks, and cypresses plus heavy undergrowth. To get a road through there, they had to remove huge trees and haul in fill dirt. At that time, the road was essentially at ground level. During heavy rains, the river would rise, covering the entire swamp and the road with water. Driving across that swamp during such times was the scariest trip I ever made. The road was covered with as much as one foot of water and was marked only by flags or flambeaus placed along the edges of the road. [My dad worked for the Highway Department, and during rainy times, he would work 24 hours a day to help ensure that people could get through this area safely.] I felt sure we were going to go off the road into a cave or worse at any minute, but we always made it safely through the swamp. Nowadays, the roadway surface is high atop a huge fill area, so crossing the swamp is no problem now.

When we would go to Columbia, we would usually see Aunt Bess. She was the treasurer for the Railway Express Agency located at the railroad station in Columbia. She was a faithful worker there for over 50 years. She would take us to various points of interest around Columbia, such as the capitol building and the farmers' market. The latter was in the middle of Assembly Street, which was very wide. Vendors would park in marked spaces in the middle of the street to peddle their produce. It was nice seeing all the peddlers and getting fresh fruits and vegetables. Then she would take us to "Five Points" to a men's and boys' place and buy us a pair of "Buster Brown" shoes. Finally, we would go to Tapps Department Store downtown where we would get a tremendous treat—soup and breadsticks. [I wish they still had it.] Aunt Ruth worked upstairs; the restaurant was in the basement. These were always great trips (except for the rides through the flooded swamp).

Another memorable adventure during this time when I was four or five was when my aunts decided to take a trip to the Isle of Palms along the beach near Charleston. I had never seen the ocean in my life. To get there we had to go across the "Cooper River Bridge." It was, at that time, a very narrow, two-lane bridge with no "shoulders." Crossing it was frightening, even for experienced travelers. [Nowadays, the Cooper River Bridge is a beautiful, wide, multi-lane structure.] Aunt Bess had rented a small beach house, and the next morning we put on bathing suits and went to the beach. Aunt Katie took my hand and we headed for the water. I thought I was fixing to step off into a very deep ocean, so she had a hard time pulling me into the water before she proved to me it was shallow. After a day or two at Isle of Palms, Aunt Bess decided to take us to Murrells Inlet, which is up the coast from Charleston and past Georgetown. We went to a restaurant there called "Oliver's Lodge." The road into Murrells Inlet from Highway 17 (the "Coastal Highway") was a two-rut, sand road. The seafood was great. The roads around there are much better now!

One more swimming story: there was a swimming pool, called "Dingles Mill," a mile or so from my granddaddy's house toward Sumter. Uncle Jim (Aunt Katie's husband) decided one day to take me to Dingles Mill and teach me how to swim. There was a platform in the middle of the pond, and he pulled me out on an inner tube and we climbed onto the platform. He proceeded to tell me how to swim and then threw me in over my head. I learned to swim very quickly and somehow managed to get back to the platform.

As alluded to previously, the Bakers attended Broad Street Methodist Church in Sumter, South Carolina. My first memory of church was one Sunday I was standing on a pew with Aunt Katie when I yelled out to say hello to Preacher Smith to the amusement of all present! Aunt Katie also taught me every nursery rhyme as well as how to read, write, and count. When I started first grade at Brogden School near Sumter at age five, I did very well because Aunt Katie had already taught me everything. (I made all A's then, and never made any more until I was in college!) My teacher, Mrs. Peake Britton, taught three different grades in a one-room school. While I was at Brogden School, we were playing baseball one day using a pine limb for a bat. I stood too close to the batter and got hit just over my right eye brow. They took me to Dr. Winter in Sumter for stitches, and I proved I had good lungs as I yelled loudly while being stitched without Novocain.

Living with my Parents

When I finished the first grade, my mother and father decided I should come home to live with them and my brother, George ("Bubba").

This resulted in some adjustment in my lifestyle. It was still during or just after the Depression, and times were still economically tough. We lived near Liston Mathis' General Store and Tourist Court, and the highlight of our day was when mother would give us a few pennies to buy candy at the store. Baby Ruths, Butterfingers, and Hershey bars were a penny each. Pepsi Cola and RC Cola, our favorite drinks, were a nickel each. Every Saturday, mother would give each of us a quarter, and we would ride our bikes downtown to the Rex Theater to watch the Saturday feature. It was always a Western involving our heroes Hopalong Cassidy, Buck Rogers, Bob Steele, Gene Autry, Roy Rogers, Lash Larue, etc. The movie would begin around 10 a.m. and on Saturday they always had a continuous serial, almost always Buck Rogers flying space ships and fighting men from Mars and Jupiter. The movie cost nine cents; popcorn or a candy bar, five cents; and a coke or Pepsi, five cents. Mother always encouraged us to see the movie several times. I think mother and daddy appreciated some privacy.

After the movie we would ride by the boarding house next to the Toumey Hospital to watch the Singleton/Watts boys perform some unusual feats. For example, two of them could run and jump over the hood of an "A Model" Ford. They did these feats every Saturday, and people would come just to watch them! Afterwards, we would ride by other places of interest and get home around 4:00. [The Singleton/Watts boys lived on a dairy on the east side of Sumter but took their cows periodically to a place on the west side of Sumter where someone allowed them to graze. Later, they would move them back to the dairy on the east side. To move the cows from one side to the other, they drove them right down the main street of Sumter, creating a western-style cattle drive which always drew a crowd.]

Bubba and I went to Miller School. My second-grade teacher was Mrs. Brooks, and she was mean. As was common then, we had a long, horizontal water pipe with holes in it so that when the water was turned on, it would spurt up through the holes so everyone could get a drink. One day when we were getting a drink, someone—not me—blew in one of the holes spewing the water out so that some people got wet. (I had done that before, but not that particular time!) Mrs. Brooks came over and slapped me in the eye. When I got home, my eye was quite red and mother asked me what happened. I told her and the next day she took me to school and confronted the teacher. She told Mrs. Brooks if she ever did that again, she would give her a red eye. I was embarrassed, but deep down I was proud of my mom.

My brother Bubba was one tough little hombre. He had straight blond hair when he was young, and mama usually kept it cut as a "butch." He was fearless and would take almost any dare. We fought each other quite a bit. Being a year and a half older, I usually won, but he was always ready for another one. Almost every day he would get into a fight with somebody at school. It was common for me to get a message from one of my cousins Virginia or Evelyn to meet Bubba "at the flag pole" to fight some other guys. One time the opponents were the Rogers brothers; unfortunately, there were three of them and only two of us. Another time, we were fighting with some brothers after school, and our cousins were there to cheer us on.

Virginia yelled to me, "Hit him in the crown of the head, Arthur."

I didn't know where the "crown" was! On another occasion, Bubba sent word that we had another fight after school. We met the boys we were supposed to fight, and, again, there were three of them. They came after me and I climbed the flag pole and kicked them down when they tried to climb up and pull me down.

Erwin Brunson, one of dad's hunting companions and a neighbor and family friend, drove our school bus and almost always had a cigar in his mouth. One day when he was driving the school bus, he told Bubba to "sit down and get quiet." Bubba looked him in the eye and reached up and pushed the cigar in Erwin's mouth while he was driving the bus. Erwin whacked him a good one.

Another incident that occurred on a bus happened when Bubba, who was in the 4-H Club of America, was picked up by a bus taking him and other students from other schools to a week-long camp at Camp Long on the Santee River near Manning. Bubba got on the bus with his "matching luggage," two brown paper bags. He put the bags down at the front of the bus, put his hands on his hips, looked the whole bus in the eye, and said threateningly, "I am George Albertus Baker, III. Does anybody want to do anything about it?" All the kids on the bus were scared to death. One of those scared students was named "Edith." She went to Dalzell School and was also a member of the 4-H Club of America. We did not know each other at that time, but years later she and I married. What a way to meet your future brother-in-law!

As I mentioned previously, I made all A's in the first grade. When I got to second grade and beyond, my grades were only average. There were so many other wonderful things to do rather than study, and besides I didn't like to study. We had wonderful neighbors and friends and there were so many things to do—play ball, play war, go sling-shot hunting for sparrows or whatever else we could hit, shoot up bottles or cans, play on nearby railroad tracks and the trestle, or go swimming.

We always had animals—especially cats and dogs. Once we had a big, black cat; he was a real hunter. He would often bring in squirrels, rabbits, birds, and even snakes. Daddy was an excellent hunter and fisherman; he almost always brought home meat of some kind. He always had hunting dogs and was especially proud of one female who had a beautiful litter of ten puppies. Daddy hunted every Saturday with his hunting companions, usually coming in late with a big bag of game. He also often came in a bit inebriated. In those days there was no way of knowing when your hunting dog(s) got lost. In order to retrieve them, hunters had old cow horns. When they blew the horns, the dogs would usually return, the dogs being able to distinguish their master's horn from anybody else's. Daddy would take us out in the swamps the next day or so, and we'd have to listen for those dogs and help him gather up his dogs. Also, the dogs had identifying collars on, so during the week people would find the dogs and call my daddy to come get them.

Sometimes, after receiving his paycheck on Friday, dad would not show up until late at night with much of the rent and grocery money already spent, causing a lot of arguing. My mother was a beautiful woman, but she had a temper. During these times we children cringed as we listened to heated arguments. Sometime mama would take us to her mother's place. Grandmother Holiday was a great lady who never missed church at Grace Baptist Church and knew her Bible from cover to cover. Her husband died at age 38, leaving her with eight children. Grandmother lived four or five doors from Robert "Bobby" Richardson, who later became an all-star second baseman with the New York Yankees.

We lived in several different rental homes on North Main, all within a good city block. I suspect we were constantly moving, seeking lower rent or maybe we couldn't make the rent. Two neighborhood friends we grew up with were Russell Sutton, who later became an all-state football and baseball player at Furman University, and Harold Odom, whose dad ran a barber shop. One year Harold got a 410 shotgun for Christmas; he and his gun were the envy of all of us. One day he was going into the woods to hunt and wanted me and another neighbor, Richard Garrett, to go with him. My mother would not let me go, and I was disappointed and mad at her. Harold and Richard went anyway. While they were back there, they sat on a log to rest and leaned the cocked shotgun on the log. Somehow, the gun slid down and went off hitting Harold in the thigh. He had a hole in the front the size of a silver dollar and in the back the size of an orange. Despite being treated by doctors for over a year, he lost the leg up above the wound. I was glad I listened to my mother and stayed home, and I learned a good lesson that mothers know best.

We lived for a while in the "long house," which had a narrow hallway that ran the entire length of the house, with all the rooms off the hall. Bubba and I would skate down the hall. One day I stopped at one of the doors and had my fingers in the crack of the door when Bobby, my younger brother, decided to close the door with my fingers caught in it. Ouch! I'll never forget that moment. Another incident there happened one day when we were helping mama wash clothes on the back porch in a washing machine with a ringer. There was a thunderstorm in the area, the porch floor was wet, and lightning struck something nearby knocking us all down.

There were, of course, no televisions when I was growing up, so every night we enjoyed listening to the radio. Favorite shows were Amos and Andy, the Hit Parade, and Charlie McCarthy, the dummy partner of Edgar Bergen.

Around 1939, daddy was working for the Highway Department, and a small house became available next to the highway department offices and shed. Whoever lived in the house was responsible for watching the equipment over weekends. We moved into that house. There was a canal just behind the house; we played in it constantly. The highway shed was on East Calhoun Street on the "wrong side of the tracks." About a block away was the Ice House and Coal Center and across from there was a huge cotton warehouse. It had long platforms all along the outside walls, and we had a great time riding our bicycles along the platforms.

Every Sunday daddy was in charge of making sure all the heavy equipment was gassed up for work Monday morning. The Highway Department was using a big "sand pit" near Dalzell to get sand for building roads, etc. So we would get to ride to the sand pit, where Bubba and I had a great time running and jumping in the sand while daddy was fueling the equipment. Afterwards, daddy would take us to Dalzell to see Mr. Sam Moore's "Hitchhikers Cabin," a small hut next to the highway. It had a cot, with blankets and water, and I think he had some basic food there also. Men could spend one night there, and Mr. Moore fed them breakfast the next morning. We thought that was very interesting. Little did I know that Mr. Moore was the grandfather of my future wife, whom I had never met.

About this time I was entering junior high school and was beginning to notice girls. There were lots of parties, and sometimes I was invited to some of them. One night I was invited to a party and one of the dads was driving us all home. East Calhoun was a nice street with nice families living in nice homes; it was on the west side of the tracks. East of the tracks was a "bad section" for four or five blocks before you got to the highway shed. I was embarrassed for my friends to see where we lived so I asked to get out at a friend's house on the west side and walked home from there.

My mother's youngest sister Martha Ann was young, pretty, and single. On December 7, 1941, my mother had invited a couple of soldiers to come have dinner with us at the request of the Military Command at Shaw Field. [Shaw Field was a newly built Army, Air Force training base near Sumter.] Mama was hoping to help Martha find a boyfriend, so we had a great dinner. Bubba and I went up across the tracks to play with some friends. It was a warm day and people had their windows open. While we were playing, it seemed everybody turned their radios up as loud as they would go. "The Japanese had bombed Pearl Harbor" we heard! Bubba and I had no idea where Pearl Harbor was, so we started running home as fast as we could, all the while looking over our shoulders for Jap bombers! As we got home the Air Corps soldiers were rushing for Shaw Field.

One day our Aunt Bess decided it was time we had our own home, so she helped us build a new house off North Main on Hunter Avenue. Uncle Fred built a house near North Main and the railroad tracks, and we built one about 300 yards away in the middle of a pecan grove and next to a cotton field. We were proud of our new home, which we moved into in 1942. It had a living room, dining room, kitchen, hall, back screened porch, and two bedrooms. The three boys slept in one of the bedrooms.

Around the time I became a teenager, I became very conscious of the fact that we were poor. However, with a few exceptions, everybody else was poor too during this time. I was also becoming conscious of my social being, clothes, money, etc. I remember one day at school a fellow student whose daddy was a rich banker told me that my breath smelled bad. I was devastated, but probably should not have been as his breath probably smelled bad too. We all had pimples, but I always thought I had more than my share. I always looked forward to "care packages" from my cousin John Ogg Baker. He was a bit older than I was and always had really nice clothes—much better and finer than we could afford. I loved the "hand-me-downs."

I also began to work at various jobs. I delivered the "Sumter Daily Item," but it was hard getting everybody to pay up on Fridays so I could get my "cut." One of my first jobs was at the "B&H Drive In" near the corner of Main and Calhoun. Drive-in restaurants were very popular then. I was a "carhop." They were similar to today's Sonic Drive-Ins. I made good money there and spent most of it on clothes. I'd work two weeks to get enough money to buy a sweater!

World War II had a big effect on my family. My father was skilled in the operation of most pieces of heavy equipment. He was drafted and inducted into the Combat Engineers, and in a few months he was shipped to the Pacific theater of operation where he participated in three invasions. He was a part of the 37th Division, which was actually a part of the Ohio National Guard Unit. One of the few stories he shared of his service during this time began on a troop ship he was on that got torpedoed. They didn't sink, but they made it to one of the uninhabited Aleutian Islands. My daddy organized the effort to catch fish and monkeys to eat until being rescued some two weeks later. Each night back home, we anxiously kept up with the news of the 37th Division and feared we would receive a telegram telling us daddy had been killed or wounded. Thank God he received only minor injuries, although he did contact malaria and jungle rot, which he never got over.

The war years were tough too on the family left behind. Everything was rationed, and you had to have stamps to be able to buy anything. There was very little driving and lots of bicycle riding. Mama got an army check for less than $100 each month. She somehow kept up with home-operating costs, and we never went hungry. Everybody had a "victory garden" where we grew fruits and vegetables. We had chickens for eggs, and young fryers and hens to eat. One night mama woke me to say she thought someone was stealing our chickens. It was summer and the windows were up. We listened and did hear a noise. I took a pistol and fired through the screen in the direction of the noise. I don't know if I hit anybody, but we never lost any chickens again.

There were plenty of trees where we lived, and Bubba and I had to cut a lot of firewood during the war. One day I had to go into the woods and cut some "fat light wood." This can be cut from an old, dead pine tree and is great for starting fires. That day my friend Harold, who, as I mentioned previously, had his leg shot in a hunting accident and was on crutches, came along. We walked a half mile or so into the woods and began gathering light wood. I got a little winded and sat on a pine log we were cutting on. Harold decided he would take a swing at the log. Fat light wood is very hard and tough to cut. When Harold swung the axe, it bounced from the wood and thank goodness turned in his hand so that the flat side of the axe hit me in the head just above and outside my right eye. Blood was really pouring. Harold couldn't help me, so I had to walk home holding the cut together with my right hand. My brother Bobby was with us, and he ran ahead to our house and yelled to our mother that "Nookie" Odom had killed Arthur with the axe! You can imagine how frightened she was when I showed up at the door covered with blood. She got someone to drive us to Dr. Winter's office for stitches. He sewed me up, again without Novocain. I still have a small "chip" hole in my skull. I learned another lesson that day: never sit close to someone who is cutting wood!

I inherited my father's love of hunting. He often took me on deer drives before he went into the army. When I was 12, he took me deer hunting in the Wateree Swamp. He left me by a large acorn tree with his double-barrel shotgun, with stern instructions not to shoot a doe because the game warden was on the hunt and the fine for killing a doe was $25. It was a warm, fall day, and I fell asleep. Something woke me up, and I looked on the other side of the tree. About 35 yards away were three deer walking through a thicket. My heart was beating so loud and so fast that I'm sure they heard me. I had never seen a live, wild deer before, so I looked very hard for horns on the deer. I could swear I saw horns on one of the deer so I shot. "She" dropped dead in "her" tracks. As soon as I discovered I had shot a doe, I began to cry. I knew we didn't have $25. Thank goodness my dad and a friend were the first to arrive and found me crying. They thought it was funny and immediately butchered the deer. When we arrived back at the cabin, they told everyone it was a "peg-horned" deer. No one questioned the story. Then they bloodied my face with the deer's blood, making me nauseous and not caring if I never killed another deer.

On another deer-hunting trip, I learned another valuable lesson. I was left on a stand and heard two dogs running and barking, apparently chasing a deer. I had a single-barrel, 12-gauge shot gun, which you had to cock to shoot. I was behind a log and cocked the gun and was aiming at the noise with my finger on the trigger. To my amazement, one of the black men who were "drivers" came out of the thicket. I was so close to shooting him. I broke out into a sweat and began to shake all over. He never saw me and I never said a word. I learned that day that when hunting never shoot at anything unless you see for sure what it is. I have thanked God many times that I did not pull that trigger.

During the war I was fortunate to get a job at Shaw Field at the Officers' Club. I worked at the food and beverage bar; my job was to deliver food and beverage orders to young officers living in the B.O.Q. (Bachelor Officers' Quarters). These officers were there to learn to fly, and most went from Shaw to the war zone to fly against the Japanese or Germans. A lot of them were only four or five years older than I was. I became friends with a lot of them. One night one of the officers happened to see me downtown in Sumter. He had "picked up" two young ladies and invited me to come along. I was around 14 and she was 18, and I was "green as grass," but nevertheless I went with him. I guess this was my first "date" but I surely did not know what to do or say. We ended up going out to the Officers' Club, and I finally got to go home. I really ate well while I worked at the Officers' Club. They had plenty of bacon, sausage, and steaks; and I drank a milkshake every night. I got paid a salary and also got many generous tips.

Granddaddy and Ma Ma lived on the Manning road, and about a half mile behind their house was the Pocalla Swamp. Aunt Katie and those had a black lady, Vernell, who helped them at the house, and she lived right on the edge of the swamp. She told me there were lots of wild ducks in the swamp and there was a small boat there too. I had never been duck hunting before—had only read about it—but I decided to go hunting one day. I got up at 5:00 a.m. and rode my bicycle through town with my dad's 12-gauge, double-barrel across the handlebars. The distance was at least six miles. I got to the swamp around 6:00, found the little boat, and "poled" out into the main stream. [I later discovered you could practically wade across the swamp except for the main stream.] It was very foggy, and when I got to a curve in the stream I pushed up against a log. Out of everywhere came hundreds of mallard ducks; all it seemed were trying to land on top of me. I have hunted ducks the rest of my life but have never seen a prettier sight. I shot every shell I had and knocked down several ducks; but having no waders or retrievers, I was able to pick up only one beautiful mallard, green-head drake. I rode to granddaddy's to proudly display my trophy and to get a good breakfast. I then rode down Main Street in Sumter around 9:30 or 10:00 with my mallard hanging from the handlebars and my gun across the handlebars. Many times later, I took friends duck hunting in that swamp with great success.

In 1944 my father came home from the Pacific theater of war and was discharged because of malaria and jungle rot in his feet as well as because of the family he had. He went to work with Boyle Construction Company as a heavy equipment operator. Almost as soon as he got home, he and my mother began to argue. Sometimes, she would take Bobby and go to grandmother's house. My mother seemed more schizophrenic than before, but nobody wanted to notice.

And Then There Was Edith

During the summer following ninth grade, I played Legion baseball. One day in June we were rained out of practice, so we decided to go to a movie. All the players sat in two rows, and I sat down beside two girls who were already there. Harry Stokes was sitting on the other side of me, and he and the girls began to talk. [Harry is given credit around Sumter with having taught Bobby Richardson how to play the infield. Harry would hit Bobby ground balls until he fielded 100 consecutive ones without error. If he missed one, he had to start over toward another hundred!] Anyway, Harry knew these girls and introduced me to Edith and Alice Edens from Dalzell. Harry asked me to change seats with him, and I did. My life changed from that day forward. Later the next week, I went to a movie by myself and saw and sat by Edith. We then began to meet in the movies on a fairly regular basis—I was in love! We had our first date sometime later.

Edith's mom and dad used to come to town on certain days of the week, and I soon learned what days and what time and would wait on them. Mrs. Edens would shop, and Edith would usually go to a movie, and I would go with her. I knew where Mr. Edens parked in Sumter, and often I would ask him for a ride to Dalzell. They lived on "Pine Hill" on Black River Road, which at that time was a dirt road. There was no phone line that ran up the Black River Road, so we had a tough time communicating. Hence, the rides I could catch with Mr. Edens were important. Often, I would get there just in time for dinner; Mrs. Edens was a great cook. I really enjoyed the meals and they made me feel welcome. At the first meal I ate with them, Mr. Edens said "Let's pray." He said the prayer very fast and somewhat slurred. I know now that he was pulling a joke on me because long after the prayer was over and he was eating, I was still bowed, waiting for the prayer to end. Edith punched me to let me know. She and I would go up to the living room where her sister Helen had a great collection of records, mostly big-band music—Harry James, Glenn Miller, Nat King Cole, Frank Sinatra, etc. At other times we would sit on the unscreened front porch with Mr. and Mrs. Edens. Edith had a dog named "Skippy." She really loved that little black and white, long-haired dog. Mr. Edens had many prize bird dogs. I would usually stay until around 9:00, and Mrs. Edens and Edith would take me to the "corner" in Dalzell where I would "hitch" a ride home. Sometimes I would get a ride fairly quickly; other times it might take me several hours.

After meeting Edith, my whole outlook on life changed. I had never thought a lot about college, but after I met Edith, I at least began to think about it. I had used bad language, and suddenly I realized that would no longer be acceptable around Edith and her family.

In August of the first summer after meeting Edith, the Edens family rented a house at Ocean Drive Beach, and they invited me to come down for a few days. At the time I was playing American Legion baseball and was doing very well playing third base and center field. I was so excited to be invited and could not bear to think of Edith down there meeting other boys, so I did what any red-blooded American boy would do—I "cut" a game and two practices and went to the beach with the Edens. The first night I was there, Edith and her sister Alice had also invited girl friends of theirs. They had a record player in the living room, and that night a good many beach boys came over to dance. After an hour or so of this, Mr. Edens stuck his head in the door and said, "Al [i.e., Alice], Edith, it's time for bed." After the third time he warned with no results, he came back and in no uncertain terms in a very loud voice said, "You boys hit the road now, and I don't mean five minutes from now. I mean now!" The other boys hardly hit a step off the front porch as they sprinted out of the house. I didn't know what I should do so I began to run too. Edith and Al laughingly coaxed me back. This was my first time to visit Ocean Drive Beach and throughout my life I have loved this spot and almost felt like it was my second home. The wide, white strand stands out in beauty over all the other beaches I have ever visited.

When we got home from the beach, football soon began, but my main interest was going to Dalzell as often as I could. I'm sure now Mr. and Mrs. Edens "wore thin" with me coming out so often, but they were really nice to me. Not waiting for a ride from Mr. Edens now, I would usually hitchhike out to Dalzell, get out on Highway 521, and walk the two miles on the dirt road to Edith's home. I would sit with Edith and her parents on the front porch in the evening, or Edith and I would sit in the living room and listen to records. We managed to get in some hugging and kissing sometimes. The Edens were nice to invite me to supper. Then about 9:00 Mrs. Edens and Edith would take me to "the corner" to hitch a ride home. Sometimes it was almost midnight before I would get home.

One time I got a "smart" idea that I would ride my bicycle from my home to Edith's home. I did and started back about 8:00. It was a "pitch-black" dark night; there was no moon or stars. I was about half way home with no cars on the road and was riding down the middle of the road. All of a sudden, I rode right between six or eight teenagers. I was shocked, and apparently they were too. They saw me and yelled, "Get that 'cracker'!" I don't know if they were serious or not. All I know is that I broke all speed records on that bike to Sumter, and that was my one and only bicycle trip to Dalzell.

Sometimes, we would have Edith come to our house and eat with us. Daddy usually cooked or grilled barbecue chickens; he was very good at it. On one occasion Edith went with us on a fishing trip to the Wateree River swamp to a place called "Green Lake." The entire family went along; and as soon as we got a "mess" of fish, mama cooked them in a frying pan on the lake bank. They were good!

Edith went to Hillcrest High School in Dalzell while I went to Edmunds High School in Sumter. We obviously had friends of our own at our respective school. From time to time we would "date" other people. Edith was a beautiful girl, and there were not many students at Hillcrest; so, I felt I had to compete with all those boys who were trying to date her. A lot of times I would get out of school early and hitchhike to Hillcrest. I would just walk onto campus and wait until school was out; then I would find Edith and catch a ride to her house with her mother. I often wondered how the boys there felt about me coming out there and "intruding on their territory" like that. One of those boys was named Wallace Myers. He was one of the toughest guys I ever knew; he was a great football and baseball player. Many years later at a class reunion at Hillcrest, Wallace, who had cancer at the time, came up to me and said, "Art, you know one thing I'm disappointed about is that I didn't get to 'kick your butt'!" At that point, I guess I found out what those guys felt about my intrusion on their territory.

Once when I was at the beach during spring break, I met a girl, Adville Baskin, from Bishopville, who was dating a friend of mine, "Crow" Bradham. I was around them for several days, and I ended up dating Adville. She was sort of aggressive and had her own car, so she would come by my house after we came back from the beach. One day she came by and talked my brother Bobby into getting her a picture of me. I did not know she got the picture. Years later, she went to Columbia College, where Edith was already a student, and put my picture up in her room. Columbia

College was a small college, so of course Edith's friends told her about the picture. I was suddenly not welcome around the college. But thank goodness, I eventually worked my way back into Edith's good graces and we began to date again.

Another time during spring break I went to the beach before Edith got there, but her sister Alice was staying at the beach house with some of her Columbia College friends. They mixed some "P.J.", a mixture of grape juice and vodka, in an old dishpan and offered me some. I thought it would be "cool" so I drank some. That night I got very, very sick with a fever and a lot of vomiting. The next day they took me to Dr. Nixon, the only doctor at Ocean Drive Beach. He gave me a shot of penicillin in my rear end—I think with a dull needle. That experience was enough for me to know I didn't want to drink any more alcohol. I've really never drunk even a bottle of beer. I have tasted liquor and drunk a small glass of wine or champagne on special occasions. I think I saw what alcohol did to my father, and I didn't want that. Then too, I knew how much Edith did not want us to drink. It was one very good decision I made.

My Early Days in Sports

Other than my enduring love of football, I played a good bit of baseball, including YMCA baseball and Legion baseball. I played pitcher, third baseman, and centerfielder; and I was a pretty good player. I love to tell the story of how I struck out one opposing player three times in one game. That player was a future major league baseball hall of famer, Bobby Richardson. I have to confess, however, that I was 12 and he was eight at the time; this age difference may have given me an edge. [Bobby has said that I was the only one other than Sandy Koufax who ever struck him out three times in one game!] Aunt Katie kept some of my write-ups (we couldn't afford to take the paper), and I actually still have records of my batting and pitching records. I played little or no basketball. We could not afford a basketball and had no place to play basketball, nor a basket or backboard.

My first interest in football was in second or third grade when we played football during "recess." In the first game I played, there were perhaps 20 kids on each side. I took the opening kickoff and ran it all the way back through all 20 opposing players for a touchdown. I thought I must be a pretty good football player.

It was not until the ninth grade, however, that I went out for competitive football, as quarterback. Our coach was Dooley Mathews—a small man who coached in Sumter only one year, I believe. Being a ninth grader, I was a substitute. The only game I played in was the Orangeburg game, which happened to be our homecoming game. We were beating Orangeburg about 30-0 when the game was nearing the end, and Coach Mathews was trying to get everybody into the game. He asked if everybody had played, and somebody said Baker hadn't been in. I was hiding because I didn't know all the plays. He looked around and saw me and asked me what play did I know. I told him some pass play and he sent me in. Our captain, Theron Cook, said, "Baker, throw me a pass." I got the snap and threw a pass to Theron. I was told it was a beautiful pass, but I never saw it. One of the Orangeburg players hit me with his fist right in my mouth (we didn't have face masks then), knocking me out. The game was over and the two teams began fighting. Somehow I got to the dressing room and some players helped me get into the shower, not knowing where I was. After that, I was jokingly called "one play Baker" by my teammates. My mother and father saw me play that game; it was the first time they had seen me play.

In the tenth grade, I was not a starter but played in most of the games as a backup. In the Orangeburg game at the Orangeburg County Fair, Jack Chandler threw me a 40-yard touchdown pass that I made a really good catch on between two defenders. [Jack later played at The Citadel and became an outstanding doctor in Greenville; he also became a member of the Board at The Citadel and recommended me as the head coach there.]

During these days we had spring practices in high school, and during spring practice of my tenth-grade year I was moved to the starting tailback position. I had a great spring practice—so good that when our team elected co-captains, my friend Benny Skinner, who played guard, and I were elected co-captains for the 1947 year. I was really proud that my teammates had honored me in such a way. That spring we got a new coach at Edmunds High School, Coach Bill Clark, who later coached at Presbyterian College and then Orangeburg High School. His teams and his coaching became legendary. That next fall I was so excited about football. This was the year you could either graduate in the 11th grade or go another year and graduate in the 12th grade. This was also the year that many of the guys who had fought in World War II returned home. Frank Singleton and Harold Owens both had been in the Navy. Harold was about 6 ft 1 inch tall, weighed 195 lb, and was very fast; and he seemed to be older than other players. Very quickly he beat me out and even though I was a co-captain, I did not start and played very little in our opening game. We lost to Olympia and its star running back, Jeepers Jeffcoat, 6-0. It was embarrassing being a co-captain but not playing.

About this time, my father had a close hunting friend who became close with our family. He was a colonel in the Air Force—Col. Kline is all I remember. He asked if I knew that if I went into the Army by October 1, I would qualify for the G. I. Bill of Rights and have my college paid for.

Well, I was in love with Edith and knew how important it was to go to college and graduate. Yet I feared my lack of playing time and my lack of size hurt my chances to get a scholarship, and I knew my mother and father couldn't afford to send me. This looked like my only chance. Besides, I could not see going out for 11 games for the coin toss and then sitting on the bench and watching Harold Owens play tailback for Edmunds High School. I was only 16 at the time and you had to be 17 to join the Army, but Col. Kline thought they would be so eager for new recruits that they might not check the records closely. So, I told Edith and my parents, and I signed up!

I did not tell Coach Clark (or anyone else on the team) and continued to practice with the team. We played Camden there, and as usual I went out for the coin toss. We were leading at the half, but Harold hurt his ankle, so Coach Clark sent me in. I was so "fired up" that I scored two touchdowns and had several goods runs in the second half. We won the game. Afterwards, I told Coach Clark I had signed to go into the Army. He was astonished and said I couldn't do that. He had seen what I could do and told me I would play a lot from then on. However, I had done the deed, and the following Sunday I reported to Fort Jackson in Columbia, South Carolina. I was given uniforms and promptly put on a train for Fort Bliss in El Paso, Texas for basic training. That was probably the longest and most miserable eight weeks of my life. Although I did well in basic training, I was really "love sick." Edith and I would call once a week, but we both spent a lot of time crying. At the end of basic training, I found I could make $100 more if I was a paratrooper, so I signed up. When my mother found out about the paratroopers, she said, "No way would one of her sons jump out of a plane." She "blew the whistle" and told them I was only 16. They discharged me, honorably, and sent me home. I can't say I was sorry because I was going to see and be with Edith again.

When I got home, I went back to school for the second semester and worked in the afternoons for the State Highway Department. In the fall we had a new football coach, Larry "Koon" Weldon, a Sumter County native who had gone to Presbyterian College in Clinton, South Carolina where he played quarterback and pitched on the baseball team. I believe he still holds the record for P.C. pitchers with 21 strikeouts in a nine-inning game. After college he ended up with the Washington Redskins as Sammy Baugh's backup. That summer several of us players helped Coach Weldon build a barn on his farm. We started practice on September 1 as usual, and it looked as if I would be one of the starting halfbacks.

After two weeks of practice, Coach Weldon called me into his office to inform me that because I had been in school for two weeks prior to joining the army, they were counting that as an entire season. Thus, I was ineligible to play. I was crushed; there went any chance of earning a scholarship. But Coach Weldon came up with a proposal I couldn't turn down. Sumter had never had a "B" team before, but he said, "If you will coach the "B" team, I'll make sure you get some help to attend P.C. You will have to study and graduate." What else could I do? I took him up on the deal and became Sumter's first ever "B" team coach at the ripe old age of 17.

A lot of the players on my team were only a few years younger than I was. In fact, my brother, who was only one year younger than I was, was on the team; he often complained to mama and daddy that I did not give him enough playing time! I was really excited though and suddenly realized that this (i.e., coaching football) was what the Lord intended me to do. I also quickly realized that coaching is important but it's not nearly important as having good players. At least four of my players went on to play collegiate football, including one who later played for SMU.

We played some other "B" teams (Camden, Florence, and Columbia), some small county schools that were then class "C" teams (Hillcrest, Maywood, Timmonsville, Summerton, Lynchburg, Bishopville) and Asheville-Central. We won all ten of our games; in fact, none of the games were even close. Our last game was against Columbia's "B" team. Their coach was Pete Borders, who later became a friend when we moved to Eau Claire. When the Columbia team arrived, Coach Borders asked, "Where is the 'coach'?"

I said, "I am the coach."

He said, "No, I mean the real coach."

I said, "I'm the only coach we got."

We beat them 40-0. I guess I thought I was some kind of head coach! The Booster Club gave me a nice leather suitcase to use at college. One of the civic clubs gave me $100 to help on my tuition at college.

In January Coach Weldon sent Joe Kervin, E.M. Watt, Jack Chandler, Bill Baldwin, and Kirby Jackson to P.C. for "tryouts" and put me in the group. I was a relatively small person to expect to get a scholarship to play football, so before I left, Coach Weldon told me to tell (P.C.) Coach McMillan that I weighed 155 lb, and to eat several bananas and put some rocks in my pockets. In those days, when you went to try out for a scholarship at a school, they kept you several days and you actually practiced with the team. All the other players from Sumter did very well; I thought I did okay. But when we were preparing to leave, Coach McMillan offered all the players scholarships—except me. I was crushed. But Joe Kervin went back to see Coach "Mac" and told him they all wanted to come to P.C., but they wanted to go together with me and was there any way he could help us. He called me back in and said, "I can give you a bed in the basement of Springs Field House, your books (from a box of used books), and an opportunity to "walk on" to the football team. And, I can get you a job in the dining room washing dishes." I jumped on it before he could change his mind.

I went home and began studying hard so I could graduate from high school, which I did in June 1948 from Edmunds High School (now Sumter High School).

2 AT PRESBYTERIAN COLLEGE

In September 1948 my mother took me and Kirby Jackson to Presbyterian College (P.C.) in our '45 Olds. As soon as we arrived on campus, we were met by a welcoming committee of upper-class football players. They sent mama on her way and promptly put us through all sorts of initiations. For example, we had to push eggs with our noses on the plaza and we were swatted with brooms in the rear when we couldn't answer questions about P.C.

The First Year

I was given a bed in a room in the lowest, darkest area of Leroy Springs Gym. My roommates—Lou Surls, Bob Stutts, and Sam Baker— were men who had fought in World War II. We had two double bunks; a thin partition separated us from five freshman basketball players from Indiana. The latter were afraid of their own shadows, but they were especially afraid of my roommates who usually came in about 1:00 or 2:00 a.m. after heavy drinking. There was a light hanging from the ceiling that was about a foot above my head, and one of my roommates would always turn it on no matter how late they came in. He was probably the scruffiest man I ever knew. We were roommates for an entire semester, and he never changed or washed his sheets. Nor do I ever remember him washing his clothes.

One of my classmates (I'll call him "Joe") introduced me and the Indiana guys to a unique system of cheating by scroll. He would get a long roll of paper like you would have in a cash register to record sales and roll the paper from both ends toward the middle. He would then record information that would be covered on the exam on the paper roll, roll it up so it looked like two wheels at the end of a scroll, and put it in his pocket. When information was needed on an exam, he would roll through the scroll till he found what he needed. The rest of us were afraid to try this system. One day we all had a biology test under one of our favorite professors, Dr. Stump, who lectured while smoking a pipe. His classroom was like a theater with the rows of seats tiered upward and a walkway going up the middle of the room. There were probably 15 steps to the top row. Joe had carried his scroll with him and his assigned seat was up near the top on the center aisle. Mine was on the lower front row. Midway through the test, I heard a commotion behind me up in the top of the room. I looked just in time to see Joe's scroll rolling down the steps from top to bottom. One of the rubber bands had broken, and the scroll rolled all the way down, unwinding as it came. Joe looked at Dr. Stump, raised his hands in resignation, and followed his scroll down the steps and out of the room. The Indiana boys and I were amazed!

And then there was a classmate who was a war hero (I'll call him "Bob"). Everyone was scared to death of him. He was built like a Greek god—about 6 ft 3 inches tall, weighed 220 lb. A friend of mine decided to break into a professor's office and get a copy of the test he would give the next day. He and another guy went through a window over the door in the dark about 2:00 a.m. They felt their way over to the metal cabinet where they had been told the tests were filed. Just as they rounded a six-foot cabinet, a flashlight came on and there was Bob with a 32-caliber revolver pointed at them. He had the same idea and had gotten there before they did. Knowing that Bob had reportedly killed a number of Germans, my friends were scared to death, but did survive the incident.

One final cheating story: My friend and fellow football player (I'll call him "Al") was taking a Spanish exam, his first in his freshman year. Al "borrowed" a few answers from the student sitting to his left. Later when the professor, Dr. Glover, graded the papers, he accused Al of cheating. Al denied it emphatically. Dr. Glover asked how he happened to have the same answers as Mr. Callahan. Al replied, "We studied together." Dr. Glover answered by showing Al the two papers; they had different questions. Neither Al nor I had ever heard of two different tests at every other desk. He was in deep trouble.

I went to P.C. to play football. I did not lack confidence in my abilities, even though there was no reason for me to be a good college player or even any kind of a player. After all, I had not played football for two years. But my best friends, Kirby Jackson, Joe Kervin, and E.M. Watt—all from Sumter and all much better athletes than I—were always encouraging me; and I was crazy enough to believe I was as good as any of them. I was 5 ft 8 inches tall, weighed 155 lb and was by no means very fast; but I was quick, understood the game, and was mentally and physically tough.

Colleges had freshman football teams back then, and we played both on the varsity teams as subs and on the frosh team. I won the starting quarterback job on the frosh team and was so proud. I could throw the ball and run the ball fairly well; we ran the option, so the offense fitted me well. We played Clemson frosh (7-45), North Greenville Junior College (24-14), Wofford (14-21), Furman frosh (7-28), and Newberry frosh (21-7). I scored a touchdown on a 60-yard run against Newberry and threw a touchdown pass in the Clemson and North Greenville games.

One memorable game for me during my freshman year was when I got the opportunity to play in a varsity game against Clemson. Being a freshman, and a lowly one at that, I worked very hard during practice to make the travel squad and somehow I worked my way up onto the kickoff receiving team at safety. When we trotted out onto "Death Valley," I saw the biggest players I had ever seen on the other end of the field. One of them (No. 77) was so big that it looked to me like he had one foot on one hash mark and the other foot on the other hash mark. They wore purple pants and orange jerseys. We won the only thing we won all night before the game started, when we won the coin toss and chose to receive the kickoff. Senior Cally Gault was one safety or deep back, and I was the other one. The kickoff went between us and he, being a senior, would make the call as to who would catch the ball. Cally was a tough guy, but he had played at Clemson before. He yelled, "You get it!" Just before I caught it, I envisioned in my mind the next day's headline in the "Sumter Item"—"Local Boy Scores against Clemson on Opening Kickoff!" As I caught the ball and started toward the Clemson goal line, a Clemson player came toward me with his teeth gritted. I gave him a little jerk; he dived at me and missed. I thought to myself, "Hey man, there ain't nothing to this college football." At that time, I made the worst decision of my college football career. I cut to my right and in front of me was No. 77. We had a collision and I began seeing stars and hearing the National Anthem in my mind. I started stumbling off the field, and one of my teammates pushed me towards the sidelines. When I got there, I grabbed a teammate and said, "Hey man, help me I can't see out of one eye!"

He responded, "Turn your helmet around you fool; you're looking out of your ear hole!"

After the game, we returned to P.C. with plenty of lumps and bruises along with a nice check for the athletic department for playing the Tigers at their field. And, so much for my envisioned headline in the "Sumter Item." [One great thing about playing at Clemson, however, was that they had a great training table; we got the best steaks and big pitchers of milk.]

All in all, I felt I had had a pretty good freshman year, and so I had high hopes for my college football career. However, in the spring I discovered my new-found success was short lived. During spring drills I found myself as the third-string quarterback, which at some big schools might not be bad but third string at P.C. was no honor. So I "ate humble pie" and resolved to work as hard as I could.

My first year at P.C. was an "education" for me in more ways than one. I was not really ready for college classes yet, and I did not have enough money to pay my fees. Every week I was worrying where I would get the money for my next payment. It cost $650 per year to go to P.C. then. While that may seem like "pocket change" today, it was a monumental amount of money for us back then. My parents were separated, and I could not count on any help from them. My wonderful sister-in-law Helen and my rich uncle Ally each loaned me $100, and somehow I made it through my first year financially. However, I now had debt to pay off and needed money for the next year at P.C., so I headed off to the beach to earn money working in the "Soda Shop." Helen and another teacher, Brownie, owned the business, and I had worked there in previous summers, but I was now a partner with them in the Soda Shop.

Things were going well until one day in July when I got a penny post card in the mail from Coach Ben Moye at P.C. He informed me that even though I had passed the required 24 hours of coursework, I had only 23 quality points, which was one shy of what was needed to be eligible to play football the next year. He said I could either go to summer school at P.C. to get the additional quality points or I could "sit out" the fall semester, live in Columbia, and take a couple courses at the University of South Carolina (USC). I couldn't afford to leave my job and responsibilities at the beach, so I decided to live in Columbia and take two courses at USC in the fall.

The Second Year

Fortunately for me, my cousin Mary Hudson was living in Columbia with her family, and she offered me a bed for the fall semester. I got a job at the South Carolina Highway Department stamping license plates. I found out about the Brookland-Cayce All-Stars, a football team that played in a semi-pro league that included similar teams of former college and high school players. There were teams in Florence, Rock Hill, Gaffney, and Charleston in South Carolina, Augusta and Savannah in Georgia, Gastonia and Wilmington in North Carolina, as well as the nearby Olympia "Green Wave." I started practicing with the team and subsequently played on the team.

My schedule was very busy that semester. I would go to class in the mornings, then to work in the afternoon at the Highway Department in a building behind the state capitol, get a bite to eat at Mary's, and then go to football practice at night. Every Wednesday Mary had chili, beans, rice, and cornbread—man was it great! She and her husband Ben were so good to me. Also, during this time, Edith was attending Columbia College, but we had decided to date others <u>some</u>.

I had a great time on the football team. We ran the single wing and I played tailback. I was at least as good as their starting tailback, so we split playing time. Both of us also played safety on defense. We really had a good team, and in fact we were the best team in the league, finishing the season 10-0. The Olympia Green Wave was 9-1, having lost only to us. They proposed an 11th game for a chance for them to tie for the championship. Such a game would mean a little more money, so we accepted and played the game on December 22 at Olympia's field. I had had an outstanding season, scoring eight touchdowns and throwing four touchdown passes. In the game on the 22nd I had a real good game, scoring twice and completing four of six passes. We won 31-14. I really appreciated being able to play on this team and keep up my skills and conditioning during my time away from P.C.

During that last game on the 22nd Bill Simpson, the principal at Olympia High School, was the referee. He was an outstanding football official. Olympia had two huge linemen whom it was said the Green Wave got out of jail to play in this game. They were slugging somebody on our team almost every play. Finally, Bill Simpson threw a flag on them. They walked with him as he stepped off the 15-yard penalty. When he reached the 15 yards, they cursed him. He picked up the flag, threw it into the air, and marked off another 15 yards. They both walked along with him and as he turned around after the second penalty walk off, one of them hit him in the mouth. That started a huge fight; both benches and both stands emptied. To be honest, two or three former USC players and I just sat on the bench and watched the fracas. The game finally resumed and as I said we won.

Little did I know that two days later, on December 24th, Christmas Eve, the worst imaginable thing would ensue. As I usually did, I was working at the Sumter post office during the holidays. I had finished my route and left for home about 6:00 p.m. It was dark and I was walking home, hoping to catch a ride. Some of my friends stopped me as I passed Mitchell's Drug Store and simply said, "Arthur, you need to hurry home." I got there as soon as I could and found our house dark, so I went back up the street to my Uncle Fred's house where I heard the most shocking news I had ever heard or will ever hear. My mother had shot and killed my father during an argument at our home. I don't remember all the details immediately afterwards, as I am sure I was in shock. I ended up at my Aunt Blanche's mother's sister's house.

Sometime later Mr. and Mrs. Edens came by, and Mrs. Edens

suggested I might want to go and see my mother. I went to see her in the city jail. I still don't know what to say. She had been suffering for some years from schizophrenia, and I am sure she finally "snapped."

After a hearing Mama was transferred to the State Mental Hospital in Columbia where she went through many electric shock treatments. I visited her there as often as I could, but I always dreaded going because it was so dismal and I felt so bad for her. I just didn't know how to handle this situation. Edith always helped me during this time. Mama was released some ten years or more later and got a job at the PX at Fort Jackson. She eventually married a retired military man, Ed Holzer, and they lived in Hopkins, near McIntyre Air Force Base. He died around eight years later, and we moved her into a senior home in Sumter where she had her own little apartment. She died some years later. We all loved our mother; she was a wonderful lady and really looked out for us, especially when daddy was away during World War II. Everybody in our family knew for many years that she was mentally ill, but in those days nobody wanted to even talk about it, much less admit a family member to the State Mental Hospital and it finally took a court order to do so. If she had come along later in time, she probably would have gotten the necessary care and medicines to treat her illness better.

After my father's death and funeral, we were all in a great deal of confusion. My first impulse was that I needed to stay home and keep my brothers together. Fortunately, we had lots of relatives who supported us and helped as they could. But it was our Aunt Bess who took charge and told me I was going to return to P.C. for the spring semester and finish my education, George (Bubba) would live with her, and Bobby would be admitted to Epworth Children's Home in Columbia.

Bubba, living with Aunt Bess, went to Lower Richland High School in Hopkins near Columbia, where as usual he made many life-long friends. After less than a year Aunt Bess made a major decision that would change his life forever. She enrolled him in Warren Wilson Junior College in Swannanoa, North Carolina. He became a student leader there and graduated from high school and completed two years of junior college. Most importantly, he met his wife to be, Irene Case.

Bobby entered Epworth Children's Home where he had a completely miserable experience. It was so bad that I promised him we would let him come live with us after I completed college and the army.

I did return to P.C. for the spring semester and moved into Laurens Dormitory because it was the cheapest dorm to live in. My roommate was Cedric Jernigan, an offensive guard from Fayetteville, North Carolina; we became life-long friends. It was very hard for me to get adjusted at P.C. again because of all the turmoil. I did not get started well with my books but finally realized that I could never graduate at that rate and went to work on my studies. My major was history, and I really liked Dr. Newton Jones, my history professor.

Almost every Wednesday Pat Donavant, who dated Edith's roommate Tootsie Springs at Columbia College, and I would hitchhike to Columbia—a distance of around 60 miles. We were allowed to sit with Edith and Tootsie only in the parlor, but we usually managed to find a dark corner where we could do some kissing. Then again on Saturday, we would hitchhike back to Columbia to see "the girls." If we could scrape up enough money, we would go to a movie. If we spent the night, Pat and I would usually stay with either Aunt Katie or Aunt Ruth. Sometimes, I would eat meals with Edith at the college; oftentimes I was the only male in the dining room, but all the girls were very nice to me and made me feel welcome. As I think about it now, I don't know how I ever graduated from P.C. after missing all those days going to and from Columbia.

When I was a freshman, I pledged Phi Kappa Alpha Fraternity, and when I returned to P.C. I became active in fraternity life. I was fortunate to have chosen the No. 1 frat on campus. The student who pledged me was Harry Dent, a student leader from St. Matthews who later became a lawyer, a political leader for the Republican Party, and a close confidant of Senator Strom Thurmond. Subsequently, he worked for Presidents Nixon, Ford, Reagan, and Bush 41.

Spring football practice began in March, and I was full of confidence since I had had a very good season with the "All Stars" in Brookland-Cayce. I started out as quarterback but soon learned I was too short to be a drop-back passer. I could throw the ball well but often couldn't see over the linemen to find the receivers. I ended up spring drills with an average performance and a third-string position. I was disappointed and disheartened, but I decided to stick it out.

The spring semester went well for me academically. I was doing really well in history and began to read everything I could about the Revolutionary and Civil Wars. Once again, however, I ran into end-of-the-year financial problems and needed $100 to complete my tuition and board payments. I did not have any idea where I would get the money and was able to dodge the financial office for a week or two. I finally got up the courage to ask Edith's sister Helen if she could lend me the money, and thank goodness she did. I paid her back in full after working during the summer. I have always been thankful for her help.

During the rest of the spring semester, we played a lot of "half rubber," a game where you cut a solid rubber ball in half and used a broom stick to bat the "ball." We also played a lot of ping pong in a third-floor room with no air-conditioning. We would be soaking wet from sweating when we finished. On Wednesday nights, we all went to the Piker frat room to watch the "Pabst Blue Ribbon Wednesday Night Fights," where we saw Sugar Ray Robinson, Jake La Motta, Rocky Graziano, and others. Another fun thing was that we had a "Heinz 57" dog on campus named "Psyco"; his favorite pastime was chasing squirrels. To our delight, he occasionally caught some! Often, he would wander into any classroom of his choosing where he was always welcomed by the professor and students.

When the spring semester ended, Mr. Edens and I headed back to Ocean Drive Beach to clean up the Soda Shop for opening around June 1. Helen and Brownie got there when their teaching was over around June 1. They had a little house behind Mr. Edens' house. I stayed in a small room off the dining room; it had an outside entrance and a lavatory in it with a bathroom just outside.

Sundays were always our big days; we had our biggest paydays then. The old crowd that had been there all week were leaving, and the new crowd coming in for the new week were just arriving. But the biggest group we depended on for Sundays were the people who came for the day only. Most were South and North Carolina people, young and old—mostly tobacco and cotton farmers. Many of them came every Sunday and were often real characters. Sometimes they would let only one particular worker take their order. One man, who was probably in his 50s and never spoke above a whisper, would only let Brownie wait on him. Brownie took a lot of teasing about this. We gave the man a nickname and looked forward to his regular visits each Sunday. They were all great customers, and we would not have made it without them.

My favorite time at work during the summer was when Edith and her family came down for several weeks. That meant I got to spend a lot of time with her even though I still had to work my usual time shift. Sometimes she would work with me. Other times we would sun bathe, walk on the beach, and occasionally have "real dates." Another good thing was that we got home-cooked meals at the house with lots of vegetables. Mrs. Edens was a wonderful cook, so Helen, Brownie, and I made the most of those great meals. During those days I weighed about 155 to 158 lb and tried very hard to gain weight. Almost every night I would make and drink a thick milkshake hoping to gain weight.

We had a good summer at the beach. I met a lot of interesting people and made friends with a lot of people from all over South and North Carolina. Some of them I still see and many of them have done well. The Soda Shop did well financially and I made enough money to pay for my fall semester at P.C. I figured I would find a way somehow to pay for the spring semester.

College football practice began on September 1. Although Labor Day was a big day for the Soda Shop, I had to leave before the weekend to get back to P.C. by the first. There was another P.C. football player from Rock Hill who happened to be at the beach, so we decided to hitchhike to P.C.

together. We caught our first ride with a boy and three girls from North Carolina who were on a "binge" to Myrtle Beach. They had had quite a few beers and were "feeling no pain." We had not gotten out of Ocean Drive before we knew we were in for a wild ride. In about five miles they had to stop at a little "road house" to get a new supply of beer and to "shag" some. After we got back in our car on our way to Myrtle Beach, the three girls in the back (we were in the front seat) began to brag about the physical attributes of one of the girls back there. In fact, they all of a sudden pulled down the girl's top to show us. I knew I needed to be somewhere else! We got to Myrtle Beach and they decided they would get rooms at a motel, and they begged us to stay with them. I knew I had to be at P.C. the next afternoon; and not wanting to get in bad with the coaches by being late the first day, I decided to move on. The player from Rock Hill said I must be crazy! He stayed; I left.

The Third Year

That fall I worked hard, but there were two quarterbacks—Lefty Harper and Lefty Hamilton—who were better than I was. So I started the season as the third-string quarterback. I played some in the Clemson game but not much after that until we lost at The Citadel and at Furman. It was frustrating for me, and I have to admit I thought about quitting several times. The height of my humility occurred when we were playing Catawba and were behind 20-0 at the half. I just knew if Coach Mac would put me in I could turn things around for our team. Coach Mac made a great half-time talk challenging us all. I was ready and sitting in the back of the room when, after finishing his talk, he yelled, "Baker!"

I jumped up and almost ran up the aisle between the lockers, stepping on other veteran player's feet, thinking he had finally wised up and was going to start me at quarterback in the second half. I got right in front of him, put my helmet on, and said, "Yes sir coach—I'm ready!"

He said, "Ben Hay Hammett, our sports information director, is not here. You know the plays; I want you to record them for the second half."

He handed me a clipboard and a form to keep the plays on. I could have crawled into a hole! But, I did what I was asked. Not only did I not get to play much that year, I got hit in the mouth during practice and my front four upper teeth were broken off at the gum. I had to have them pulled out and later got a plate. It just was not a good year for me football-wise. However, I did start to study harder and learned to love my history major and professor.

As soon as football season was over, we went into intramural basketball. The Laurens dorm entered a team nicknamed the "Laurens

Eskimos." We also got a couple married guys from "Vetsville" to play on our team. We were pretty good. I got to where I was pretty good with the "two-handed, set shot" from outside, which was similar to today's three-point shot. I also played softball with the Pikers, and we usually won the President's Cup for most points in intramurals.

During this time I was a member of ROTC. I had had ROTC in high school and had been in the army for three months, so I knew the military pretty well and was made a sergeant. I liked the military, but the next year I did not stay in for the advanced ROTC program because I let my roommate talk me into sleeping in the mornings instead of "marching." Later I regretted this decision when I volunteered for the "draft" after graduation and went into the army as a private, while most of the guys who had been of lower rank in ROTC than I, went in as second lieutenants.

I went home for Christmas and again worked at the post office as a substitute carrier. I would work about a ten-hour day and for that time made good money. Edith worked at a department store, and we would eat lunch every day at a boarding house. When I was home for Christmas, I would spend nights with my Uncle Fred and Aunt Madge and my two favorite cousins Evelyn and Virginia who were several years younger than I. Madge was a super cook, and the girls and I had a wonderful time.

After the holidays and working at the post office were over, my good friend Hugh "Tiger" McLauren and I would usually go into the "swamp" for several days to hunt ducks, hogs, deer, squirrels, and so on. So on the Monday after Christmas, we were ready to go hunting. Unfortunately, I hadn't bought my hunting license or duck stamps. You had to get your duck stamps at the post office, but it didn't open until 9:00. Tiger was impatient, so we went out to a small lake just outside of town. Ice was on the lake but there were some ducks coming in and we shot several. We had to wade out into the icy water to retrieve them. While we were out there, a man stopped and shot several more ducks. We waded out to pick up his ducks for him. When we came in and gave him his ducks, he queried, "I guess you boys have your hunting licenses and duck stamps?"

Tiger did not have his either, but he looked the game warden straight in the eye and said, "Oh, yes sir."

Then the warden looked at me and asked me the same question. I couldn't tell him a lie; he used to hunt with my dad. I said, "No sir but I'm waiting for the post office to open."

He responded, "Boy, I ought to lock you up, but I'm going to give you one hour to get that stamp and license and show them to me. Now go!" I did and was sure glad he had known my dad.

During the summer I met a new friend from Charleston whose name was Drew Cade. Helen and Brownie had decided they would not lease the "Soda Shop" that summer, so I was looking for a summer job where I could make some good money and still not be too far from Edith. Drew's mother, Mrs. Smith, worked for the Corps of Engineers office in Charleston, and she convinced her boss, Mr. Blair, that he needed two strong, survey-crew members that summer. He hired Drew and me, and we were assigned to a survey crew that operated in South Carolina and did surveys on proposed construction sites at military bases. If the work was in Charleston, we earned $7.00 per hour as a temporary federal employee. If our work was out of town, we got salary plus $10.00 per diem. That was a pretty good salary then. Drew and I were assigned to a three-man crew; our crew chief was "Big Jake." He read the instrument, while Drew and I cleared right-of-way and put in "tack points" for runway construction at Shaw Field and Donaldson Air Base in Greenville, South Carolina. We also did several surveys at Fort Jackson in Columbia for proposed construction of barracks, and we worked for several weeks at the Charleston Air Base. It was very hard work, especially in the swamps around Shaw Field and the phosphate mines around Charleston. We battled the heat, snakes, alligators, and hornets in clearing right-of-way.

When we worked in Charleston, Drew and his family graciously allowed me to stay with them. They lived in an old Charleston house— long and narrow, two-story. They were very nice to me. Drew's mother and grandmother fixed us great meals and a sack lunch each day. When we worked in Sumter or Columbia, we stayed at my Aunt Katie's house. She was like my "second mother" and could cook better than anyone I've ever seen. She too would fix us a sack lunch. When we worked in Greenville, we had to stay in a boarding house.

For a two-week period during that summer, Drew and I had the most interesting job. We worked on a ship in Winyah Bay near Georgetown, South Carolina. We had bunks on the ship and a cook who fixed nice meals. The Corps of Engineers' mission there was to clear the channel of stumps to make the channel deeper. Our (Drew and I) job was to drag a metal beam along the bottom of the channel until we found a tree stump, at which time we would drop a buoy to mark the spot. Subsequently, the Corps would use their barge with its towering crane with a bucket on it to pull up the stump. When the bucket took hold and they began pulling up the stump, the barge would almost stand on end! We would often fish during our spare time. One day we hooked a 40-lb sea channel bass; it took us over an hour to land it. Sometimes we would go into Georgetown for a movie or some dancing.

The Fourth Year

When I returned to P.C. for the fall semester, I faced the same situation as I did the previous year—I was still the third-string quarterback.

We played Clemson in our first game, and as usual we all played some in that game. However, I could see the "handwriting on the wall" and realized I was not going to play very much again this year. I really loved playing football, though, and I enjoyed contact. I hustled so much that my teammates chided me for going too hard. Two young coaches had joined the coaching staff as assistant coaches right out of college. One was Sid Varney, who was a great guard at the University of North Carolina where he played with Charlie "Choo-Choo" Justice. He was tough and appreciated tough, hard-working players. The other was Norm Sloan, who had played football and basketball at North Carolina State University. He came to P.C. to coach football (assistant coach) and basketball (head coach). He too appreciated hard-working players.

Our third game was against Davidson. As we began our preparation for this game on Monday, both of our left halfbacks had minor injuries— neither could scrimmage—and we didn't have a third halfback. Coach MacMillan yelled for a third halfback. I was so tired of being a benchwarmer—even thinking of quitting—that I jumped into the huddle and yelled, "You've got one!"

He said, "You don't know the plays."

Having been a quarterback, I knew all the plays and I assured him that I did. I had been waiting so long for this chance that I had a great day at practice. I was "possessed," scoring several touchdowns and making some very good runs. Coach Mac was impressed, and Coaches Varney and Sloan had the tough, hungry player they were looking for, and they supported me. On the opening kickoff against Davidson, our first-string left halfback, E.M. Watt, hurt his ankle. The second-string left halfback was still hurt, so on the first series I was in the game as left halfback. Coach Mac could not stand for a back to fumble. Lefty Harper, our quarterback, called my play on a straight-ahead hand off. I gained four or five yards—but fumbled. Not about to lose my chance on a fumble, I recovered it. I went on to lead all rushers that day, and we won.

E.M. Watt nursed his sore ankle the rest of the season, and Curtis Freeman and I shared the job as starter. I had new life; I was playing, contributing, and getting better. I had my best game against Newberry College in our annual Thanksgiving game at Newberry. I once carried the ball six times in a row on the same play, moving the ball over 50 yards and setting up a touchdown. We won 27-0. I won my first letter and was a "happy camper."

After spring practice, I was a projected starter for the Blue Hose. Up until this time, I had had a small scholarship, covering books, room, and job in dining room. I went in and asked Coach Mac for more scholarship money. I told him Edith and I planned to be married in August. He said,

"You know, I usually don't give scholarships to married players."

I said, "Coach Mac, just because I'm getting married will not make one bit of difference as to my play. You know you will have a player who will be loyal to you, the team, and the school; and I think you know nobody will work harder or hustle more than I will."

He said, "Alright, I'll take a chance on you."

Years later when he was retired and living in Clinton, I wanted Edith and our four children to meet him. He had lost a leg to diabetes then, but he welcomed us graciously. He said to my wife and children, "Your daddy wasn't the best player I ever had, nor the fastest, but I can truthfully say he was one of the toughest players I ever had at P.C." I was very proud of what he said to them.

I worked again with the Corps of Engineers during the summer, but this time they assigned me to the "H-Bomb Plant" in Jackson, South Carolina. My first assignment was to keep a written log on a well-drilling rig. The building site near the Savannah River Nuclear Plant was underlain by limestone caverns. The rigs dug deep holes, which were filled with cement, as a part of the process to form a foundation for the buildings. I worked there all summer, receiving a salary plus per diem. I stayed in a boarding house in Aiken where we had good meals. Almost every weekend, Edith and I were making wedding plans, so it was a busy summer.

Toward the end of the summer, August 24th to be exact, Edith and I were married. She attended a small Methodist church in Dalzell. We didn't know it at the time, but her mother was sick—later to be found to have pancreatic cancer. She had asked Edith if she would agree to a small, high-noon wedding following the regular service at her church; if she did, Mr. and Mrs. Edens would give us our silver and china. Edith had a beautiful wedding gown she had worn earlier that spring when she was crowned the May Queen at Columbia College. Alice was her maid of honor, and my brother George was my best man. After the wedding family and friends were invited for lunch at Edith's home.

Something unfortunate happened that weekend. I always received my pay check from the government on Fridays. On this particular weekend, however, they changed the pay day to Mondays. Unable to get my check and cash it on Friday, I had only $50 or so in my pocket pending our departure on our honeymoon after the wedding and lunch. While I was dressing to leave, my brother-in-law, Van Newman, came into the room and asked casually if I needed some money. He said he had $20 in his pocket, which he loaned me. Then Mr. Edens came in and said, "Arthur, do you have enough money for your trip?" I told him my sad story and he loaned me $100. I don't know what we would have done if they hadn't loaned us the money. Fifty dollars would not have gone very far!

Mr. Edens had us park Edie's car, a Plymouth her parents had given her for a graduation present, in front of their house and told all those hooligans (my friends) not to mess with that car. We left and headed for Charlotte, North Carolina, where we were to spend the first night of our married life. About half way to Camden, a highway patrolman pulled us over and said someone had called in to say we were driving dangerously. [We later found out it was my friend Tiger McLauren who made the call.] The patrolman soon realized what was going on and wished us well and sent us on our way.

We spent our first night in what then was a nice motel in Charlotte, but today it is in a "bad area." We suddenly realized we were married, and we believe we must have been the least knowledgeable young married couple that ever started out. The next morning we had pancakes for breakfast and headed for Boone, North Carolina. Riding in the hills/mountains and the shock that she was actually married proved too much for Edith, and she became nauseated. We stopped and spent the night outside Boone. As we were checking out the next morning, we were shocked to see Mr. and Mrs. Edens pull up—they recognized our car. I was really glad to see them, as I had never had a sick wife before! I said, "Mrs. Edens, Edith is sick."

She looked at me and said, "Edith knows how to take care of herself."

I hushed up. Later we went to see the outdoor pageant "Horn in the West" with Mr. and Mrs. Edens.

Edith got to feeling better and we headed back towards home. We stopped in Linville Caverns at a real-elegant-looking lodge. We went in to eat lunch, and man was it expensive! We were too embarrassed to say we couldn't afford these meals. I noticed they did not have oysters on the menu, so I asked for oysters. When they said they didn't have any, we said we would go somewhere else to find oysters. I guess that set a precedent for us for years ahead. We still will not pay too much for a meal. In fact, we usually get one meal and split it. We spent the last night of our honeymoon in Marion, North Carolina, and then drove back to Dalzell.

The Fifth Year

Football practice at P.C. began the following Monday. Mr. Edens and my aunts, Katie and Bess, helped us furnish our apartment, and he used one of his farm trucks to move our furniture up there before the wedding. Hence, when I reported for practice, we were already moved into our little army hut, #12 Vetsville, to begin a new and exciting life. I don't know how we expected to live. I had no job; and although Edith was a certified teacher, there were no teaching jobs available. She did manage to get a job as a receptionist at an architect's office. She was making $20 per week and that was our total income. She had to help keep the architect's little girl, act as receptionist, and be a secretary, and she was in the office all day with his young nephew. This was all new ground for Edith. I got three meals from the dining room and usually brought them home so Edith and I could share them.

We got along okay for several weeks when Edith got a chance to teach second grade at Hickory Tavern, some 25 miles away. They got more students than they had expected and needed one more teacher. A lady teacher down the street knew Edith was looking for a teaching job and told the principal about her. She got the job, and several women carpooled every day. But man, going from $80 a month to $150 was big time. Edith had it pretty rough. She had to get up early to catch the carpool; then she had to build a fire in the stove in her classroom. After teaching all day, she got home mid to late afternoon.

As soon as we had gotten there, I started two-a-day practices. My work during the summer at the Savannah River Plant had involved primarily sitting near a pump. That along with the time required for the wedding and honeymoon had given me little time for physical conditioning; hence, I was not in the best of condition when practices started. However, I was in about the same condition as everybody else, and practice was really not that bad on me.

I had rotated at left halfback the previous year, but I was starting halfback when we began this season. We had a pretty tough schedule, and I was holding my own doing okay but not seeming to do as well as I wanted. We played a game at Troy University in Alabama. I was sick with a fever and couldn't work out on Friday. I wanted to play really bad, though the doctor advised me not to. I did play, however, and ran well; the coaches jokingly said I should get sick before every game. About mid-season, I hurt my knee and missed playing several games. When I returned to practice, a freshman was playing more than I. The Catawba game was homecoming, and guess who was homecoming queen—Edith! She was a beautiful queen and made me so proud. I missed scoring a touchdown in that game by less than a yard.

I played pretty well in the Appalachian State game and at our final game in Newberry. I was given a chance to run the ball on three consecutive plays.

When the season ended, I was very disappointed with my football season. But as we all know, things don't always work out the way we planned it. A year later while playing regimental football in the army, I performed much better than my last year at P.C. I was more confident and more poised, and enjoyed much more success. My senior year at P.C. was a big disappointment to me; though I started more than half the games, I just didn't play with the fire I felt in the past.

The second semester (January to June) when football was over, I really had little to do except intramurals and sleep; so afternoons when Edith got home after teaching all day and found me in the bed, it did not always sit well with her! She sometimes cooked supper, but usually I went over to the cafeteria, got my tray of food, and brought it home to share with her.

Edith and I started going to church, attending the Presbyterian Church during the fall; but since we were both raised in the Methodist faith, we began to attend Clinton Methodist Church on a regular basis. During the second semester, I again played intramural softball for the Pikers and did well. And Cedric Jernigan, my former roommate, and I began to play tennis every time we could. Tennis Coach Leighton liked us—we helped him with the courts—and he let us play in two P.C. matches and we even competed in the state championship.

Because I was in my ninth semester, I had more than enough hours to graduate, but there was one big obstacle. Trigonometry was a required course for graduation, and I was failing this course in my last semester. I never really had a good math teacher and I never learned any math. Enter serendipity. It just so happened that my trig professor, Dr. Sheridan, also moonlighted by doing surveying on a commercial basis, and I found out he needed a rodman. And I needed a "C" in trig. As noted previously, I had worked as a rodman on a survey crew, and I knew a good bit about surveying, topography, etc. So I maneuvered myself to work for him in the afternoons when he was surveying, doing anything and everything he wanted. We never mentioned salary, and I never received any pay. But when grades came out, I had a big "C" in trig and was thereby cleared to graduate in June.

Graduation from college was a wonderful miracle in my life. I never dreamed I could or would go to college, much less graduate, until I met Edith and began to realize the need to be able to support a family. There were many people who gave me encouragement and helped me financially along the way. My parents were not able to help me financially, but they were happy that I would try. Aunt Bess and Aunt Katie were most encouraging, and Aunt Bess helped with money as much as she could. Mr. Hugh McLauren got his civic club to give me $100. Uncle Ally and my sister-in-law Helen each loaned me $100 when I really needed it desperately. But Mr. Edens was my greatest encourager and provided money, especially the last several years. He would lend me money when I needed it, and I would work and pay him back during the summer. I know that God's plan for my life was to finish college, and that motivated me all along the way. And of course, Edith was with me all the way and was my constant encourager. Graduation day itself in June 1953 was a wonderful event. Aunt Bess, Aunt Katie, Aunt Ruth, and Mr. and Mrs. Edens were all there.

3 AT FORT JACKSON

I had been deferred from the draft until I finished college. Now I had finished. Rather than just wait to be drafted, I volunteered right away so I could get out in two years at the right time hopefully to begin a coaching job. I reported to the Army at Fort Jackson in the latter part of June and went through the Induction Center. I began basic training in the 13th Regiment Company "C" during the first week in July, and for eight weeks I went through basic training for the second time in my life. I was appointed "Guide on" for the platoon.

While having my medical examination, they found that I needed to have all my upper teeth pulled. I had had four front teeth knocked out in practice one day; and in my last game in college I had two jaw teeth knocked loose, and they became abscessed. The army dentist gave me a choice: I could go into the hospital and have them pulled all at once and then have to begin basic training all over again, or I could go every week to have a few pulled each time. Not wanting to begin basic training for a third time, I chose to have them pulled by the week! They would pull several and then cut open the jaw, scrape the jawbone, and stitch the gums, and then I would head back to basic training for another week while I had to eat "soft" foods. When my gums got back to normal, they took moldings from which false teeth were made. They made me a great upper plate (I still have the originals although I don't wear them now) and a partial plate for the lower jaw. They really did a great job, and I made it through basic training again.

During basic training we did not have the first few weekends off, so Edith came over to the fort on Sundays. We had one weekend where she could come on the base, and we stayed in the Guest House. She applied for and got a second-grade teaching job at Jackson Heights Elementary School, which was on the post at Fort Jackson. We found and rented a one-room apartment near the fort.

After finishing basic training, I was given some choices as to my next assignment. One, I could stay with "C" Company as the "clerk," which I turned down, having seen all I wanted to of basic training from a company standpoint. Two, because I had played football in college, I had a chance to play for the Post team, made up of college players from all over the nation. The third choice was to be a member of the Physical Fitness Committee. I wanted to be on the Committee and accepted the invitation. The first thing I had to do was attend a Physical Fitness Instructors' Course for six weeks at Fort Bragg in North Carolina. We wore either shorts, tee shirts, tennis shoes, and caps or sweats, and we learned how to teach every exercise the army way and to teach every phase of physical fitness.

When I returned to Fort Jackson to work on the Physical Fitness Committee, it was about time for football practice to begin. There were eight of us on the Committee, which included men who had played college football at Florida State, USC, Oklahoma, California, P.C., and The Citadel. It soon became evident that not all of us could play football; some of us had to teach physical fitness classes. The lieutenant in charge of the Committee asked me if I would be willing to give up football. If I did, he said he would recommend me for every promotion I could get as soon as rank could be made. [I was a private and in 13 months I was a sergeant.] I have always worked hard at any job I had, and I have always taken a lot of pride in my work, whatever it was. I took my job seriously. I once figured that in my almost two years in the Army, our Physical Fitness Committee trained some 15,000 to 20,000 trainees. I know I was in the best physical condition of my life then; on one medical test, I had 0% body fat.

We gave the training from a platform and had to not only identify the exercise we were about to perform but also to count the repetitions out loud and be sure every man did the exercises according to army regulations. The companies had to take and complete 12 exercise periods, all one-hour long. Each exercise was more difficult than the last time they took it. They also had five periods of bayonet training, three periods of disarmament, and two periods on the "confidence course." The disarmament involved taking on a man with a knife and disarming him. The confidence course was a group of 15 obstacles trainees had to complete, including climbing to the top of a 150-ft tower and then down, coming down a rope 50 ft high hand over hand, climbing and jumping over a nine-ft wall, and hand over hand and using feet to go over a 40-ft rope above water.

Before we let the companies of basic trainees go through the course, we would demonstrate how each obstacle had to be completed. One of the guys on our Committee, Bill Rotezhiem, was a gymnast; he had been on the Florida State University gymnastic team and on the Pan-American Games team. He was very good. Bill always demonstrated the 150-ft tower climb; he would climb to the highest bar and then do a one-handed hand stand, which was very impressive. But you can be sure we ordered the trainees not to try Bill's feat.

We got many trainees the first week of training who were quite overweight—many from "up north" who did not get outside as much. By the end of the eight-week basic training period, many of these trainees' pants sizes (i.e., waist sizes) had decreased by 10 to 15 inches; their pants would double over. Physical training was a good and necessary conditioner, but it was another way of emphasizing discipline. If one man did not complete an exercise properly, the entire company had to do it over.

In addition to PT instructor, we were asked to be "chaperons" for the Fort Jackson Teenage Club, which was located on Forest Drive exactly where Shannon Baptist Church is presently located. Our duty was to supervise the activities for the Post teenagers. The club had pool tables, ping-pong tables, a game room, a serving room, etc. We also had access to an army bus and took the teenagers on field trips. Our pay for this was free housing attached to the Teenage Club. The Club was very popular, and we had a great time with the young people. We met Sgt. Frye, the USC groundskeeper, and his children there. Even today, we still see some of our "teenagers" or their children around Columbia.

One funny thing happened to us there. Like every other part of Fort Jackson, when the Army ordered a 3rd Army Inspection, the Teenage Club was included. We had been told when the "big General" would be by to inspect our club, and as luck would have it I had to give a PT class just before the inspection. It was in July and hot, and I had to change into my khaki dress uniform. I rushed home after class and put my best khakis on, still sweating profusely even though I had just stepped out of the shower. Edith "operates on her own clock," and she was not ready with a three-star general waiting on us. We finally rushed out and went and met the general. I saluted and said very nervously what I was supposed to. As most people are, the general was enamored by Edith; and as usual, she wanted to know where he was from, and about his wife and children. Meanwhile, my knees were actually knocking together. Due to Edith's charm, we got a top rating.

While we lived at the Teenage Club, our nearest neighbors were where the colonels lived. We had one couple who lived the closest to us, and Edith had her first experience of dealing with an alcoholic. The wife stayed on booze and wanted Edith to listen to all her problems.

Sports in the Army!

During this time, I participated in almost all the regimental sports. We had a good flag-football team; I was the quarterback and really threw and ran the ball well. Besides completing 15 of 19 passes, I returned a punt 70 yards for a touchdown. We didn't win the Post championship, but we beat the team that was the champion.

I also played basketball. We had one great basketball player from High Point College, Jack Powell; he was 6 ft 4 inches and could shoot the eyes out of the basket. One night in one of our league games, the score was 61-60 in the other team's favor. I was pretty quick and stole a pass with three seconds left to go. I dribbled down for a layup that could win the game, but I was fouled. I made the first free throw but missed the second, sending the game into overtime. I think they won in overtime. As I mentioned previously, at P.C. I developed a very good two-handed, set shot, so I got my share of points. [The first jump shots I ever saw were by the Indiana boys at P.C. Even though I worked hard on a jump shot, it took me a couple years to develop a good one.]

Additionally, we had a very good fast-pitch soft-ball team. We had a lot of strong football players on the team. Hugh Ballard played first base, Howard Derrick was a great catcher, and we had a black pitcher, whose name I can't remember, who was the best in the league. I played centerfield and during those days I was very quick. I felt if the ball was in the air between right centerfield and left centerfield, I would catch it. I batted left-handed, and I perfected the ability to beat the ball anywhere I wanted to. If I got it on the ground, it was going to be a hit. I batted .375, and we won the Fort Jackson championship.

I had a brief chance to play baseball. Games were played on Sundays, and one time the regular centerfielder was out; so they asked me to play. I was used to seeing and catching softballs in centerfield, but I had trouble seeing and catching the smaller baseball, misjudging several fly balls. I did, however, hit a homerun over the right-field wall. Unfortunately, they didn't have the designated hitter then, so they let me know they didn't need me anymore!

My participation in sports seemed to never end. Somehow, Fort Jackson decided to enter a Pony League team (for teenagers) into the local league; and somehow one of the boys, Charlie Funk, was the son of a colonel who was looking for a coach for the team. Charlie told his dad to hire me, and he did. I got out of my PT job every day at noon during practice and play time. We were provided with an army bus to take us to and from games. When we started the program, it was the first time the Fort had a team so there was no pony league regulation field available. No problem! The General asked if I had men, could I build a pony-league team. I said yes, and they gave me a corner on Jackson Boulevard and a platoon of men waiting to go into basic training. They also gave me a dump truck and plenty of picks and shovels, and promised to build two dugouts and put up an outfield fence. Jerry Frye (Sgt. Frye's son) was our catcher, Charlie Funk, the Miles boys, and a wonderful little fellow named

Smith were good players. Russell was a tall boy who was our best (and only) pitcher, and we had a Mims guy who could hit. We had a good team but did not win the championship; but we did win more games than we lost. And, we had a lot of fun.

While I was at Fort Jackson, Todd and Moore Sporting Goods was a local sporting goods dealership on South Main Street in Columbia. I had been told that most of the high-school coaches and athletic directors "hung out" there on Saturday mornings. When I graduated from P.C., I knew exactly what I wanted to do for my profession. Edith and I had both long planned for me to be a teacher/coach in South Carolina. I truly felt I was "called" to do that. So every time I could, I went on Saturday mornings to Todd and Moore to hobnob with the coaches and athletic directors. I got to know Charlie Todd and George Moore, the owners, very well; and they were on the lookout for a job for me when I left the Army. While I was at Todd and Moore one Saturday, I met Coach Harry Perone, the locally well-known coach at Dentsville High School. At that time Dentsville was a small, class "C" team located near the Fort. Harry asked me if I would like to come out in my spare time and help him coach his team. I was very excited and accepted, and got some valuable experience under Harry.

Incidentally, Dentsville back then (1953-1955) was a very small community outside Columbia with sand hills, scrub oaks, and pine trees. One wealthy man whose daughter asked him to consider buying some of the Dentsville-area land said, "Those sand hills and scrub oaks will never amount to anything." Today, the Dentsville area, now Northeast Columbia, is probably the most affluent area of Columbia. If only I could have bought some land back then!

Our First Baby

Our first baby was due in December 1954. Because I was in the Army, the delivery would be in the Army Hospital. Edith's pregnancy was a new "wonder world"; neither of us knew much about having babies and in those days fathers only "got in the way." But as in almost everything else in our lives, Edith took it all in stride; and though she didn't know a lot more than I, she acted like she did.

During this time, it just happened that I was ordered to attend a special NCO leadership school. It was a "spit and polish" school where each man was pushed to the limit. School began at 5:00 in the morning, and every NCO who had attended from our regiment had finished either first, second, or third, so the pressure was on. The school tested you on every phase of army life. It lasted six weeks and after three weeks, I was doing really well.

This was about the time that Edith's "time" was coming due, and as it would happen her "water broke" on a Sunday afternoon. I drove her to the Fort Jackson Hospital maternity ward. This was our first child, and I was really nervous. Edith seemed her usual cool, calm, and collected self. When we arrived at the hospital, a nurse colonel came to me and said, "We don't need you. You can go home and we will call you."

I asked, "Wouldn't it be okay if I sat around?"

She said, "We don't have husbands sitting around now. Corporal, I'm ordering you—MOVE!" So I went back to our apartment and waited and waited and waited for that phone to ring.

I had to be at the leadership school at 5:00 the next morning to conduct a class on how to dismantle a carbine rifle in 30 seconds and put it back together in working order. I can tell you my mind was not on that carbine rifle. I had not heard a word from the hospital since I took her there at 5:00 the previous afternoon. Finally, after the presentation about 10:00 a.m., I was ready to go AWOL or whatever I had to do to find out about Edith and our baby. I went to our captain in charge and told him the circumstances and also told him he could have my corporal stripes or he could send me to Korea, but I was going to that hospital. He said, "Just a minute now. Let me make a call." He did and found that our baby, Arthur Wellington Baker, Jr., had been born at 8:00 a.m. and no one had called to tell me.

The captain gave me permission to go to the hospital, and when I got there Edith was in her room with "Artie." I didn't have a mirror to look in, but Edith said my face lit up like a big lamp. I thought Artie had to be the prettiest baby I had ever seen. Edith looked great too. After several days, Edith and Artie came home. We had his crib and room all fixed up, and our lives would never be the same again. From that day forward, everything we planned had to include not just the two of us, but Artie too—then later, of course, his sister and brothers.

The Remaining Time in the Army

During my time in the army, Mrs. Edens became ill will pancreatic cancer. She had been so good to me during my courting years; I loved her dearly and had great respect for her. Along with my Aunt Bess and Aunt Katie, Mrs. Edens taught me so much about class and how to treat others. Her faith in God was an inspiration to me. She was always trying to care for me and to gently guide me in the way nice young men were expected to be. She suffered greatly with pain the last several months; it hurt all of us to see her suffer. Mr. Edens did everything he could to get her help, but in those days there were not the treatments for cancer that we have today.

She and all her children were close, but I thought she and Edith were especially close. She called Edith "Hun-Baby." When Mrs. Edens passed away, I was deeply saddened. She was such an encourager to me and always knew just what to say to me to make me feel better or even to make me aware of something I might be neglecting. I enjoyed eating Saturday lunch when Mrs. Edens was cooking. She was a wonderful person, and I know I am a better person because I came under her influence. At her funeral, I was very emotional, having lost a wonderful friend and encourager.

My second year in the Army was easier than the first. You must learn to do things "the army way" and I had learned that. I was now a sergeant but still had to pull my regular "Sergeant of the Guard" duty when it came my turn. We also had to stand inspections, usually on Saturday mornings where we had to be sharp, have clean and pressed uniforms, haircuts and shaves, and polished brass and shoes. We each had a weapon assigned to us, and that weapon had to be spotless. We knew we had to be sharp on those inspections; a bad grade went on our record. Sometimes the Regiment would have a parade, and sometimes the entire Post would have a parade on "Tank Hill," which they still use today. It was a great sight with Regimental flags and the bands playing. It was about a three-mile march from the 502nd Regiment to Tank Hill—a long march.

During our last months in the army, we lived in a duplex on Munson Springs Road off Devine Street near the Veterans Hospital. My Aunt Katie had lived close by on Munson Springs. When we moved, my old friend and roommate from P.C., Cedric Jernigan, moved into the other side of the duplex. He and his wife Betty and Edith and I had a lot of fun, and we had our first-born there—Artie (for us) and Cliff (for them). Another friend from P.C., Al Campbell, lived down the street from us, and we got together with them also. Al often made catfish stew, but he made white stew, and we preferred red stew. [Mr. Edens fixed the best red catfish stew I ever ate.]

One of my best friends from Sumter and P.C., Kirby Jackson, signed with the Cincinnati Reds right out of college. While I was at Fort Jackson, he played for the Columbia Reds, a Cincinnati Reds farm team. He was a very good outfielder who could hit and run, but he stayed hurt a lot. He played with quite a few major leaguers—Ted Kluszewski, Frank Robinson, Johnny Temple, and Wilmer "Vinegar Bend" Mizell, among others. After the season Kirby came to live with us, and we did some things together. Sometimes the three of us would go out to eat and to a movie. Kirby was not married at the time and dated some but was trying to decide whether to stay in baseball or get out and teach and coach. When he moved out, he started coaching and teaching in Marion, South Carolina. He later met his wife Patricia while we were all at the beach, and they remained our friends over the years.

My two years in the army were a good and important part of my life. I was honored several times by my Regiment and once was the "NCO of the Month" for the entire Post. When I met with my Regimental Commander, Col. McCowan, for my final annual review, he asked me to consider staying in the Army. He said he would send me to Officers Training School and that with my education and record in the army, he was sure I would be commissioned a second lieutenant. I thanked him but told him that my whole life had been planned—indeed it was God's plan—toward a career in teaching and coaching. Thus, I left the Army in August 1955. The discipline and physical fitness training I learned in the army served me well during the rest of my career as a football coach. Edith and I looked forward to the next phase of our lives, which we knew would be very different.

4 AT MCCOLL HIGH SCHOOL

As I mentioned in the last chapter, during the spring of my last year in the army, I went by Todd and Moore Sporting Goods store in Columbia each Saturday morning looking for possible coaching jobs becoming available. Charlie Todd and George Moore were very helpful to me and were constantly on the lookout for a good job for me. Because they had one of the biggest sporting goods stores in the state, they knew everybody in the schools. We preferred to stay in Columbia but were looking for anything available.

My former P.C. coach, Ben Moye, was coaching at the time at Brookland-Cayce High School in Cayce, South Carolina, next to Columbia; and he really wanted me to become one of his assistant coaches. But, they had no coaching supplement. And, I learned that Belton High School in Belton, South Carolina, was looking for an assistant coach and they were going to pay $4000.

But in early June Messrs. Todd and Moore told me about a job coming up at McColl High School in the town of McColl near Bennettsville in northeastern South Carolina. The principal, a Mr. Bristow, was a highly respected man from Summerville. I got in touch with him, and he invited me to come and bring Edith to McColl for an interview. It turned out that the coach had been fired after a 1-9 season. Mr. Bristow showed me around. The fields were in poor shape, the equipment was in poor shape, and the old gym was an antique. He offered me a job. I would be the only coach for football and would also coach boys' basketball and baseball. Additionally, I would teach a full load of physical education plus eighth-grade science. For all of this, the salary would be $3600.

After I got back home to Columbia, the principal at Belton called and offered me the assistant coaching job at a salary of $4000, and I would coach only football and basketball. Although the latter offer was for more money and less work, I decided I would rather start my coaching career as a head coach rather than an assistant coach and accepted the McColl offer. I have never regretted that decision.

The Army paid for our move to McColl after my discharge in August. We rented a small, two-bedroom home on South Main Street, which the agriculture teacher, George Seaborne, was vacating. We were very excited about my job and moving to McColl, even though the salary would be less than I was making in the army. But I was a head coach; in fact, I was the only coach! And, Edith was pregnant with our second child, due in January.

As I mentioned in Chapter 2, after my father's death my younger brother Bobby entered Epworth Children's Home where he had a completely miserable experience. It was so bad that I promised him we would let him come live with us after I completed college and the army. It was now time to fulfill my promise. To do this, Edith and I had to become his legal guardians. Because he was still a minor, he received a social security check of around $20 a month. When we finally moved in, we had a one-year-old boy and a sixteen-year-old boy in the house together with "one on the way."

The First Year

Bobby and I moved to McColl in August right after I was discharged from the Army; we went early to get ready for football practice and to get the stadium and playing field in good shape to play football. We were allowed to stay in the unoccupied teacherage (a building providing living quarters by a school for its teachers) until Edith arrived with Artie and our furniture. We had to laugh when Bobby and I arrived and some of the people said they didn't know which one of us was the coach and which one was the player.

Due to the circumstances of the previous coach leaving and a new principal other than the one who hired me, the football facilities were in a mess. The little stadium was badly in need of repair, and the playing field was at least hip high in weeds. I had a tough time getting the school district to cut the "grass." Finally, one of the player's father who was a farmer, C.S. McLaurin, sent out a tractor, cut the grass, and fertilized the field. By the time of the first game, the field was in good shape. The equipment was really in bad shape too. No one had properly cleaned it up and stored it. I was really disappointed, but Bobby and I got some players to help us and we went to work.

McColl was primarily a mill town. The mills did not pay big salaries, so both parents often worked at the mill on different shifts. Thus the mill children were often unattended and led pretty difficult lives.

This time was in the mid-50s before integration, but McColl was ahead of the times! There were three distinct classes of people whose children all went to McColl High School. (1) The merchants and farmers were the relatively well-to-do citizens. (2) The mill workers lived in poorly kept mill villages. It was hard to discipline this group of young people; they generally didn't even want to go to school. (3) The third group was comprised of Pembroke Indians, who lived throughout this part of South Carolina. Because McColl was only a few miles from North Carolina, some of these students lived in North Carolina. These proud people were usually farmers, laborers, etc. They had often married white people and black people, but as long as they were Pembroke, they attended the segregated white schools. My first big job was to get all three of these groups to play together as a team, since none of the three were all that socially compatible. Actually, I was real surprised at how well they ended up working together.

C.S. Williams, the new Superintendent of McColl Schools, was a mild-mannered man who really didn't know a fullback from a wide receiver, but he was very supportive. He was much more interested in school budgets, daily attendance, and keeping teachers and parents happy. Charlie Fitzgerald was the new principal of the high school. He had come to McColl to play semi-pro baseball. In South Carolina and North Carolina back then, semi-pro baseball was very popular, and there was a very strong semi-pro league among cities and towns that had mills. There was great competition between the mill owners to have the best team. In fact, Mr. Johnson, the owner of McColl Mills, once had Billy Joe Davidson, the first "big bonus baby" in the majors. Billy Joe signed the first big bonus $100,000 before he pitched for the McColl team. Charlie Fitzgerald was lured to play on that team.

Charlie was from Manchester, New York, and a college graduate, so when baseball was over he became the principal of McColl High School. He also coached the girls' basketball team; I coached everything else. Charlie was a tall, nervous, fidgety man, but a wonderful principal who worked well with the teachers. As I look back on those years, he was a very good friend to me and was probably the only man who could have handled the situation that existed at McColl High. Students were constantly breaking into the school office or cafeteria. They hardly ever got away with their deeds because he would track them down. The students nicknamed him "Charlie Spade" after a prominent television sleuth of those days. Students would occasionally get in all kinds of trouble—cut school without an excuse, disrupt a class, get in a fight. In most every case he would give them a choice: two licks or two weeks' suspension. He had the shop teacher thin the big end of a baseball bat down to a paddle on both sides. In those days you could paddle students (at least the boys), but you had to have another teacher present. Charlie always came to my class to get me as a witness. He would make the guys bend over putting their hands on the desk, feel their rear ends to see if they had anything extra–magazines or newspapers—inside their pants, and then ask them if they were ready. You have to remember Charlie's forte in baseball was as a hitter; he always hit over .300 and led the team in homeruns. When the young man said he was ready, Charlie would spit on both hands (baseball habit) and hit a left-handed homerun off the boy's rear end. Two licks were about all one could stand. I saw football players in the shower after two licks and there were some awful-looking bruises on those cheeks. Today, he would surely be fired and sued, but you must remember these boys were used to, and led, a very tough life, afraid of nothing. So Charlie had an "equalizer" at school.

When Bobby and I began cleaning equipment getting ready for the season, I needed equipment managers. I didn't have any coming back that I knew of, but a little fellow who lived up the street and worked selling popcorn for his daddy at the only movie theater in town showed up to help. John Marcus Geddie, who was an eighth-grader at the time, not only helped us but also became a good player; and he and his family became life-long friends of ours. He later picked up the nickname "Moose." Between us we got the equipment in about as good a shape as we could. I knew that if we were going to build pride in the "Red Devils," we had to get some new equipment and uniforms.

Dusty Johnson was the son of the owner of one of the mills who was a strong supporter of our program. His wife taught at the high school. He suggested that we might convince the school and town to help us collect paper products. His mill had a cotton press we could use to bale the paper, Sonoco would pay for the paper, and Dusty would provide a truck to haul the paper. We were way ahead of our times with recycling. We had an old room where we stored the paper until we had a load to send out. I got tired of handling paper, but we raised enough money to buy new uniforms the second year.

The first day of practice was very exciting for all of us, trying to fill out eligibility sheets, getting sizes right, and so on. We had a lot of different uniforms that first day. Obviously some helmets and shoes didn't fit just right. John Marcus came out for football the first day with some other younger players. I was so busy getting my schedule up and trying to coach all positions that I hardly listened to complaints about equipment. For the first several days it seemed like every time I turned around, John Marcus was complaining because his shoes didn't fit. I would say, "Shake it off, John Marcus; your feet are not used to football shoes." After two days I decided to look at his shoes and thereby learned a valuable lesson. He had on two left shoes! I learned that day to not get ahead of things, take your time, and stick to fundamentals. I got him a pair of shoes and listened to all complaints after that.

I found out that some good potential players could not come to practice. These included some of the Pembroke Indians and some of the sons of truck farmers who lived in the area. The boys were needed to work on the farms or other family businesses. So I went to see one of the fathers whose son Gary Woods was a big fullback and I knew one of the best players available. I said, "Mr. Woods, I need your son on my team; he's the best player we got."

He said, "Well, I've got to have him to work."

I said, "Well, what does he do?"

He said, "He helps me cut timber and I'm way behind."

I said, "How if I send a few boys over to help you and we practice at night, would you let him come?"

He said, "Well, I guess so if we can work it out." So we started practicing at night and I picked up a few good players.

Our first game was with nearby Clio. They were a strong class "C" team; we were a very questionable class "B" team. Their coach was a long-time, local legend, "Tito" Swann. He ran the single wing and had some tough country boys. We played in McColl and had a nice crowd, but we couldn't stop the single wing and lost 13-7. From that disappointment we went through the season winning two games, losing six, and tying two. Our team improved each week and at the end of the season we were a pretty good team.

There are two things I remember about the season. We tied Cheraw 21-21. Bobby (my brother) ran a punt back for a touchdown and after the game all the old-timers came up all excited saying it was the first punt return for a touchdown in ten years. The other thing I remember was one night we were playing Charlotte Catholic High School in Charlotte, North Carolina (why I don't know). J.C. Griffin was our captain and our tailback and held for extra points. In the third quarter we scored a touchdown. Our center who snapped for extra points was hurt, and we had to put our second-team snapper in to snap. Just before the play, I saw J.C. having a heated discussion with the referee. Finally, the ref brought J.C. over to me and said, "Coach, your captain insists he would like a practice snap before the play. Would you please tell him that is not legal?" I learned another lesson: Don't leave anything untaught!

J.C. went on to USC where he did not play football but did earn a BA, MA, and PhD in English. He has written two football books on the history of South Carolina football. He dedicated one of the books to me, which was a great honor, and he was very generous in including me as one of the people he wrote about.

I was disappointed after my first season that we didn't have a winning record, but I couldn't mope for long because basketball season was next and I was the head coach. While I didn't play college basketball, I was fortunate enough to play in a good intra-mural league. And in my senior year at P.C. Norm Sloan, one of the top basketball coaches in the country, had only nine players on his team. I knew I would probably have to coach basketball in high school, so I asked Coach Sloan if he would allow me to come out and be his tenth practice player. He did, and I learned his system which subsequently served me well.

Our basketball talent was better than our football talent; actually, we had a pretty good team. We used Norm Sloan's program intact. We pressed from the opening whistle and won a lot of games. We won the huge "Tobacco Belt Tournament" and went to the finals of the district where we lost to Latta whom we had beaten twice during the season. Leon Maxwell, the Latta coach, taught me another coaching lesson in that game. He played man defense in a zone and I didn't have a good answer for it to help my players. From then on, I made sure I had a contingency plan—I never again wanted my players to look at me during a game for a solution and I didn't have one. Sometimes, I just had to say, "Son, you've got a player in front of you who just might be too good for you to block." Even then I tried to be prepared to tell him what and how he could help himself.

My first basketball season, we had a game in Gibson, North Carolina, which was not far from McColl. One of my former P.C. classmates, Bev McIntyre, was their coach. I sensed we were in trouble when some of our fans told me the referees were the local druggist and auto mechanic. They let everything go, and at half time we had 21 fouls called against us and three against them. There were several pushing contests and near fights. Even though seven of our good players fouled out, I believe we still won. After the game we were dressing in a dark room behind the gym. About the time we were half dressed, in burst about a dozen Gibson "town toughs." Our players were huddled in a corner like a covey of quail. I will always remember that night. I walked over to the town toughs and said, "Men, we're trying to get dressed and back to McColl to see Sugar Ray Robinson fight Rocky Graziano." One of the big boys said, "Coach, we're fixing to have us a fight right here." Just at that moment Coach McIntyre came in the door and grabbed a big push broom. He faced the "home crowd" and said, "There is not going to be a fight here tonight." He and some other school officials got us to our bus; but as we left, it was bombarded with rocks, bottles, and bricks. We did get back to McColl and I think Sugar Ray won the fight.

We went on to have a very good season in my first as a basketball coach, winning 20 games.

In January Edith was coming up on her ninth month of pregnancy. We were having exams at school. Early on the morning of January 18, she woke me after she had been up sometime to calmly say that she had begun her birthing pains. She was calmly doing all the little things so that Artie's food and things would be ready for him. We had two wonderful neighbors who lived across the street, the Betheas and the Fouches. Jinx Fouche, Sam's wife, had offered to stay with Artie while I took Edith to the Bennettsville Hospital eight miles away. I was so nervous and couldn't believe Edith was calmly taking her time. I was frantic; Jinx was pleading with her to go, and I was too. We finally left and I drove as fast as I dared to get to the hospital. Her doctor was Doug Jennings, Sr. When we got there I remembered that my first class had a final exam that morning and I had to be there or call someone to give it for me. The nurses said for me to go on back to McColl; Edith would not have the baby for several hours. I learned from that experience not to listen to nurses when it comes to delivering babies. I had no sooner gotten back to McColl and given out the exam when the principal, Charlie Fitzgerald, came running to my class to say your baby has come, get back to Bennettsville. When I got there, Edith was fine (she always made having a baby seem so easy—I think I had a harder time than she did) and our brand-new, beautiful daughter, Kimberly Edens Baker, was fine too!

Next came baseball and we had a rather average team. Bobby was a very good baseball player—pitcher/centerfielder--and he could hit the ball a mile. Over the season, we won a few more games than we lost.

With another member of our family present, we needed more room. One of my athletes Penny McLaurin's folks had a nice, three-bedroom, frame house several blocks nearer town. Among other things, they farmed and ran the local grocery store (this was before grocery chains came to McColl), and we learned another valuable lesson in our married life: don't charge groceries! We did and it took us until a year after we left McColl to get our grocery bill paid. We rented this house and put up a fence to keep Artie and "Flip," our cocker spaniel, in the yard. Flip was named after Al "Flip" Rosen of the Cleveland Indians.

In spite of the fence, sometime Artie and Flip would get out. One day our mailman, Coleman Jones, was delivering mail to our house and Flip, who was sick, bit him. The big joke around town was that our dog bit Coleman and the dog died a few days later.

When we moved to McColl, I remembered the teachings of my P.C. athletic director. When you move into a community, (1) join a church, (2) join a civic club, and (3) contribute to the community. So we joined the McColl Methodist Church, and I joined the Lions Club and participated in many community projects.

Our "new" home was closer to town, and it was on the way home for John Marcus every night when he finished his pop-corn job at the movie theater. He would come in the front door (we didn't usually lock doors in those days), walk back to the kitchen, and ask Edith what she had to eat. He would get out what he wanted. Often the refrigerator would be almost empty—especially if it was near the end of the month (we got paid monthly). The next night he would often get his mother to bake us a pie or a cake. John Marcus was our "guardian angel." Toward the end of the month when our groceries were running low, Edith cooked biscuits, and we would eat biscuits and syrup for dinner. It's still one of my favorite meals—she can really cook good biscuits. One other interesting thing about food: hardly a day went by without one or more of our students bringing us a "mess" of greens, or beans, corn, or whatever from their gardens. Sometimes they would bring something like a bowl of cooked rutabagas. Many of them lived on small truck farms. These gifts of food helped us get through the month food-wise.

During the summer, I got a job with the U.S. Government measuring land. It was a hot job that paid a little—but at least enough to help out. I spent a lot of time improving our facilities at school. Bobby played American Legion Baseball for a nearby Laurenburg, North Carolina, team, and again he was very good. He played against Sonny Jergenson and Roman Gabriel, who played for a Wilmington legion team. They both became famous professional football quarterbacks. Bobby was pretty tough and one night he went over to Laurenburg for a dance. Seems he was dancing with a little girl, and her boyfriend didn't like it. A fight ensued, and Bobby was hit by a pair of "brass knuckles." He had ten stitches in his lip. All his McColl buddies who brought him home around midnight told us it wasn't Bobby's fault.

Also during the summer, the county sent me to a physical education seminar at Kings Mountain State Park. When I returned we had a county-wide teachers' meeting in Bennettsville. Without warning the superintendent called on me to give a report on the seminar. That taught me to be sure to be prepared for any occasion.

The Second Year

We were much better prepared for our second football season than our first. I had used students to help me get the fields in much better shape. Our gym was an old antique; the paint on the floor had been painted-over time after time and was almost black. Charlie Fitzgerald and I decided I could use student help to scrape the floor. We even managed to scrounge some paint remover. It took us three or four months, but we had us a nice, new playing surface for basketball season. And, with the money we had earned on paper sales to Sonoco, we purchased new uniforms for the varsity.

One thing I have always felt strongly about is to have a good youth program to teach young guys the fundamentals before they get to the varsity level. McColl had never had enough players to field a "B" team. I spent all spring and summer recruiting every seventh, eighth, and ninth grader I could find to play football on a "B" team. I scheduled five or six games for the "B" team that fall. We didn't even have a set of uniforms for them. But I knew that two of the "B" team players, Whit and Ray Wilson, were grandsons of Mr. Johnson, the mill owner; and I knew he would be there to see them play their first game. I put the worst torn, mixed-up uniforms on the players for the game. The next day Mr. Johnson called me and asked me to have lunch with him. He said, "Coach, those are the worst uniforms I have ever seen [I had put Whit and Ray in the worst jerseys]. Don't you have any better?"

I said, "No sir."

He said, "How many boys do you have on your "B" team?"

I said, "24."

He said, "How much will it cost to get 24 uniforms?"

I told him I would find out, which I did. Three weeks later we were the best dressed "B" team in eastern South Carolina, thanks to Mr. Johnson and the McColl Mills! Thus, I learned early on the value and importance of having a strong booster group.

We had many players back our second year and a few new ones who didn't play the first year. One of the latter was a wonderful athlete, Bobby Gause, a big bruising fullback/linebacker who was fast and tough. We were really excited about having him. He was maybe 6 ft 1 inch, 200 lb. I learned another lesson early. Bobby met a nice, young girl whose husband had been killed in the service. Before I knew what was going on, he let that girl talk him into marrying her. In those days you couldn't play high-school sports if you were married. So I learned that (as Coach Howard would later tell his staff at Clemson) anytime there's a contest between football and girls, girls will win every time!

When the season started, we beat Clio and their single wing 24-0; and from then on we won six games and really played well—even against larger teams, including Bennettsville, Dillon, and Marion. Bobby again was outstanding as were the Dudley boys and the Crow brothers. Gerald Quick was an outstanding player who would later play professional baseball in the Chicago Cubs' organization. He later became the head of the "March of Dimes" in the state of Missouri.

Basketball was also much improved this season. The trips to away games were a pleasure. The boys and girls traveled together on one bus. The girls would bring food—fried chicken, sandwiches, ham biscuits, cookies, and cake, and in those days I could eat a lot and never gain a pound. Boy, did I enjoy that food. We played some really big teams, such as Sumter, which game we lost by a point or two at the end. We beat Dentsville and again won 20 or more games.

On one occasion Charlie Fitzgerald, the principal who coached the girls' team, got the flu, and he told me I would have to coach the girls for him for a week. Now I had never coached girls and obviously did not know how to deal with them. If I yelled at them, they cried. If they did well I caught myself a number of times almost hitting them on the rear telling them "good job." I was sure glad to see Charlie return!

In the spring, with Bobby and Gerald we had a pretty good baseball team. They could both pitch well and could usually get on base. We just had to work to get them in to score when we got them on base. The rest of the players on the team were not consistent hitters, so we worked hard on the "squeeze play" for when we got Gerald or Bobby on third base. We had a right fielder, Carol Jones, who wore thick glasses. In one game we had Gerald on third with no outs, and I gave Carol, the batter, the "squeeze signal." So Gerald is racing for home plate as the pitch is thrown, but Carol swings hard and hits a line drive right at Gerald's head as he raced with his head down to home. Fortunately, this was during the time when Elvis Pressley was popular, and Gerald had an "Elvis haircut," i.e., thick! The ball hit Gerald in the head, and he fell in the baseline face down. I ran out thinking he must be dead. Meanwhile, Carol is in my ear whining, "Coach, you didn't give me the squeeze signal, did you?" I could have choked him, but I was so concerned about Gerald. I slowly turned him over, and he had sand all over his face and his eyes were closed. Suddenly, he opened one eye and said to me, "Was I inside the foul line or outside?" [For the uninitiated, if a runner is hit by a batted ball in fair territory, he is out. If hit in foul territory, it would only be a foul ball.] We had instilled this rule in our players while practicing the squeeze play during practices. At that moment, I felt sure Gerald was okay.

Sometime in May, Rosser Thrash from Todd and Moore in Columbia called and told me about a job at Denmark High School in Denmark, South Carolina, that would not only pay me more but also furnish a free house. I visited the principal, Mr. Hannah. He was just back from taking the seniors to New York where he was "rolled" (beaten) and robbed on his way to get coffee early one morning. As I talked to him, he had a "black eye." I was excited about the new possible opportunity, but I also did not want to leave all I had worked to accomplish at McColl.

Meanwhile, my brother-in-law, Van Newman, who was sports editor of the "Columbia Record," contacted me to say he had learned that the football coach they had hired at Newberry High School had died during the summer of Rocky Mountain spotted fever, and they were looking for another coach. It was then about two weeks before football practice was set to begin. Harry Hedgepath was the long-time athletic director there, and Mr. J.V. Kneece was the principal. Urgently needing a new coach and having someone available with two years of experience (me), they offered me the job, but it paid less than Denmark. McColl offered me a small raise to stay. Van pointed out that the Newberry job would probably be the best place to move upward from, so we decided to take the job and move to Newberry, South Carolina, about 50 miles northwest of Columbia.

A Few Parting Remarks

Before we leave the McColl story, I want to make a few parting remarks. One of my favorite classes I taught was seventh-grade general science. I had a group of bright, young students. I've always felt that teaching/coaching is a "calling" whereby we have the opportunity to influence the lives of young people we teach and coach. There were three or four young girls in this class who played basketball and were very good students. My favorite was a young girl named Gwen Burrough; she was pretty but had cavities in her front teeth. When she smiled she would put her hand over her mouth, I'm sure to hide her cavities. I encouraged her almost daily to get her teeth fixed. She finally did and turned out to be a beautiful lady whose husband coached at Bennettsville and whose son also coached and taught. Gwen worked at the local dentist's office for many years, and she has thanked me many times for insisting that she fix and take care of her teeth. She had three cousins—all girls—who were very good basketball players too.

During the 1950s the famous Jim Tatum was considered one of the top five coaches in the nation. He was from McColl where his sister was the postmistress and his brother ran a gas station. Occasionally, "Big Jim," who coached at UNC and Maryland, would come home to McColl to visit, and his sister would make sure we had a chance to meet Coach Tatum. What a thrill that was for a young coach in his first year of coaching!

Either my first or second year at McColl, Kirby Jackson, who was coaching at Marion High School; Melecue Metts, who was coaching at Orangeburg High School; and I decided to go to a coaching clinic at Florida State University where Tom Nugent had introduced the "I" formation. This was before Interstate Highways, so we went across South Carolina, Georgia, and northern Florida all on two-lane highways. We arrived in Tallahassee and registered for the clinic at Florida State to learn about the "I" formation. Coach Nugent dressed up in a silk suit for each presentation; he was also the emcee for all other speeches. It was a pretty good clinic, and I was impressed by the fresh-orange juice dispensers that were everywhere and free! One day we were riding in downtown Tallahassee, a city about the size of Columbia. We were looking for a restaurant and stopped at a stop light on top of a hill with the sun shining in our face. This beautiful young lady walked across in front of us with the setting sun behind her; she had a great figure and looked like a model. Kirby, who was then single, jumped out of the car and ran after her, trying to meet her. Melecue and I pulled over and about died laughing as Kirby tried unsuccessfully to meet "Miss America."

In later years Tom Nugent became the head coach at Maryland; and after Clemson beat Maryland, Clemson Coach Frank Howard, who was always great for a memorable quote, said, "I guess we dotted Nugent's "I" today!"

While I was in McColl, I really wanted to pursue a commission in the Army National Guard, but the nearest unit was in Hartsville, and I would have to go there every Saturday and Sunday for a year to get the commission. I was already away from my family too much, so I decided not to pursue a commission. Many of my friends did and later added to their retirement after 20 years in the National Guard, with many reaching the rank of colonel.

One thing I really looked forward to each summer around the 4th of July was going to Ocean Drive Beach. Mr. Edens would let each of his children have his beach house for a week and because of my coaching would let us use it during the July 4th week. I would save up my land-measuring money, and we had a black lady go with us to help cook and mind the children. During these times we would invite Jess Neely and Nita with their two children. Jess was head coach at Marion. We also invited "Frog" Weldon and Deanie with their two children, and Kirby would come and sleep on the couch. It was mayhem with all the children, but we managed to have a great time together. Later we would invite Susan Sheriff after her husband Tommy was killed by a grenade in the army in Germany. We didn't actually get the rest we needed, but we were young and enjoyed each other. Besides we had all played football together at P.C.

Dick and Jess liked to drink a beer occasionally, while Edith and I did not. One night we were at the famous "Pad" sitting at a table and shagging a little when a guy at the next table slammed his beer can down and it spewed all over Deanie, Frog's wife. Frog jumped up and went over to the guy and said in a loud voice, "Did you know you spewed beer all over my wife?" The guy stood up and he was about 6 ft 3 inches tall. Frog, around 5 ft 8 inches tall, was very impulsive and would fight at the "drop of a hat" but he was no fool. He looked up at that big guy and, trying to think of something conciliatory to say, said, "Where are you from?"

The big ol' guy said, "Loris."

Thinking very quickly, Frog said, "Well, that's where my wife is from. What's your name?" Thank goodness Frog diffused the situation and avoided a fight!

Another summer, a fight broke out just outside our beach house, and there was a big crowd as three or four boys were beating up on two guys. Jess and Frog jumped into the fight on the side of the two guys. After some shoving and pushing, the four boys apparently decided they didn't like fighting evenly and walked away. There was hardly ever a dull moment at the beach in those days, but when we returned home all tanned, we had to put full attention to our imminent football season.

Before I finish this chapter, I want to relate one amusing (some might call it hilarious) story that took place at McColl. Early on, I noticed a little boy, whose name I don't remember and if I did I wouldn't tell it, who was walking around all bent over at football practice; I thought he was going to hurt his back. I asked some of the other boys if they knew what was wrong with him, and they said they didn't and that he walked around straight-up during his classes. So I called him over and said, "Son, is there something wrong with your back?"

He said, "No sir."

I said, "Why are you all bent over all the time?"

He said, "Well coach, you told all those older boys who've played a lot before to show us younger ones how to put our uniforms on. They showed us how to put our pants on, our shoulder pads, and helmets—how to fit them and tighten them up. But coach, I'd never seen a 'jockey strap' before. So I asked one of the boys how to put this thing on. He said, 'You wear bib overalls, don't you? You put the jockey strap on just like your bib overalls'." He had the straps up over his shoulders. Oh, the shenanigans that go on in locker rooms!

In those early years I was so excited about coaching and learning anything and everything I could about the game. I must admit that even in those days I thought I could be a college coach. God had given me the desire to learn and the confidence to believe in myself. However, I clearly understood I had much more to learn in order "to get there."

In June 1957 the McColl era ended as we moved from McColl across the state to Newberry. We had enjoyed our stay in McColl but looked forward to whatever the future held for us.

ARTHUR W. BAKER and JACK B. EVETT

5 AT NEWBERRY HIGH SCHOOL

The previous football coach at Newberry High School the year before I went there had written an article in the "Newberry Observer" criticizing the Newberry High School Board for being "backward" in their support for football. They fired him despite the fact he was an excellent coach and would later win many games and state championships; he became a unique and famous high school coach in South Carolina.

Newberry High School was an old-fashioned, Latin high school, meaning it was very tough academically and very strict in tradition. Harry Hedgepath, a legend in South Carolina high school coaching, was the athletic director and baseball coach at Newberry, and he had hired a successful football coach from Laurens to replace the former coach. However, as I noted in the last chapter, just a few weeks later the newly hired coach died from Rocky Mountain spotted fever, they said. Van Newman, my brother-in-law, had a friend, Sonny Gray, whose father-in-law, Mr. Murry, was chairman of the School Board in Newberry. Through this association, Van recommended me and through Mr. Murry, I was hired as football, basketball, and track coach at an annual salary of $4100.

The move was rather sudden. I went to Newberry and carried Edith and the children along with my brother Bobby. I took Harry Hedgepath's offer to find us a home to live in. He arranged for us to rent a house from an old, eccentric guy who had rental properties, ran a second-hand furniture store, and loaned money to poor people at high interest rates. The only good thing about our rental house was its location about two blocks from the high school—obviously close enough for me to walk to work.

The First Year

I immediately began preparations for the 1957 football season. Unlike when I arrived at McColl, Harry had all the equipment cleaned and stored, and shoes were in brown paper bags with the sizes written on the bottom. However, the equipment was very old, and the uniforms, very plain as well as old. Harry had taken advantage of all the old army-navy sales, and we had plenty of old, gray, wool socks, jocks, and sweat shirts—all World War II leftovers. He was very tight about what we could buy. I did have an assistant coach, Donnie Layton, who was a teacher. He didn't play college football, but he worked hard and was loyal, and did a good job.

Bobby would be a senior on my team, and he could play quarterback or running back. We had some pretty good players coming back from the previous year. We played a very tough schedule, including Lancaster, Clinton, Laurens, Belton-Honea Path, Eau Claire, Batesburg-Leesville, Brookland-Cayce, and Mid Carolina. Bobby was very consistent and very good. We had a pretty good team, but not good enough. We won four games but lost six. Our best win was against Brookland-Cayce, 14-7. In the Eau Claire game, I was on the sidelines, of course, and one of their players, John Boulware, made a tackle and spun around and kicked me in the thigh. I had to go to the hospital after the game. I still see him from time to time, and that happening is always mentioned with a chuckle.

I remember one thing from my first game, which was against Lancaster, the state champs. They had a great team; we were just getting started. At the half, the score was 30-0 Lancaster. I figured they would play some second-stringers in the second half, but they seemed to still be playing with a passion. When the play was near me, one of their players would jump up and say, "How do you like that, coach?" I was confused as to why they were so fired up but I didn't say anything. I just wondered why the Lancaster coach would embarrass our team. Three or four years later while I was taking a class at USC, the sports editor from the Lancaster paper told me that the coach had quoted me to his team as saying we would beat Lancaster so bad that I was going to bring my rocking chair and rock. I never said anything like that my entire career and certainly hadn't talked to anybody from Lancaster. I was furious when I heard what had happened. Some years later when I was at Eau Claire, we scrimmaged Lancaster. I remembered but didn't say anything to my team, but they got the message. We shut them out—a little revenge!

The best thing I did that first year was to go all out recruiting a "B" team to, hopefully, ensure a stream of good players coming up to the varsity each year. As I had done at McColl, I tried to recruit virtually every eighth- and ninth-grade boy to come out for football. I even went to the junior high schools recruiting. We had a good turnout and a good, winning season with the "B" team. Most, if not all, of these players moved up to become outstanding varsity players.

Upon arriving in Newberry, I realized that Harvey Kirkland was a fine coach at Newberry College. I greatly admired him and sought every opportunity to get to know him. He was a man of strict habit, and I knew when he would go to the gas station, dry cleaners, and so on; and I tried to be at as many of these places as I could so I could "bump into him" and talk. We became friends. His son Benji was quarterback on our "B" team. I tried to learn everything I could about coaching football, and he saw a willing student in me. His subsequent mentoring of me was a most important part of my coaching career and life.

We joined Central Methodist Church and went to Sunday School where Coach Kirkland was the teacher. He was very good and I hung on his every word. Edith and I became directors for the Methodist Youth Fellowship and enjoyed our work in this endeavor. One Sunday night we were to have the MYF put on the church program, which included us singing a few songs. The choir director was directing and I was part of the singing group. We were practicing for the program and she stopped us and said, "Somebody in this group can't sing; you all keep on singing." She then moved in front of each of us as we were singing; when she got in front of me, she said, "You are the problem; you can't carry a tune." That ruined me for life. I still have a bad feeling about people hearing me sing.

The first summer in Newberry I decided to begin work on my master's degree in Administration at USC. I was eligible for the G.I. Bill of Rights benefits. I went to school in the mornings and worked at a job in the afternoons in the basement of the Employment Security Commission in Columbia, where I worked for a supervisor named Ed Zobel. [He would come into my life later when I was at Eau Claire High School.] There were two or three other teachers who traveled the 90 miles or so roundtrip to Columbia, and we formed a car pool, taking turns driving.

Around August or September, our children began to have bites all over them. We discovered the house we were renting was full of fleas. We contacted the landlord about the problem, and he said it was our problem. We had signed a six-month lease, but I told him we were moving out and would not pay him another cent and I meant it. Mr. Murry, the School Board chairman, found out that I meant it. He owned a group of four very nice apartments about a block up Spears Street from where we were living, and he offered us one of them that was vacant. He furthermore asked me to pay the owner the remaining rent that was due and in return he would give us the apartment rent free for the same number of months. In doing this, he probably saved me a lot of potential trouble. It was a nice apartment across the street from the "Teen Age Club." We became close friends with our other apartment renters—Jim and Elinor Beard and the Foyes, who lived under us. The family below grilled steaks every Friday while we were eating hotdogs. Man, did they (the steaks) smell good!

There was a canal that ran just beside our apartment complex. Artie was about three years old and he loved tractors. Often we would walk the five blocks to "town," stopping by the tractor dealership and then the 5- and 10-cent store for popcorn or a candy sucker. One day we realized that Artie was missing. I panicked and just knew he had drowned in that canal. I set all kinds of sprint records running down that canal—no Artie. Then we remembered the tractor place and hopped in the car and drove there. Yes, they had seen him. About that time one of my players drove by and told me that Buddy Threatt, another of my players, had Artie at the 5 and 10 store buying him popcorn and candy. Boy, were we thankful! Artie was having a great time eating popcorn and candy, while his mom and dad were trying to overcome shock!

Now, back to sports. As I said before, we had a so-so football season, but basketball season was different. Led by Bobby Baker and Melvin Bouknight, we were very good. We "pressed" from the opening whistle and played good man-to-man defense. We could shoot and pass very well. We went to the finals of the district tournament, playing Lancaster, which also had a good team. They had the two Davis twins—both about 6 ft 4 in. and good athletes. We led 58-57 with a few seconds to go, having just scored. There were no timeouts left, and I'm screaming to the team not to press, but this team was like a group of animals and they smelled victory. The Davis twins were smart, however, and they set a pick on Buddy Threatt. He ran into the twin, and they had one-and-one foul shots. He made both shots with no time left on the clock, and we were in shock. I learned another good lesson. While it's good to have the enthusiasm and momentum of the "press," you've got to have a quick way to call it off. Prepare for every situation that can happen. Incidentally, Lancaster went on to the state finals.

At Newberry High I had an unusual eighth-grade science class. In those days they often put the best students together in one class, and I really had a good one. They were the most inquisitive and challenging students as a whole that I can remember. We had all kinds of science projects in which we learned together. Many of the girls in the class babysat for us from time to time. One of them was Jane Henderson, who later became the wife of the famous UNC/USC basketball coach, Frank McGuire. This class was an outstanding group who were great students; they did superb projects. I think I learned more from them than I taught them.

During winter months, Harry Hedgepath and I often hunted quail together. He had a couple dogs, but when we hunted around Newberry, it was one covey shot and the birds went over the next hill. We hardly ever found the "singles." Sometimes, Billy Odell, the famous Baltimore Orioles pitcher from Newberry who had played for Harry in high school, would hunt with us. One day I actually saw him kill five quail on a "covey rise"—a very difficult feat. He and Bobby Richardson are the two best quail shots I've ever seen, although Edith's dad, Mr. Edens, and her brother, Curt, were also very good.

Newberry had never had a track team, but in the spring I decided we would have one, mainly so I could get the football players out running in the (football) offseason. We had a lot of football players returning. The only problem was there was no track at the school. There was an old, dirt track at the fairgrounds that had been used for horse racing. I asked the players to furnish their own transportation to the track, which was several miles from town. The school district refused to drag the track or fix it up at all, but we made the most of the situation. We even had one player, John Miller, qualify for the 440 in the state meets in Columbia. But most importantly, most of the players got in a lot of running to keep them in reasonably good shape during the offseason.

Bobby made All-State in football, basketball, and baseball, and had several scholarship offers including Newberry and Clemson. However, he failed to score high enough on his SAT scores to qualify. He was offered a scholarship to Gordon Military College in Georgia. He was selected to play in the annual North-South game in Columbia in August. We went to the beach intending to return for his game in Columbia, but on Tuesday he separated his shoulder in practice, requiring surgery. The coaches with Gordon stuck with their offer, however, and Bobby enrolled there in September.

During the summer, Coach Kirkland and his family "took us in." Coach and I would fish together in nearby ponds and Lake Murray. We were often invited to the Kirkland's backyard for a fish fry and "Red Horse Bread" (hushpuppies). Coach would cook fish in his cooker that were really good. Almost every time, the main topic of conversation was football; thus began my "main course" in football. More importantly, he taught me that no matter how many good things I did, no matter that I did not drink alcohol or curse, that unless I accepted Jesus Christ as my personal Savior, I could never enter the gates of heaven. He did not teach me this during any one day or occasion, but over the years that he was my dear friend and mentor. He changed my coaching knowledge and philosophy that always stood me in good stead. Wherever I coached, I had an advantage, for I had learned the right way.

Also during the summer, I often went out to fish on the various ponds that were all over Newberry County. I would wear old blue jeans and high-top tennis shoes, have a fish stringer and a bait can on my belt, and fish with a fly rod. I would put a generous portion of worms on a hook with a small weight and cast it out, letting it go to the bottom, then pulling it slowly to me. Mostly, I waded up to my waist while fishing, and I usually had good luck. Edith loved cooking and eating fish and would even help me clean them. Talking about the country around Newberry, we also bought eggs and milk from farms there.

One day, Rev. Truesdale came to our house after making an appointment with Edith. She thought he wanted to talk about Bobby who was dating a girl in the church. When she realized that was not the case, she told him I was not home. He told her he didn't want to see Art; he wanted to see her. He offered her the job of Director of the Kindergarten at the church. She accepted it and began work in September 1958. As usual, she enjoyed her work and did a great job.

The Second Year

During the summer, Harry allowed me to buy some new uniforms and equipment. I knew our football team would be much improved in 1958. We had three quarterbacks who were pretty good at that position but who could all play other positions. Lloyd Brigman was No. 1; Charles Hazel was No. 2 quarterback and No. 1 running back. Benji Kirkland, an eighth grader who was Coach Kirkland's son, was our third-best quarterback. We had some good, young running backs too. Melvin Bauknight was a very good player who later became an outstanding coach at Newberry.

We opened the season against a very good Batesburg-Leesville team and played them even for three quarters, when tragedy struck. First, Lloyd Brigman, who was proving himself as a first-class quarterback, tore a ligament in his knee while returning a punt. Then Charles Hazel, our No. 2 quarterback, had a finger poked in his eye, and he was in bed for eight weeks with a damaged retina. Another available quarterback, Jerry Davenport, had a broken leg (worst I ever saw) and missed the rest of the season. I made a tough decision by deciding to play Benji Kirkland at quarterback. He was small (120 lb) but very good and very tough. He was our quarterback the rest of the year, of course with some limitations, but he did well. Our team was much better in 1958 than in 1957, but with the three key injuries we were not near good enough. Our record was 4-6-1, but we played some good ball games—Brookland-Cayce 14-7, Eau Claire 6-7, and Batesburg-Leesville, 7-14. When we played at Eau Claire, we lost the game late in the fourth quarter on a long run. The Eau Claire principal was impressed with our team.

Basketball season was another good year for us. We played the same style I learned from Coach Norm at P.C. But the most exciting thing to me about this time of the year was the development of our "B" team football program. The core of this group would later play for the Upper-State Championship, although I myself would not be there.

I had joined the Newberry Chapter of the Junior Chamber of

Commerce; I enjoyed the projects and the fellowship, and I attended most of the meetings. One day at school, my principal, J.V. Kneece, told me it was "Boss's Night" at the JC meeting, and he wanted me to be sure and go with him. Upon arrival and during the ensuing program, much to my surprise and delight I was named the Newberry JC "Man of the Year," a great honor that my wife and I appreciated.

Again this year I worked with the track team, and this time we qualified four for the state meets. I fished some more and played some baseball for the Newberry team in the Dutch Fork League. On away games we had to furnish an umpire, and the home team furnished one. One day, we were playing at Peak, South Carolina, and I was the base umpire because I wasn't playing in the game. Behind first base was a high hill where the "local boys" sat, chewing tobacco, drinking beer, and seeming to be there for one purpose—to "bait the umpire." The baiting was okay but they started throwing rocks and pecans at me. I got mad and went storming up the bank. Four or five of them stood up, all over 200 lb with bib overalls on. They looked at me as if to say, "What are you going to do about it?" I looked at that big group of mean men trying to decide what I was going to do or say. Finally I said, "The way some of you are hitting your target, maybe you should be pitching for your team." (Their pitcher was bad.) They looked at me and, thank goodness, we all had a good laugh.

During my 1958 season, Danny Doar, a graduate of Newberry College, came over to do his practice teaching, and I talked him into helping Donnie Layton and me coach the football team. Around that time I met for the first time another life-long friend—Steve Robertson. A Newberry College graduate who played center on the football team, he was in the army at Fort Jackson. He was dating a beautiful majorette in our band; thus he came back to Newberry often. Coach Kirkland recommended him highly as a possible future assistant coach, and we began to talk about 1959 when he would get out of the army. In fact, he had agreed to come to Newberry High, and Mr. Kneece had a spot for him to teach; but that was not meant to be.

We continued to go to the beach each summer around July 4th. In the summer of 1957 we invited the Kirklands to go with us and we started a tradition that lasted over 20 years. We would go and sometimes stay at least a week. Coach Kirkland, we soon learned, loved to get up early and fish off the pier, and he loved to "body surf." Then while the wives and kids sunbathed or swam, he would take me on the beach and give me a football clinic. At first I was a little embarrassed, but after a while I was so engrossed with his every word that I forgot we must have looked very strange going over "steps," "techniques," etc. on the beach. But I learned a mountain of knowledge about football, discipline, and teaching that is still in my foundation of the game today. Then we would go up from the beach where his wife Libba would have his sandwich laid out with his tea in exact proportions.

Coach had had a heart attack back in January or February but was such a disciplinarian that he did everything exactly as the doctor had told him. Libba waited on him hand and foot. After a nap, he was ready to fish again. He and Libba always stayed out in "Helen's little house" out back. Edith and I stayed upstairs in the corner bedroom nearest Helen's house. Every morning about 6:00 and then again around 2:30 or 3:00 p.m., he would throw rocks against our screen to wake me to go fishing. At night we would go to Calabash or some such place to eat seafood, and when we got back home we would always walk down to the Pavilion and let the children play the game machines. Then, on the way home we would stop by the ice cream place for a cone of ice cream. This was a ritual we would follow for years with the Kirklands because it was what he wanted to do and he had me completely sold. As I said earlier in this chapter, Coach was a man of strict habit.

After Libba and Coach went to bed, we would stay upstairs and sometimes play games with the children. It did not take too much persuasion for Ki Ki, Coach Kirkland's daughter, to get out her ukulele and sing "This land is my land"; she would later become "Miss South Carolina." Benji would throw passes on the beach, and he and Artie would fish with us until they got tired. One of the first times we went to the beach with the Kirklands, Artie was four or five. We were unpacking; the Kirklands were already unpacked. Artie was so glad to see Coach Kirkland that he ran to him and, not meaning to, ran head first into Coach's stomach. Coach Kirkland said, "What you say Artie?"

Artie said, "Put your head on the motor and drive." Coach laughed about this for years and always reminded Artie of it whenever he saw him.

Occasionally, Coaches Frank Singleton and his wife, Jackie, and Jim Satterfield and his wife, Anne, and sometimes Steve and Linda Robertson would go out with us to eat. One time Frank was with us and we went out to "Jack's Seafood" back in the boondocks but a great place to eat. Frank always loved to kid the waitress, while Coach Kirkland and Libba were always very proper. The waitress that night was a sassy thing dressed out in a clinging bodysuit. Frank was really teasing her and she was giving him "tit for tat." She began to take orders and got to Libba for her order. We had choices as to whether we wanted shrimp, flounder, and oysters—either one, two, or all three of them. The waitress asked Libba what she wanted, and she said, "I'll take the platter."

In the mode that Frank had teased her, the waitress said, "Lady, do you want anything on it?" It was very difficult for us to keep a straight face. Frank laughed for several minutes, but Steve and I didn't have guts enough to laugh in front of Coach Kirkland. Coach and Libba didn't appreciate it one bit. Incidentally, Jack's had an open window at the end of each table where you could throw oyster shells out during steamed-oyster season.

Oftentimes, I went on scouting trips with Coach Kirkland. He had a hard-and-fast rule—never stop at a gas station or anyplace else that had beer signs outside. He said if something happened while he was there, people would say Coach Kirkland was in a beer joint. He would have a hard time finding one today.

In the fall of 1958 I would have my game on Friday and get up early on Saturday and wash out our dirty uniforms. Then I would go to the college game wherever Newberry was playing and be on the sidelines where I learned more about sideline management. Once I was coming back from Catawba with Coach Kirkland, Red Burnette, and Hubert Setzler, and Coach asked me if I would drive. We were talking so intently about football that I got lost. It took us a long time to find our way back to Newberry. For some reason, he never asked me to drive again.

During our McColl and Newberry years, we loved to visit with Mr. Edens, my mother, Aunt Bess, Aunt Katie, and Aunt Ruth. They all meant so much to us and we loved them all dearly. Mr. Edens would always be glad to see us. I loved to hear his stories, and he loved to tell them. He would always cook country sausage and grits—wish I could find some of these sausages today. Then he would sometimes cook catfish stew and rice as only he could do it. Sometimes I would get to hunt quail with his dogs. Often I would find 10 to 12 coveys of quail in the "Hills" where Mr. Edens had planted lespedeza and bicolor patches to feed them. He would always want to hear about every dog point and every shot I took. Edith's brother Curt had a wagon built with air tires so his dad could still hunt. They had an old, gray mule and a driver who worked on the farm. The mule wouldn't bolt when the shooting began. What a great arrangement! It was said that Shorty and the mule could find a covey better than the dogs on occasion.

When we went to visit my aunts, they usually had something for the children; they often made dresses for Kim. One thing we could always count on was great meals. They could cook vegetables, meats, and desserts better than any I have ever tasted. If they knew we were coming, Aunt Ruth would always bake one of her pound cakes, and Aunt Katie would bake a sweet potato pie for "her boy."

After basketball season, I again had track and we progressed somewhat. As before, it served mostly as a conditioning program for our football players. We were going to be a good football team in the fall of 1959. However, things changed for me again.

During the spring, Van Newman, my brother-in-law, came by Newberry one day and missed me, but he left word for me to call him. When I called, he told me that he had run into Coach H.B. Rhame, the athletic director for the District I schools in Columbia. It seemed that Buddy Hodge, the football coach at Eau Claire High School, was resigning to return to Sumter and enter business with his brother. Mr. Rhame told Van to tell me to get in contact with him if I was interested in the job. I did and from there a series of weird events came together.

Edith's sister, Helen, had once coached the girls' basketball team at University High School where Mr. A.R. Hafner was the assistant principal. Mr. Hafner knew that Helen grew up on a farm full of quail, and he and Mr. Rhame loved to hunt quail. Ed Zobel, for whom I had worked the previous two summers, was president of the "Green Backer Club," the Eau Claire booster club. The "deck was stacked." Ed met with us, and we met with Mr. Hafner, who remembered my Newberry football team had barely lost to Eau Claire the previous year, even though Newberry was a lower classification school. He offered me the athletic director, head football coach, and physical education teacher position for $5100.

Newberry was paying me $4300 at the time. I had really worked very hard to build up the football program at Newberry, and I knew we would have a very good team in 1959. Eau Claire had never had a winning season in the nine years of its existence. I, of course, had told my principal and the chairman of the School Board at Newberry of my contact with Eau Claire. I asked what my future in terms of salary, teaching loads, number of assistants, and budget for football looked like. The response was, "We don't want you to leave, but we are spending all we can on athletics at Newberry High School right now."

Once again, I was faced with a difficult choice—stay at Newberry where the fall football team looked very good, or move on to Eau Claire, which had never had a winning season. Van's advice was that if I expected to reach my goals in coaching, he felt Eau Claire in Columbia, the capital and largest city in South Carolina, with news coverage in the two local newspapers—"The State" and "The Columbia Record"—would help me get there quicker. All things considered, we decided to go to Eau Claire.

6 AT EAU CLAIRE HIGH SCHOOL

Eau Claire High School is located in the Eau Claire section of Columbia, the capital and largest city in South Carolina right in the middle of the state. Unlike when we moved to McColl and Newberry, we were familiar with Columbia. I had lived there and attended USC four or five months back in 1949, and Edith had attended and graduated from Columbia College. And, we had lived there together during our two years at Fort Jackson. We were excited about moving there.

Our First House

With a salary increase as a result of moving from Newberry to Eau Claire, Edith and I decided we could afford to build our first house. We decided on a new development, "Northwood Hills," in the Eau Claire section of Columbia not far from the school. One of my football player's (Billy Ward) daddy worked with E.D. Sauls, who at that time was building a lot of homes in Columbia, and he assisted us in this endeavor. Our home was a three-bedroom, old brick, one-story house trimmed in "Dallas Green." We were so excited; we could hardly wait for our first home to be completed.

We stayed in Newberry until our new house was completed and moved into 15 Glenlea Drive around the middle of August. The children, Artie and Kim, were about as excited as we were. New neighbors who had kids about their age were the Murphys (Kim's best friend Cindy), the Rollinses, the Lucases, the Lingles, and the Ballews (Artie's friends James and Mark). Our house was on a steep hill falling away from the house in the front, so it was a daring feat for Artie and the boys to go downhill on a skateboard (there were many falls). Artie and James and Mike Murphy loved building forts behind our house in the woods. One day our friends "Frog" and Deanie Weldon were visiting and sitting in our family room looking out the back. Frog jumped up and yelled at Edith (I was not there) that she better run out back because Artie had a hatchet after Kim (who probably had Cindy with her and was bothering the boys). Edith, who is famous for her low-key demeanor, walked slowly to the door and calmly told Artie to put the hatchet down. He did, and she calmly returned to her seat, much to Frog and Deanie's surprise.

Aunts Bess, Katie, and Ruth gave us advice, helped with curtains, and gave us some shrubbery for our yard. They were about as happy with our move to our new house as we were. Edith was happy to be coming back near Columbia College. Being Methodists, we joined College Place Methodist Church, which is adjacent to the Columbia College campus. As in Newberry, we became involved with the Methodist Youth Fellowship.

That First Summer

During the summer between Newberry and Eau Claire, I continued to work on my master's degree at USC and to work with Ed Zobel. One of my classes was an English vocabulary class taught by the famous author and long-time USC English professor and head of the English Department, Havilah Babcock. He wrote such books as "My Health is Better in November," "Jaybirds go to Hell on Friday," and "I Don't Want to Shoot an Elephant." He also wrote many essays and short stories that were published in newspapers and hunting magazines. And, he wrote the textbook used in our class—"I Want a Word." His classes always filled up quickly, and this class was filled when I tried to sign up for it; but I told him I was a quail hunter and he let me in. This class was one of the most interesting I ever took. We usually had about 300 words a day to learn. He would give us a test each day by saying, "I want a word that means [fill in the definition]," and we had to give the word. He sat up on a desk above everybody's head, always with a cigarette dangling from his lips with ashes falling all over his suit. I sat right in front of him, and often he would come to class and say to me, "Mr. Baker, pass this around and have everybody look at it." It would usually be a check from "Sports Afield" or some other hunting magazine for an article he had written. The check would usually be around $5000, about the same as my annual salary at the time. He would say, "That check was the result of insomnia; I couldn't sleep one night and got up and wrote an article for them." He was always telling us hunting stories by saying, "Bernard and I killed 30 birds last week." [Bernard Baruch was a well-known American high-ranking diplomat.] Or, he would say, "Winston [Winston Churchill] shot birds with me last month." Or, "Matt Dillon is coming down this week; he may never miss a shot on

"Gunsmoke," but he can't shoot or kill as many birds as I can."

One day a television filming group interrupted our class to ask for two students to act as brother and sister in a film advertising a local savings and loan association. The boy had to have a coat, but none of us had one. Dr. Babcock offered me his coat because he thought it would fit me, which it did. Thus, I was the "brother" in the tv ad. Another time, I missed a class. He asked me the next morning where I was the day before. I told him we were building a new home in Eau Claire, and I had to go mark the trees we did not want them to cut in our yard. He said, "Mr. Baker, I have been teaching a long time and as you can imagine I've heard every excuse; but this is the first time I've ever heard that excuse—congratulations!" Dr. Babcock would rank among the top three or four professors I ever had.

Another course I took was "International Relations." We had to read Russian, Chinese, and several magazines. Dr. Ochengy was referred to by the students as "Dirty John." Almost every day, he would have partially eaten sandwiches in his various pockets and would invariably pull one out and finish it in front of the class. He was brilliant and often the local television news reporters would interview him about current world situations. I enjoyed him and his class very much.

The First Year

People in the coaching profession had warned me that Mr. Hafner, the Eau Claire principal, was an eccentric, old bachelor, who would not spend much money on athletics. One good break for me was that Frank Singleton, whom I had known since my childhood days in Sumter, was already teaching nearby at Heyward Gibbes Junior High School. Additionally, Paul Stephens, a former star lineman at USC and former football coach at Columbia High School, came to Eau Claire as assistant principal the same time I did. Between us Mr. Hafner became our strong supporter. They allowed me to hire two new assistants. Steve Robertson, who had agreed to join me at Newberry High School, would come. And, I persuaded George "Buddy" Sasser, a former University of North Carolina quarterback who was completing his master's at USC, to be my No. 1 assistant. Cy Havird was already there as "B" team football coach, head basketball coach, and baseball coach.

One thing I remembered about Eau Claire teams was that they had the plainest uniforms I had ever seen. They wore green stockings, green pants, and solid green jerseys with plain white helmets. When we scouted them at Newberry, we thought they looked like grasshoppers, so I was determined to do something to "dress up" the uniforms. I had a friend from McColl, Freeman Sligh, who was a commercial painter in Columbia, and he wanted to help. This was before helmet decals of any size. I knew the shamrock emblem was a three-leaf clover, so I asked Freeman to paint a "shamrock" on both sides of our white helmets. He did a great job and we had the neatest-looking helmet decals in the state. We were allowed to buy new green and white jerseys and one nice set of white, game pants that would go with either jersey. Coach Kirkland had impressed on me the vital importance of having good shoes that fit, the best head gear we could buy, and the best shoulder pads.

I was very excited about my first season at Eau Claire. I had coached against them while I was at Newberry, and I knew they had some great players. Nevertheless, I still sought some more players. The Halford twins were Jake (6 ft 2 inches, 175 lb), who played football, and Jack (6 ft 7 inches, 220 lb), who played basketball and was in the band. Jack needed the half credit in band in order to graduate; I needed Jack to play football. I first, after lengthy assurances, got Mrs. Halford to agree to let Jack play football; and then I got Band Director Tom Isbell to let Jack play. Jack was a good player, and Tom became a life-long friend. Incidentally, there was another set of twins on the team—Billy and Paul Lomas. They were identical twins and both were halfbacks. When they lined up with one on each side of the quarterback, the defense must have thought they were seeing double!

Football practice began after the summer coaches' clinic and the North-South all-star game. Our players were eager to go but were not in very good physical condition, so we had our work cut out for us. There was a steep bank about 20 to 25 yards up at a 45° angle. We started pushing them on fundamentals and ended every day with sprints up the bank. Even today when the Eau Claire bunch gets together, they still talk in reverence about "the bank"; but they are proud of the fact that they ran that bank. I think I convinced them that although running the bank was very tough, it led to winning games.

The schools in the Columbia area that were established with winning football records were Dreher, Columbia, and Brookland-Cayce. We would also play Lexington, which was very good; Newberry, which was good with the players I had built on; Bishopville and Olympia, which were always tough; plus Aiken, Winnsboro, and Camden. Our season ended at 5-4-1, the first winning season in the school's ten-year history.

During the spring, I was the track coach, and we required all football players who weren't playing baseball to come out for track so we could improve their speed, quickness, and strength. During my first year as track coach, we had a very weak team. I let Melecue Metts, the track coach at Orangeburg High, talk me into scheduling a tri-meet at our city track (one of the best in the state) with Orangeburg and Beaufort High (the previous year's state champ). Orangeburg was loaded. The meet was a great one for Orangeburg and Beaufort! The final score was Orangeburg 85, Beaufort

84, and Eau Claire 13. I was so embarrassed and had my head down walking off the field. George Martin from Olympia High (we all helped each other among the city schools as judges and timers) walked up to me, put his arm around my shoulders, and said very seriously, "Art, tell me, do you coach your runners to run in the back of the pack?" That day really embarrassed me. The shamrocks could do better than that. It inspired me and our players, and we did get better, doing well in the rest of our state meets.

Buddy Sasser had made a wonderful contribution to our program as a first-year coach, but the football coach at Conway High School in eastern South Carolina near the coast convinced Buddy to "come home" to Conway and eventually become the head coach after a year or two. He moved and became a very successful coach at Conway before moving on to become an assistant coach at Wofford College and Appalachian State University and later head coach at Wofford and at East Tennessee State University. We have remained good friends through the years and spent many wonderful days hunting together in and near Conway. His wife Sara Jean always reminded me of Edith.

After Buddy left, I decided to put greater emphasis on our "B" team and youth program. I asked Frank Singleton to become the head coach of our "B" program (seventh, eight, and ninth grades). Frank taught science and physical education at Heyward Gibbes Junior High School and was therefore able to observe each boy in our junior-high system and recruit them for football.

Coach Cy Havird also left Eau Claire High that year. One funny incident happened while he was the baseball coach. We had a baseball game versus A.C. Flora High School. Jim Pinkerton, the Flora coach, came over after he and Cy were "having words" prior to the game. Since I was the athletic director, he sent for me and Paul Stephens, the assistant principal. The problem was that the foul lines were really crooked. I asked Cy why the lines were so crooked. He said he sent two students to line off the fields, and he guessed they lost their string. I had to laugh; a roll of string would have cost ten cents.

I was left with two coaching vacancies, but I had to find coaches who could also teach the subjects Mr. Hafner needed to be taught. I offered the varsity backfield coaching position to Steve Satterfield, a former quarterback at USC who was the backfield coach at Sumter at the time. He felt he would be the next head coach at Sumter and opted to stay there. However, he asked me to interview and consider his younger brother Jimmy, who was graduating from USC and had been part of the football team. I met with Jimmy and, even though he hadn't played a lot at USC, he was quite knowledgeable about football and eager to be a part of our program. His major was English, and the vacant teaching position at Eau

Claire was English. To consider him for the teaching position, Mr. Hafner attended one of his practice-teaching classes at Columbia High School. Jimmy was tall and skinny then and wore horn-rim glasses; he looked like a "nerd." Mr. Hafner thought he taught okay, but said his voice was "too high." Nevertheless, we hired him and he made an excellent coach, later becoming head coach at Furman and winning a national title there. He married his high school sweetheart from Lancaster in the fall, much to the displeasure of her father, but after a few years he and Jimmy made up and were real close.

The other coaching vacancy allowed me to hire Leonard Shealy, who had played baseball at Clemson and was already a shop teacher at Eau Claire. He wanted to coach football, and I convinced him to join Frank Singleton as a "B" team coach. Leonard also succeeded Cy as our baseball coach.

We came up with a summer workout program, printed it up, and gave it to our players. We had the seniors lead the program, and we would call the ones missing to encourage them. One day I called one of our players, Mike Moore, who later coached at Irmo High School, and was really getting on him for missing a workout. I didn't know they had two phones—not common at that time—so when I paused to catch my breath, Mrs. Moore came on the extension and said very calmly, "Coach Baker, Mike didn't come to your workout because I've had him doing some work for me around the house."

Jimmy Satterfield still laughs at how I changed my voice to say, "Oh Mrs. Moore, that's perfectly alright as long as you had him working." The players responded to the program well, with most of them showing up for the workouts. During the coaches' clinic in August, several coaches from outside Columba asked to ride out and watch. This was the beginning of our great year in 1960.

The Second Year

The second year at Eau Claire, we had most of our team returning— Thomas Ray at quarterback, who later started two years at quarterback for Clemson; Billy Ward at fullback, who later started three years at fullback for Clemson; and Buddy Robinson at offensive and defensive tackle, who later played at Clemson for four years. Probably the most talked-about game we played that year was the first game of the season against Brookland-Cayce. We were picked to lose by 30 points, mainly because of their All-America running back, Mike Derrick. However, we beat them 30-6 and thereby jumpstarted our 10-1 season. We were a "well-oiled" machine, losing only the last game to North Augusta and Coach Cally Gault 15-19. Cally was another wonderful friend from my P.C. days. We thought we had the game won when we thought Butch Williams had caught a low pass around their two-yard line with about a minute and a half left in the game. However, the officials ruled the pass incomplete. We almost had a riot after that game when some of our disappointed fans followed my lead in charging the officials after the game. Actually, it taught me a lesson, and I tried to do better after that.

It was a great year for us and brought great coverage to Eau Claire. The players were not only good, but they played like the gentlemen they were. At mid-season, we installed a wing-T offense, which gave us a great attack. That winter I was asked to lecture at several clinics. My topic was "Motivation Shamrock Style." Steve Robertson saw the movie "Hitari," where a rhino attacked a truck with John Wayne driving and almost tore the truck up. With Steve's suggestions we initiated the "Rhino Club." We had special jerseys and put them on the players when they earned them on the field. We even stopped a "Sportsarama" game to put one on Bobby Cole. [The Sportsarama game was a preseason event where eight area teams played one quarter each. There was always a packed house, and our cheerleaders usually won the spirit award.] We gave them tee shirts to wear at school. Soon the Rhino tradition became a known factor all over the Midlands area. The following summer I was fortunate to be named a head coach of the annual "North-South game" played in Columbia. I coached the North team with Coach Willy Varner. We lost the game 0-7.

We made great strides too this year with our "B" team. Frank and Leonard made a great coaching team and began several years of undefeated "B" team seasons. We had over 100 seventh, eighth, and ninth graders playing. Frank and Leonard used our offense, defense, and terminology. I asked them to limit the offense to four running plays and three passing plays and to have just one defense, while really emphasizing the fundamentals. They were great motivators, and our "B" team always had great enthusiasm. One great moment each day was when the "B" team left their practice field below ours. The entire "B" team would stop on the sideline of our field where the varsity was practicing and give a long cheer "Go-oo-oъ Shamrocks!" It would give me chill bumps. Then they would go in. I insisted that they practice only one and one-half hours—no more. I also asked Frank and Leonard to play every player in every game. They would usually win the game in four quarters and then, by prearrangement with the opposing coach, play a "fifth quarter" so everyone could play. We never ran a player off and hardly ever had one quit. It was the "meat" of our success at Eau Claire.

Frank Singleton's supplement for coaching was $350. He taught physical education at Heyward Gibbes Junior High and often played with the students, sometimes "swapping licks" on the shoulder. [He had played football and boxed at USC.] One day he was swapping licks with some students when a 17-year-old ninth grader decided he would swap. He meant to hit Frank on the shoulder, but the lick slipped off Frank's shoulder into his chin. Frank didn't even know the lick was coming and reacted by punching the over-grown junior high student, knocking him several feet on his back side and knocking out four of his teeth. The parents complained the dental bill would be $350. Frank lost his whole supplement!

Mr. James Webb, the Director of the S.C. Wildlife Commission and father of Smokey and Jimmy Webb, would every year have his game wardens and other Eau Claire parents barbecue several hogs and have a huge benefit meal to help supplement the athletic budget. The "Green Backer" club, our support group, sponsored the banquet. After our outstanding 1960 season, they surprised me at the banquet and announced they were presenting me with a shot gun. I unwrapped the package, and it was a very old, badly damaged gun that was held together by black plumber's tape. After everyone had a good laugh (they all knew what was happening), they presented me with a beautiful Browning Gold Finger, 12-gauge shotgun. It was the first gun I actually owned. Mr. Edens had always let me use his Remington 12-gauge.

Around this time, Aunt Katie began to bake me a sweet potato pie every time we won a ballgame. What an incentive that was because her sweet potato pies were "out of this world." If she knew I was coming to see them, she would also have Jell-O and custard with one of Aunt Ruth's pound cakes. Aunt Bess and those would occasionally keep Artie and Kim for Edith and me to slip away to the mountains for a weekend. These were wonderful "change ups," but Edith would cry when we left the children and cry when we got back. But we had a wonderful time together and enjoyed a little time to ourselves.

The Remaining Years

After several years at Eau Claire, as physical education teachers we began to participate in the President's Council on Physical Fitness program. Through this program, we administered fitness tests to hundreds of boys. We expanded it some by adding tests in the 40-yard dash, long jump, vertical jump and others that would indicate the skills used in football. Through these tests, we were able to identify a number of football prospects who might otherwise have gone unnoticed.

Through this program, I got to know former USC head football coach Warren Giese, who had become dean of the College of Physical Education there. USC physical education majors were required to do practice teaching in area schools. Dr. Guise began to send the students who were also interested in coaching to Eau Claire for their practice teaching. One he sent was Dan Reeves, who, after starring at USC, went on to play for the Dallas Cowboys, and later to coach for the Cowboys, Denver Broncos, New York Giants, and Atlanta Falcons. But the one Dr. Guise sent who was most important to me was a skinny young man from North Augusta, South Carolina, who was eager to become a teacher. His name was Dick Sheridan. I was so impressed with him as a person and because of his willingness to work so hard; he was just a real solid citizen. I felt that with Steve Robertson and Jimmy Satterfield on board, if I could convince Dick to join us, we would have a great staff. The only problem was that he taught only physical education, and I was the physical education teacher. However, Mr. Hafner needed a history teacher. Well, I was a history major, so Mr. Hafner and I worked out a deal. Dick would teach physical education and I would teach history. Little did I know that Dick and Jimmy would become college head coaches and play for bowl games and national championships.

During our last three years at Eau Claire, we lost some games but averaged around eight wins a season. One year we ended the season tied for No. 1 with Lancaster, according to "The State Newspaper." Another time in 1963, we beat undefeated North Charleston in Charleston 34-7 for the Lower State Championship. The next week we were playing Chester for the state championship. They had a big, 250-lb fullback and a great option quarterback. We had a quick team and could throw and run well. The game was scheduled for Friday, but on Friday the worst storm of the year came through Columbia—15° and about 25 mph winds. Mr. Hafner let me make the decision with Paul Stephens as to whether or not to play that night. I was to report to Charlotte on Saturday to be one of the coaches for the South Carolina Shrine team. I hope I didn't let that influence my decision, but I decided we would play on Friday night. The weather and Chester's strong ground game beat us 13-7. Our passing game was nonexistent, and Chester put their players all up on the line of scrimmage. My old friend "Ears" Wilson was the coach at Chester. We later played Winnsboro when they were on a 25-0 winning record and beat them 7-0. We also had some great wins over Dreher, A.C. Flora, North Augusta, Camden, and Greenwood.

But the game that "sticks in my craw" more than any other was in 1964 when we played Camden in Camden during the regular season. At the time we were ranked No. 1 in the state, and they were ranked No. 2 and were unscored on. I've never coached a game that was more "on the line." There was lots of hype in the newspapers and on television and radio as well as in the streets. We had a wonderful offense and defense. It was a classic matchup. When we got to the field, the stands were packed. People were "wall to wall" around the field right up to the sidelines; others were sitting in every available space on top of the concrete-block wall around the stadium; others were sitting in tree limbs and on top of busses outside the stadium. I could not believe what I was seeing; there was "electricity" everywhere.

We received the opening kickoff and drove to Camden's four-yard line. I did not do a good job of calling plays. We had a great fullback, Johnny Johnson, who was absolutely the toughest player I ever coached. We called him "John Henry"; he was "all business." We had a great tailback in Ray Wieble who won the state 100-yard dash that year in 9.8 seconds, a record at that time. Our other back was Sam Haskell, who was an average back but could block and catch passes well. I ran John on the first play for two yards. Wieble ran twice for no gain. On fourth down, I ran Sam Haskell on a counter, banking on fooling them—no gain. We were stopped, and it gave Camden the spark they needed. They scored later and beat us 7-0. In the fourth quarter, Ray Wieble did score a touchdown on a 60-yard run, but we were called for a clip on a questionable call, negating the touchdown.

Camden's quarterback was Billy "Pecan" Ammons, whom I would later coach at Clemson. He scored the game's only touchdown. Art Hudson, my cousin Mary Baker's son, was a 6 ft 5 inch, 235 lb tackle for Camden, who would later play at North Carolina State University. My Aunt Katie was his aunt too, so after the game his dad, Ben Hudson, came up to me and could hardly hold back his joy. He told me, "Oh, oh, this time we get the sweet potato pie!" That was nearly as disappointing as losing the game. The Camden game, I think, would rank as one of the all-time best games in South Carolina high school football.

The Camden team has had several reunions (they went on to win the state championship) since then, and often the newspapers will call me for a quote. Some years ago, I was saddened to learn that my tough fullback, "John Henry" Johnson had cancer and was in Richland Memorial Hospital on his death bed. I went to see him one day and he looked me in the eye and said, "Coach, if you had given me the ball on all four downs at Camden in 1964, we would have won the game." With tears in my eyes, I hugged him and said, "John Henry, you are absolutely right." Till this day I still "kick myself" for not having done just that.

Without meaning to brag, I felt certain we had the best football program anywhere. Steve Robertson, Jimmy Satterfield, Dick Sheridan, Buddy Sasser, Leonard Shealy, and Frank Singleton all contributed greatly, but I had great confidence in myself and felt so sure I knew what I was doing. Frankly, we were way ahead of our times. We "computerized" scouting (long-handed, that is) and always knew what our opponents were going to do, and we worked so hard on fundamentals and techniques that no one ever "out fundamentalled" us. I believed in Vince Lombardi's philosophy that in order to run a play successfully in a game, you had to run it 500 times correctly in practice.

Miscellany

Beginning with our first season at Eau Claire, I had a daily prayer and always had a spiritual speaker before the game and a prayer after the game. Rev. Eben Taylor of College Place Methodist Church was our favorite speaker; he was so good. His talks were always an inspiration to each of us. One day someone asked one of our players how we would do. He replied, "I don't know but it looks like all of us will go to heaven." I thought, "What a compliment!"

In a similar vein, one day in 1962 I ran into my boyhood friend, Bobby Richardson, at a meeting in Columbia where he was speaking. He told me about the Fellowship of Christian Athletes (FCA), which was founded in 1954. He encouraged me to send several of our players to an FCA camp in Black Mountain, North Carolina. It cost about $150, a sizable amount back then. I raised enough money from Sunday School classes, civic clubs, and individuals to send three players—John Henry Johnson, "Beetle" Cauble, and Sam Haskell—to the camp. It had a great impact on them and, when they returned, on our team. So we established an FCA chapter at Eau Claire.

During the years, I umpired little league and pony league baseball games, which were played in Brookland-Cayce or Earlwood Park. The games didn't pay that much—$6 to $8—but in those days a few extra bucks came in handy. It was not an easy job; the coaches and parents hardly ever agreed with my calls. One day at Brookland-Cayce, I called a third strike on a little fellow for the third out of the inning. It was hot and I was leaning on the backstop between innings when I heard this lady using the worst language I had ever heard from a lady. I looked to see who she was talking to and she said, "I'm talking to you; you know that last strike you called on my son was not a strike!" She was mad.

Each summer at Eau Claire, the coaching staff would have a three- or four-day seminar planning our coming season. We covered everything from A to Z, and it paid off because we were all on the same page. Our cameramen, Charlie Montieth, whose son Rock played fullback-defensive back; and Vernon Williams, whose son played tight end-defensive end and would later star for USC; plus Dr. Gene Payne, our team doctor who allowed us to use his Lake Murray cabin so we would stay overnight and have 10 to 15 hours a day to work, were also involved. They also taught us to water ski, and we fished some too. Charlie and Vernon would usually cook for us; we ate well.

Steve Robertson lived in a room in the home of a wonderful lady, "Mama Butler," who ran a hamburger café across Monticello Road from

Eau Claire High. She fixed the best hamburgers I have ever eaten. She would feed our team the pre-game meal, and she loved all the coaches and players. She was great! We would often go over to Steve's room to look at film at night, and would you believe she would usually serve us cake and coffee. Her husband was president of the Eau Claire Exchange Club, and they were among the Shamrocks' strongest supporters.

Each year I coached at Eau Claire, Mr. Hafner made my teaching schedule in the fall and winter so that I got out of school after the 11:00 class. Each Thursday, we would eat lunch, change into our hunting clothes, and leave for Dalzell to hunt quail on Mr. Edens' farm. He had some prime quail territory up above a pond he had built. Called "the Hills," it comprised some 500 acres of pines, broom straw, lespedeza, and bicolor patches. It was nothing for us to find ten coveys in one afternoon. Sometimes Mr. Rhame, the athletic director for the District 1 schools in Columbia (who was instrumental in my getting the job at Eau Claire), would go with us. Sometimes we would use their dogs; sometimes, Mr. Edens' dogs. When we left school, Mrs. Dot Moffat, the school secretary, would ask Mr. Hafner what she should say if the Central Office called him. "Tell them I've gone to a meeting," Mr. Hafner would reply.

"What if they ask what kind of meeting?" she would ask.

"Tell them we've gone to a wild-life meeting," he would respond.

Mr. Hafner shot a double-barrel, 12-gauge gun. If he missed several shots, he would always blame it on his shells and switch from #8 to either #7½ or "brush loads."

We had so many outstanding young people at Eau Claire High. It would be hard to pick out individuals, but Dickie Walters was a little fellow about 5 ft 7 inches, 135 lb, but he was one tough individual. Though he never started on offense or defense, he was our "sparkplug." It never got too tough for him, and he never, ever gave up, no matter what the score was. If we had told him he had to run through a brick wall in order for us to win, he would have found a way to do it even if it took all day. Dickie's older brother, Don, played defensive back for us and was also tough. Dickie was always on the front row when I talked to the team, and he made me feel good, for he "hung on my every word." He was very strong in his religious faith, too. One day he and one of the non-playing Eau Claire students who was a bully got into an argument on the bus going home. They decided to fight when they got off the bus. Dickie got off the bus with his brother Don, and Don heard his brother pray, "Lord, I love you and your son Jesus Christ, and I pray that you will let me beat the hell out of that S.O.B."

Dickie and Don had a great mother and father. She was about five feet tall and 100 lb. She often had to get on Dickie for various things he had done wrong. He would usually grab her in a bear hug and say, "Mama, you are my horse and if you never win a race, I'll always love you." After graduation Dickie joined the Marines and fought in Viet Nam where, unfortunately, he lost his life. Over 40 years later the "Eau Claire Bunch" presented his mother with a nice green, orange, and white plaque in his memory.

Two More Children

Our third and fourth children were both born at Providence Hospital in Columbia while we were at Eau Claire High. Hugh Ryan Baker was born February 5, 1963, in the middle of the night. I was officiating basketball games during this period to make extra money, and I had officiated a game the night before. Edith had arranged with our neighbor Chris Murphy to come over and stay with Artie and Kim if I had to take her to the hospital during the night. When Edith began her labor pains, we called Chris and she came right over. As I was rushing Edith to the hospital, she realized there was no milk and bread for breakfast; she made me stop at a convenience store to purchase these items for breakfast. I just knew she was going to have that baby in the car! In those days, dads still had very little to do with the birthing process. I was told to wait in the waiting room for expectant fathers—a harrowing experience. There were all types of fathers-to-be there. Some said nothing; others talked all the time. Some were stoic; others were near panic. I was somewhere in between all of them. I drove Artie and Kim to the hospital several times, and Edith waved to them from her window. We were all crying. Artie and Kim were mostly concerned about getting mommy (and brother) home.

Aunt Bess and Aunt Katie had helped set up Hugh Ryan's nursery, and the Eau Claire ladies had had several showers, so he was fixed up with clothes. Artie and Kim were "taken" with having a baby brother after seven years with the house and attention to themselves. Sometimes they would even "help" me or Edith change diapers. That was never my favorite chore. Diapers for Artie, Kim, and Ryan, were the cloth variety, requiring that they be "cleaned" prior to laundering them. Edith was a stickler for hanging them to dry in the sunshine and fresh air. One thing that I really enjoyed doing with all our children was rocking them to sleep at night. Sometimes I would feed them Gerber's baby food; it took a strong stomach to do that chore.

We hardly had the novelty of having a new baby in the home wear off when Edith woke me up early one morning throwing up. When she came out of the bathroom, I asked if she thought she had a virus. She replied, "I'm as pregnant as a jaybird!" Actually, we never planned any of our children; the Lord planned them for us. Curtis Kyle Baker was born November 27, 1964, just before we accepted the Clemson job. Edith's labor pains began in the afternoon, and I took her again to Providence Hospital. Our football season was over, and I was already into basketball officiating at the time. The nurses checked her into a room and came back to tell me I could go eat some supper because she would not deliver for quite some time. I went and got a hamburger, but when I got back she was already in the delivery room. [I guess I didn't remember my lesson from when Artie and Kim were born.] The doctor allowed me to stand outside the door to the delivery room, rather than wait in the expectant fathers' waiting room. I could hear all the conversations going on around the delivery room table. Edith sounded as if she were carrying on a conversation at a dinner party. I heard the doctor say, "Well, you've got another boy." We never knew before birth what gender they would be; we just prayed for a good delivery and a healthy mother and child. I also heard Edith giving instructions to the nurses as to how to take pictures of Curtis, the doctor, and her. She had it all planned.

Hugh Ryan was named for my life-long friend Hugh "Tiger" McLauren, with whom I spent so much time in their home when we were growing up in Sumter. I even stayed in their house the night before my wedding. Ryan's middle name came in honor of my beloved Aunt Katie Ryan, who influenced my life so much. Curtis was named for Edith's dad, Henry Curtis Edens. He too was a great influence and encourager to me in my life. I doubt if I would have graduated from college had it not been for the help and encouragement he gave me. Most of all, he allowed me to "court" and marry his baby daughter and helped us "get on our feet." I used to love hearing him tell all his stories when we would visit him. We came up with Kyle for a middle name and started calling him Kyle, which we both liked. It was not a family name, just one we liked. The first months of Kyle's life we would often visit Mr. Edens in Dalzell where he lived by himself. He would (I realized later) purposely say, "Now what is that baby's name—Beyle or Lyle?" We finally realized he wanted us to call Kyle, Curtis. So from that day, when Curtis was three or four months old, Kyle became Curtis. One day some time later while we were living in Clemson, Ryan asked his mother, "What happened to Kyle?"

The Six a.m. Call

With the "B" team (grades 7, 8, and 9), "JV" team (grade 10), and the varsity team going great guns, and with the best coaching staff in the state in place, as a staff we began to attend different clinics and coaching meetings at other schools and in other states. We planned to attend a clinic put on by Coach Bobby Dodd and his staff at Georgia Tech. We were to leave school on a Tuesday in February 1965.

On the previous Thursday morning about 6:00, the phone rang, awakening us. I answered, and a voice that most everybody in South Carolina—at least most sports fans—would recognize, that of Coach Frank Howard from Clemson University, was on the other end. I instantly thought he wanted to talk to me about some of our prospects. They had already signed a number of players from past years. Because we had one of the top high-school programs in the state, I thought maybe he was calling about some technical problem or how we taught tackling. Instead, he said, "Al, what I'm calling about is that I need a freshman coach—do you want the job?"

I was flabbergasted and said, "Well, first of all my name is Art."

He said, "Hell, I know that; I just don't have my glasses on."

Then, I said, "Well Coach, I have a great job here at Eau Claire, but I would like to bring my wife up there and talk to you about the job."

He said, "Well hell, I ain't hiring your wife," but continued after a slight pause, "Well, bring her up here and we will talk."

Edith and I drove up there when I got out of school the next day. Coach Howard and Mrs. Anna, his wife, took us to lunch at the "Clemson House." Mrs. Anna ordered a fruit plate but ate only a few bites. Coach Howard and Edith and I were almost finished with our meals when Coach Howard looked at Edith and said, "Honey, do you like fruit?"

She said, "Yes."

He said, "Well, here, lets you and me "half-up" Anna's plate," and he scraped off half in her plate and half in his.

He eventually offered me the job of freshman football coach at $7500. [I was making $6800 at Eau Claire and was due a $700 raise for the next year.] We returned home and said nothing to anyone.

As planned the Eau Claire coaches and I went to Atlanta the next Tuesday to attend Coach Dodd's clinic. At the clinic was none other than Coach Howard. He pulled me aside and said, "Art, I can't ask you to take a job for less than you are making. I talked to the President, and we can pay you $8000." I would have taken the $7500 but was glad to get the 8K. Mr. Hafner was both disappointed I would leave but happy for my opportunity. My new job would begin in July, so I would complete my school year at Eau Claire. Mr. Hafner let me off for spring football practice, but I still had to coach track.

Our track team developed into a competitive group and we had some talent. Coach McMillan at P.C. always told us to build your track team around quarter-milers (in those days, tracks were measured in yards, not meters). We qualified a good number for the state AAAA meet in Columbia. With five events remaining in the meet (1) the medley relay 880, (2) the 880-yard run, (3) the quarter-mile (440-yard) run, (4) the 220-yard dash, and (5) the mile relay, we figured up the points and learned that in order to win the meet, we would likely have to take first place in all five events. The players thought they could do it.

(1) The medley relay 880 was a four-man relay with tenth grader Tommy Vermillion being the anchor and having to run a 440. When Tommy got the baton, he was 35 to 40 yards behind the leader. He ran it in 47.5 seconds and caught up and won the medley.

(2) The second race was the 880-yard run. Our one runner, Buery Gantt had qualified the week before in eighth place with eight being in the race. He was not a speed merchant, and I had always coached him to get out front and depend on stamina to win. He said, "Coach, I am a senior, and this is my last race. Let me run the race like I want to, and I'll win." I told him to go to it, thinking what can we lose. He laid back the first 650 yards in sixth or seventh place; then he put it on coming around the curve, ran his best 880 ever, and won the South Carolina title. So much for my coaching!

(3) The event we had to win was the 440-yard run, and we knew we had the best in the state, Harry Vermillion, Tommy's older brother. We had won the state 440 for five straight years. Harry won in 47.4 seconds with no trouble.

(4) The fourth event was the 220-yard dash, and again we felt very confident because Ray Wieble, our sprinter, had already broken the state record in the 100-yard dash in 9.8 seconds earlier in the same meet. But as can happen in sprints, he got a bad start and finished third.

(5) The mile relay was a must, and Tommy and Harry Vermillion had to come back from grilling races earlier. I didn't know if they could do it so soon after pushing themselves so hard, but they did, breaking an old state record and setting a new one.

Even though we didn't win all five events, we still had a chance to win the meet because there was still competition in the high jump. The score at that point was Greenville High 39 points and Eau Claire 38¾ points; even ¼ point would tie. We had one jumper who competed in this event. They had a winner and a second placer, but five jumpers were tied for third. However, our jumper had passed at a lower height, and neither he nor I realized they awarded the places by the number of jumps at each level. We lost the meet! That track meet was perhaps the greatest effort I can remember for any team I ever coached.

A Few Parting Remarks

In the six years we lived in Eau Claire, it was like living in a dream town. The people were wonderful; when the Shamrocks played, everybody came to the games. When we traveled to play, everybody traveled to the games; and often we had more people in the stands than the home team. One fan told me recently that he remembered driving to one of our away games leading a long line of Eau Claire fans. He had forgotten something and turned around to go back home and get it, and the whole line of Shamrocks followed him thinking he knew the way.

After we established our program, we got good coverage from the media. My good friend Bob Fulton, a well-known sports radio and television announcer, even broadcast our games in the early years. He has since told me that he loved doing the Shamrock games because of the type team we had.

Our church, College Place Methodist, was very important in our lives. In the 1960s we were a large church with 2000 members. In fact, Eau Claire was a wonderful community where almost everybody went to church. [The "other" church in the Eau Claire community was Eau Claire Baptist Church; most everybody went to either College Place Methodist or Eau Claire Baptist.] It was often said that if burglars had been active in Eau Claire in the 1960s, they could have "cleaned up" on game nights and on Sunday mornings because everybody would have been at the game or in church.

The players and students were wonderful young people. Eau Claire was a special school where all the students were made to feel special, and they were. The cheerleaders were a special group that could never do enough to support our teams. It's a joy to see them and ball players and students I taught at reunions and on the streets and at businesses in Columbia. So many of them have gone on in their chosen businesses and professions to do exceptionally well. We get together every month or two, with sometimes as many as 50 to rehash the "old days."

The staff and teachers were also very special. As a teacher myself, I attended faculty meetings; and not only were the teachers excellent at their craft, they were good people. Leila Lucas was the chorus director, and we shared many students. The band members were great supporters; we even had a couple football players who also played in the band. I enjoyed teaching physical education and history, and often played volleyball, softball, basketball, etc. with students (probably one reason my joints are in bad shape now).

Another thing I enjoyed while coaching at Eau Claire was the relationship I had with other coaches in the area. Some of us met every Sunday afternoon to play half-court basketball. They were Harry Perone, Charlie Stuart, Van Newman, Earl Dunham, Cy Szakacsi, and others. We looked forward to our "games" each Sunday; the only rule we had was "don't drive." You could be sure that after your first "drive" you wouldn't do it again, for you would surely be "marked" pretty good if you did.

I also enjoyed playing fast pitch softball. College Place Methodist had a team in the City Church League. We had a really good team; Paul Ashley was our pitcher and he was one of the best. I played centerfield and could cover the outfield really well. I bunted a lot and in those days could get down to first base as well as anyone in the league. I usually batted over .400 and sometimes hit the long ball. Every year we either played for the championship or won it except for a couple years when Paul didn't pitch for us.

As we prepared to move from Columbia to Clemson, there was one more hurdle to get over—selling my house. As this was our first house, I had no experience in selling one. However, as luck would have it, before the school year was over, a friend, Everette Taylor, called and wanted to buy our house for slightly more than we paid for it. I had used a G.I. loan to get our mortgage, and I thought it would be easy to transfer the loan to another veteran. However, we went through all kinds of problems transferring our loan, but we finally did it.

I was both sad to be leaving Eau Claire but excited about our future at Clemson and college coaching. I had always felt, or even known, that I could coach effectively in college. Coach Kirkland had prepared me, and God had included it in his plan for my life. God had blessed me with a special feeling for young people and the ability to communicate with them in a special way, and God had given me a keen sense of choosing the right people to work with and the ability to organize and utilize them for maximum results. It was now up to me to do it. I was full of confidence and couldn't wait to begin my college coaching career.

7 AT CLEMSON UNIVERSITY

Previously, I have referred herein to my wife Edith, as "Edith," which is her given name. However, when we moved to Clemson, she became known as "Edie." So to be historically accurate, from here on I will refer to her as "Edie." In the same vein, when I was growing up in Sumter, I was known as "Arthur," which is my given name. However, when I went to Presbyterian College, I became known as "Art." Whenever someone calls me "Arthur," I know they knew me from Sumter.

Our Second House

Having just sold our first house in Columbia, our first task at hand as we moved to Clemson was to obtain our second one. We had had to move out of our Eau Claire home but were fortunate to be able to rent initially a student pre-fab from a Clemson student who was away for the summer at ROTC camp. The coaches at Clemson had told me there was a "big Clemson" builder, Lewis Merck, who would build us a house for a little over cost. Edie had saved all kinds of house plans; she had a box full of plans and ideas out of magazines and newspapers, and some she had prepared herself from observations. She knew exactly how she wanted that house built—corner fireplace, bricked-in range and oven, and sewing room with a built-in sewing machine and ironing board. Every day Edie would carry the children out to the new home site to make sure Mr. Merck was doing everything according to her plan. His dad, a very nice, older gentleman, did most of the finishing work. Lewis Merck finished pretty much on time. Soon after the house was completed, he pulled me aside and said, "Coach, you've got a wonderful, beautiful wife, but she has gotten me out of custom-home building!"

About that time, we had to decide what kind of lawn to have. Bill McLellan, the assistant athletic director, told me they were going to dig up Bermuda grass around the hedges in "Death Valley" stadium; and if I wanted the sod for our lawn, I could hire the twins who worked for the athletic grounds crew to haul the sod to my house and help me put it down, which I did. That Tifton Bermuda grass made a beautiful lawn, but boy if we missed cutting it every four or five days, it would get so high and thick that it would choke the lawn mower. Not many people could say they had a lawn from "Death Valley"!

Another plight we had to deal with at this time involved our driveway. Our house was built on a sloped hill, so we had to cut a bank into the high side of the slope. The driveway was paved with asphalt; however, we were told that the bank would not hold up during heavy rains, and all that red clay would wash down on our driveway. Hence, we had to build a brick retaining wall. Because our house was "old brick," we needed to find several thousand old bricks to build the wall, which would be about six feet high at the end sloping down to 18 inches at the driveway entrance. Again, Bill McLellan to the rescue! He told me that Clemson University had demolished two, old, classroom buildings, and they had hauled the old bricks, beams, and all the trash to one location. I got permission to gather the old bricks and began to haul several hundred to the house each day. Somebody told me it would be easy to clean them for use; he lied! I got some tools and supplies to clean them and got Artie to help me. It was a slow, tedious process, but after several weeks we had at least enough clean bricks to begin the wall.

I asked around about a good brick mason, and the guys at the gas station said the best one you could get was a guy named "Melvin." They said he was the best if the fish weren't biting. He always carried his boat in the back of his pickup truck just in case the fish happened to start biting. After looking at the job to be done, Melvin agreed to do it. He worked "by the job" rather than "by the hour" because if the fish started biting, he would leave. We agreed on a price, which I thought was high, but everybody said not to worry because he would do the best job of anybody around.

First off, he would not begin the job until there were enough bricks to do the entire job; and, second, I would have to dig the trench for the foundation since he did not dig trenches. It took me 12 hours on a Saturday to dig the trench to Melvin's specifications. He would come by for several hours to work on the wall whenever the fish were not biting. Then one Saturday, I was off and Melvin said he could finish the wall Saturday if he had an assistant. I asked how much an assistant would cost, and he said $5 an hour. I'm not great at math, but I quickly figured that would cost me $50 extra. I said, "What will your assistant have to do?"

He said, "Mix cement, fill the wheelbarrow, and have it there when I need it."

I said, "Well heck, I can do that."

He said, "I don't think you can."

My pride was really stung because I felt I was in my prime physical condition, and I sure didn't have an extra $50, so I took the job. Melvin was still reluctant. It was a hot, 96° day. He showed me how to mix the cement and off we went. Melvin, I found, could mortally lay some brick, and I soon found out he wanted to show this "smart-aleck coach" he couldn't mix cement fast enough. Each time he would say, "Come on, you're holding me up!" Each time I was becoming more and more "bushed." I was about to pass out and he was yelling, "Faster." Edie either saw or sensed what was going on, and she avoided a disaster by showing up with a pitcher of lemonade and several glasses of ice. I quietly signaled "thanks" with my eyes and finally made it through the day—one of the longest days of my life. Melvin did a great job on our wall. People said his cement and brick laying were so good because he spit some of his ever-present "chew" of tobacco into the mix!

Speaking of bricks, one day while we lived in Clemson, a lady came by the house to see some of the brickwork in our kitchen. Ryan was standing in front of her as Edie showed off her fold-in ironing board. Ryan kept looking at the lady and finally said, "Mom, her breath smells bad." Thank goodness, she wasn't the wife of some bigwig at the university—at least I don't think she was.

While I was recruiting in Andrews in the mountains of North Carolina, I met a fine gentleman who was a friend of the family whose boy I was recruiting. He had formerly been in the nursery business and found we were just moving into a new home. He said, "I've got around 100 azaleas; if you want them they are in cans and you can have them." I borrowed a pickup, loaded the flowers, and planted 100 azaleas in our backyard. I bet they are still beautiful now after all these years.

Also around this time, "they" were going to fill the Keowee-Toxaway Lake, and they notified people they could go in and dig up mountain-laurel. We got some, and they turned out well.

We didn't have air conditioning in the house, but we had an attic fan that would pull the sheets off the bed. So we stayed pretty cool, at night at least. We had plenty of hardwoods and pine trees in our back yard for shade during the day.

After we had been there a few years, Edie decided we needed to remove a few trees in the back yard. I knew Jimmy Howard, Coach Howard's son, cut trees down for a fee. I contacted him about cutting down our trees. He said he would do it, but I'd have to pay a helper. I said how much; he said $50. I said, "I'll be your helper."

He shook his head and said, "Well, it's your house."

Everything went well with the first tree. We had a swing set for Curtis and Ryan in the back yard. Jimmy said on the second tree he would climb up and attach a rope and I would have to pull the rope so the tree would fall away from the house and away from the swing set. He cut while I pulled. That tree started to fall right toward me. I pulled hard, but it was still headed right for me. I panicked and took off running, only to see the tree land right in the middle of the swing set. So much for saving a few bucks!

We had great neighbors—two families of Andersons in our back and Dr. Hunter up the street. Kim's best friend, Susan Mulligan, remains so today. At age four, Curtis loved to dress up in a Batman outfit with a cape and jockey underwear. His best friend was Terry Anderson, who later became a beautiful cheerleader at Clemson. All the children played together. We had a great time living there.

We had several dogs while we lived in Clemson. First was Sam, a male beagle. He would disappear for days at a time, either chasing girl dogs or rabbits. Every time he came back after being away several days, he was all beat up like he had been in a fight. He finally went off and didn't come back. One day during the early fall practice, Edie took the children to Columbia and Dalzell to visit Mr. Edens, Aunt Bess, and others. When they came back, I was in the bed asleep and they put a little female beagle about as big as my fist on the pillow by my head. "Bonnie Blue" was a registered beagle Edie and the children bought from a kennel in Brookland-Cayce. Our lives for the next 14 years would be touched each day by Bonnie. We loved her dearly, and she was a great addition to our family. When she was about a year old, we let her out where she slept in our carport, and about 5:30 a.m. we were awakened by her howling. Edie awoke with a start and said, "Oh my, something's wrong with Bonnie!" Upon closer inspection, however, Bonnie was just chasing a rabbit. But mostly, she was a "house dog" spoiled rotten.

We lived four different places with Bonnie, and each time when we moved the neighbors asked us to leave her with them. She loved to visit all our neighbors, and too many of them had a "Bonnie plate" so she ate a lot. When she passed away, she was outside our "quarters" at The Citadel. She had been sick and lay down in the straw near our back door. I had gone to work, and Edie called me to come home, as she thought Bonnie was near death. When I got there, Edie was rubbing Bonnie's head, and Bonnie held her head up and seemed happy to see me. In a few minutes, she passed away. We always thought she stayed alive until I got there; she was that kind of dog.

As I think back, I am thankful for all the people who helped us build our new house, move in, and get settled. Certain things—the lawn, bricks, azaleas, and mountain-laurel—showed up for us "on a silver platter," thanks to the individuals involved.

Initiation!

When I first accepted the job at Clemson, Mr. Hafner allowed me to go up for Clemson's spring practice. My first day there was a wonderful, exciting day. I was a college coach and was really feeling full of myself. After practice we all went into the old dressing room in the field house. Actually, it was a regular old room with captains' chairs and hooks screwed into a board 5½ feet above the floor where we hung our clothes. There was a regular, tiled, shower room with eight or so shower heads. It was said that the Clemson staff of Bob Jones, Banks McFadden, Bob Smith, Whitey Jordan, Don Wade, and Charlie Waller had over 100 years of combined experience, so I really felt like the rookie that I was. As I entered the shower the first time feeling very naked, I got under a shower head, turned it on, and began soaping up. Coach Jones came in and said, "Boy, that's my shower." I moved to the next one, and Banks McFadden pulled the same trick. This continued with the rest of the staff until there weren't any showers left for me. So I felt very out of place waiting for second place at any shower, but those guys took a long time showering.

I thought, or at least hoped, that the "shower room experience" would complete my initiation into the staff, but it didn't. During our early staff meetings at Clemson, we usually met in a large room with a very large meeting table. When I attended my first staff meeting, I was so excited to be coaching in college at Clemson. When I got to the meeting, all the other assistant coaches were already seated. I knew the seat at the head table was for Coach Howard. The seat to his immediate right was vacant, so I thought, "Well, isn't that something? My seat is at the right hand of the head coach—what an honor!" I sat down and soon found out why my seat wasn't all that important or as big as I first thought. Coach Howard always chewed tobacco, and between my chair and his was his spittoon. Now Coach Howard didn't spit with a "stream," as many did; he "sprayed" his spit toward the spittoon! Needless to say, a good bit of his spit ended up on my khaki pants. Edie had a hard time washing the "specks" out of my pants.

Coach Howard also liked to write out the practice schedule on a large sheet that was broken up into lines representing five-minute segments for practice. Everybody in coaching was using this type of practice scheduling at that time. A lot of other staffs were allowed to fill in the slots according to the assistant coaches' needs, but Coach Howard liked to fill in every slot himself. He would sometimes ask an assistant coach what he wanted, but mostly he wrote what he wanted each coach's group to do. He always had several pencils sharpened and ready to go. Every day, after some of the schedule had been done, one of us would notice where we needed to change something because two groups might be scheduled at the same area or some such problem. Coach Howard would look at me and say, "Now Art, that's why you should always use a pencil," whereupon he would erase the area on the sheet to be changed. At the end of the meeting, he would have a lot of eraser rubber on the sheet, and he would look at me and brush every speck into my lap.

An Adventure Every Day

During the five years I coached at Clemson, working with Coach Howard was like an adventure every day! One incident happened in the same shower room mentioned above. One day after practice, Coach Howard was talking to defensive coordinator Bob Smith about a particular defensive stunt and how he wanted it changed. In the steam that was on the tile shower, he drew the offense and defense and the stunt he wanted changed. Then he said, "Hell, that's not what I want" and he tried to rub it off to make a change, not realizing that the steam was now gone.

Another time we were sitting in the dressing room before going out for practice. We were playing North Carolina next. They had a favorite pass they liked to throw, called "curl and flat," and they had had great success with that route in games prior to ours. Coach Howard told Banks McFadden, our secondary coach who ran the scout team, "Mac, make sure you run that route a lot in practice today. Our secondary's got to learn how to cover that pass."

McFadden said, "Oh yes sir," and he held up the card for Coach Howard to see, and said, "We plan to run it at least three out of every four times during practice."

Coach Howard responded, "Oh hell Mac, that's not enough; run it at least every other play."

Coach Howard got a lot of calls from alumni and boosters about prospective players. One day a booster called him and said he had a prospect who was fast, strong, and a great competitor. Coach Howard said, "What's his size?"

The booster replied, "Well Coach, he is 5 ft 9 inches, but his granddaddy is 6 ft 4 inches and his uncle is 6 ft 3 inches. I know he'll grow up some when he gets on that good training-table food."

Coach Howard said, "Well I'm not recruiting him for breeding purposes."

After the first year, we discovered we had signed three players too many. You could sign 50 new players, and we had signed 53. We were trying to figure out what to do when Bill McLellan (the assistant athletic director) reported that we would be fined $2000 for this oversight. Coach Howard said, "Heck, I'll do that every year. Three extra players are worth $2000."

One day Coach Howard and I were talking to our trainer, Fred Hoover, about a player whose back was bothering him. Coach said, "Boys, sometimes you have to just use your head." He said when he was hired as offensive line coach he was told he would also be the "trainer" (in those days we didn't have trainers). He had a big farm boy from lower South Carolina who was a key player. He came to Coach Howard one day saying he didn't see how he could play against South Carolina because "his back was killing him." Coach Howard said, "Listen, I've got some miracle medicine. Get up on that table and I'll take care of you in a minute." He called over a student assistant from the next room, gave him a dime, and told him to go to the drug store and get a dime bottle of Sloan's Liniment. The boy came back with the bottle, Coach Howard took the cork out, and put the bottle under the player's nose. "Smell that," he told the boy. "It's a new medicine that will get you well quick." The player smelled the liniment and was satisfied. Coach put some in his hands and began to rub it in.

The young man said, "It begins to feel better already."

Coach put the cork back in the bottle, wet his hands with water, and really began to massage the player's back. After a while, he asked the player how it felt. He said, "Man, that is some great medicine! My back feels great; I think I can play." Coach hit him on his back and went to the student assistant and told him to take the bottle back to the drug store and get his dime back.

Even though we had really good running backs, there were times on passes where the backs had to pick up (block) a blitzing linebacker or defensive end. Coach Howard at every staff meeting got on me about working on the blocking by the running backs. Bob Smith, our defensive coordinator and linebacker coach, sat on the opposite side of the staff table; so often while Coach Howard would be getting on me and I'm trying my best to be most attentive, Coach Smith would have his hands up by his ears waving his fingers and sticking his tongue out. I came close to laughing many times but managed to "accept the advice I was being given" without ever laughing. I could have been fired if I had laughed.

Once in a Maryland game, they had a very good running back we had tried to recruit to Clemson. During the game this back was tackled out of bounds on our sideline and collided with Coach Howard. They both landed under a big table behind our bench. The crowd was very silent, thinking Coach might be injured. They stayed under the table quite a while. I was in the press box and asked one of the coaches on the sideline if Coach was hurt. He answered, "No, he's just asking that running back why he didn't come to Clemson!" He may have been right about that.

One day during spring practice, we were practicing on a wet field. Coach Howard was watching the offense. We were practicing a play where Jacky Jackson, a running back, was going in motion from the I formation. Coach Jordan, the offensive line coach, had his eyes locked on the linemen. Jacky ran into Coach Jordan, knocking him down. Coach Howard yelled out, "That's right; run over these coaches getting in their way and picking their noses." Coach Jordan turned red and was quite mad.

Practice went on and Coach Howard made one of his infrequent visits to the defensive field where they were working on pass coverages. He was in the secondary watching. Linebacker Billy Ware ran into Coach Howard while going to his assigned area to cover. Later after practice, Coach Smith asked if we had seen what happened on their field. We all said we hadn't. He told us about Coach Howard getting knocked down, saying he landed head first in the mud and had mud all over his ears, head, and face and had a hard time getting up. As usual after practice, we coaches were walking off the field chatting, and Coach Howard looked at Coach Jordan and told him about getting knocked down. Coach Jordan said, "Well Coach, were you picking your nose?" Coach Howard could also laugh at a joke on himself.

While at Clemson, many college football programs were getting into stretching and agilities, and many were also into lifting weights. Coach Howard said weights got you all tightened up; and asked regarding stretching if we ever hunted coons. He said, "Have you ever seen coon dogs stretch before they hunt? No, they just start running!"

We had a great offensive tackle on our team, Wayne Mass, from Sumter, South Carolina. We were playing N.C. State for basically the Atlantic Coast Conference championship. They had a great defensive tackle, Dennis Byrd, playing in front of Wayne. Both were about 6 ft 5 inches, 260 pounds, and both were All-Conference and All-State. Before the game there was a lot of hype about the game in the news media. Coach Howard called Wayne into his office on Friday and said, "Wayne, 'Sports Illustrated' called me today and said they will have a camera that will be on you and Dennis Byrd all during the game and the film will determine whether you make their All-America issue." Of course 'Sports Illustrated' hadn't called Coach Howard, but his ruse got Wayne's attention and he played his best game and we won. [My nephew, Art Hudson, played offensive tackle for N.C. State in that game. Because we (Clemson) won, I got Aunt Kate's sweet potato pie.]

My first flight with the team as a varsity coach at Clemson was to Tuscaloosa to play Coach Bear Bryant's Alabama team. When I got on the plane, I found that my assigned seat was on the seat next to Coach Howard. I thought he must want me there to go over the game plan with me, but I became leery when I noticed the other coaches trying to hide their smiles.

As I mentioned previously, Coach always chewed tobacco, and he carried a "spitting cup" onto the plane to expectorate in. He put the cup in a container between me and him. We were flying on a "prop-plane" and having a very bumpy ride. I was getting sicker by the minute. He got up to walk around the plane and handed me his cup, asking me to "take care of it." Then I had to go to the restroom—several times. I was glad to finally hit terra firma. From then on, I made sure to avoid having to sit beside Coach on airplanes.

There was one story that Coach Howard himself used to tell quite often. It was a hot, summer day and he was cutting his lawn at his beautiful home across from the "Clemson House." A lady drove up in a big, long Cadillac, stopped, and rolled the window down, motioning Coach Howard over to her car. She said, "That is the most beautiful lawn I've ever seen. How much do you charge for your work?"

Coach responded, "Well, the lady who lives here gives me three meals a day and lets me sleep with her." Whereupon, the prim lady squealed off in a cloud of dust!

As I said, working with Coach Howard was like an adventure every day.

Football Talk

I, of course, was hired at Clemson as the freshman football coach. While the won-loss record for the freshman team was certainly important—especially for the coach—the team was also an important training ground for the new recruits. I had an "average" team that first year, but we went 6-0-1, with the tie being against Georgia. In that game we scored what would have been a winning touchdown (in my opinion) at the end of the game. Our runner was caught in a "pile" and spun around and ran all the way for a touchdown. The officials, however, ruled he had been stopped back at the pile, and the touchdown was called back. But it was a good season; in fact, it was Clemson's first undefeated freshman season in 30 years.

After my first year, Charlie Waller, our quarterbacks/running backs coach, got a job with the San Diego Chargers. Coach Don Wade and I were hunting down in the lower part of the state. Coach Howard got his secretary to track us down and tell us they were having an IPTAY meeting at the Jefferson Hotel on Main Street across from the State House at 6:00 p.m. and for us to be there. [IPTAY is an acronym for "I Pay Ten A Year; it is the Clemson booster club founded in 1934, although prices have risen somewhat since then.] So Don and I were sitting out in the audience listening to all the things going on, when Coach Howard got up to speak and said, "Ladies and gentlemen, this afternoon at 5:00 Charlie Waller left us to go to the San Diego Chargers; at 5:05 I hired me a new backfield coach and there he sits." He was looking at me, and that was the first I heard about it. He told me to come to his room after the meeting and we "would talk." I thought he was going to tell me about the big raise I was going to get; I'm not sure but I don't think I got any raise—just a promotion, I guess. What he did tell me, however, was that he wanted me to go with him, Whitey, Don, and Fred to Tallahassee to study their passing game down there. I said, "Yes, sir." That turned out to be a very interesting and informative trip.

The week before we played Alabama, Coach Bryant had been saying all week that nobody on his offensive line weighed over 200 pounds (Danny Ford, later to become the head football coach at Clemson, was one of them). Coach Howard quipped, "If none of those guys weighs over 200 pounds, I want to weigh on their scales."

As we worked out in Tuscaloosa on Friday, a number of sports writers had come out for our workout. When we finished, Coach Bryant called Coached Howard over to their dressing room. They had a set of scales there, and Coach Bryant said to Coach Howard, "Okay Big Boy, let's see how much you weigh." They had "fixed" the scales and Coach Howard, who was rather portly, weighed exactly 200 pounds!

Later, Coaches Bryant and Howard came over to where we assistant coaches were waiting for Coach Howard, and they began to tell one tale after another. [They were roommates at Alabama in 1929.] What a great opportunity this was to listen to those two legends spinning their tales—unforgettable. Incidentally, we lost to Alabama the next day 27-7.

Later in the year, we played Southern California (the "other USC") in Los Angeles. Coach Howard knew it was a "money" game and planned for the team to have a good trip. We left on Thursday for California. Don Chuy, an All-American at Clemson, was playing for the Los Angeles Rams but spent his off-season at Clemson. He knew all the Clemson coaches and had a good time planned for us. One of the highlights for us was a visit to MGM Studios to watch a popular series "Lost in Space." The cast members were very friendly and spent a lot of time with us. Actor Bob Cummings, a South Carolina product, helped arrange some very nice stops for us. We all had our pictures made with the cast members. June Lockhart was the leading lady and was nice enough to have her picture made with me. When we got back to Clemson, Bob Bradley, our Sports Information Director, had all the pictures and gave them to us. In several days my wife received a large manila envelope from Los Angeles. Inside was a 5 by 8 picture of Ms. Lockhart and me with a hand-written note to her friend, "Arty" Baker, telling how she enjoyed meeting me. Of course, Bob had arranged for someone in Los Angeles to send the picture. I still have the photo. The game was not very good for us; they beat us 26-0.

Our best running back, Buddy Gore, fumbled three times. I was in the press box the third time and I threw my pen down in disgust. It skipped across the table and fell quite a distance down into the crowd. I was relieved after the game that nobody arrested me.

Coach Howard let us call most of the plays during games. One day we were playing N.C. State in Raleigh and were behind 18-17, needing a field goal to go ahead. Thus, we needed to get the ball in the middle of the field for our place kicker to have the best position to kick from. I called the isolation up the middle and got the word to Ray Yauger to run the ball on his rush to the right so it would end up in the middle of the field. Coach Howard had told me several times to make sure he runs where you want him to. Well, Ray ran right up the middle where State was waiting for him. Fortunately (for me and for Ray), he cut to the outside and scored a touchdown from the 20-year line. Later, Coach told me I better be glad that boy scored or he would have fired both of us. So much for play calling!

Charlie Waters was from North Augusta, South Carolina, where he played quarterback. Everybody wanted him, including Georgia, Duke, and N.C. State as well as Clemson. His recruiting went right down to the wire. His mother was a beautiful lady, but she dominated the recruiting conversations while Mr. Waters would let her. I noticed that while he didn't talk a lot, he did like to be included. I spent a lot of time with him, and on Christmas Eve Charlie told me he was going to sign with Clemson. He wanted to have a "signing party," and the television announcer in Augusta wanted it on television with about 20 people in the group. I got back to Clemson and went by to tell Coach Howard he was signing. Then I told him Charlie wanted the party.

"How many?" Coach asked.

I said, "About 20."

He said, "What!"

I said, "Well Coach, do you want to sign him or not?"

After some thought, he said, "Okay."

Charlie started out at Clemson playing quarterback and showed good promise. However, in his sophomore year in a game against Duke, we had an injury at wide receiver and decided to move Charlie to wide receiver just for that game. In the second quarter we decided to throw a deep route to Charlie. He ran right by the Duke defender, and Jimmy Addison threw him a "perfect strike" for a 60-yard touchdown. Coach Howard got right on the phone and said, "Art, you can forget about quarterback Charlie Waters!"

Later as we began to find Charlie's talents, we began to run him on the reverse, and he was great at that. Coach Howard usually let the offensive staff call the plays, but if he got fired up about one certain play, he would grab a player and send that play in by the player. Well, Coach got fired up about the reverse to Charlie and began sending it in so often that when the opposition saw Coach send a player in with a play, they would start yelling, "Reverse! Reverse!" Coach finally figured he better change his calls. Charlie had a great career as a wide receiver at Clemson; he was drafted by the Dallas Cowboys and moved to free safety. He made All-Pro on several championship teams.

If you coach long enough, you will see some strange things happen. Once when we were playing the Gamecocks, we ran a "sweep," which was one of our best plays. The opposite guard pulls and leads the back into the hole. On one such play, our All-America guard Harry Olszewski was pulling, and our quarterback Jimmy Addison fumbled the snap. The ball popped right up in front of Harry who caught it and scored a four-yard touchdown. We hadn't worked on that play in practice!

I have had the opportunity to work with some great coaches and men. Each one was his own man but fit into the puzzle just right. Many were unusual. Fred Cone was our recruiting coach while I was at Clemson. Coach Howard liked to brag that he recruited the best player he ever coached for a 3-cent postage stamp. His sister in Alabama wrote him on a post card that there was a pretty stout boy in Pine Apple, Alabama, who had played some football in the service and maybe he would get in touch with him. Because he was a veteran, he would qualify for the GI Bill. Well, Fred Cone showed up in the late 1940s without anyone ever having seen him play football. He played full back and place kicker, and he was an awesome player. Comedian Jerry Clower, who played football at Mississippi State, told a favorite story in a comedy routine about trying to tackle Fred in a game between Clemson and Mississippi State. [That routine can be viewed on YouTube.] Fred went on to star for the Green Bay Packers and still holds some records there. After a year with the Dallas Cowboys, he went to Clemson as recruiting coach. He is the strongest man I have ever seen who never lifted weights. One day one of the coaches was moving, and all of us coaches were helping him. He had a big refrigerator-freezer, and we were really struggling with it. Three of us got on one end and Fred easily handled the other end!

Coach Howard had a standing rule to discourage fighting among players during practice. If players got into a fight, he would call the team up in a circle and make the fighters take off their helmets and finish their fight. Sometimes, it got one-sided and he would always stop it before somebody got hurt. One of our fullbacks was "John Henry" Johnson, who had played for me at Eau Claire and whom I had recruited to Clemson. He was around 5 ft 9 inches, 205 pounds and, as I first noted in Chapter 6, he was the toughest player I ever coached. [His brother Bobby followed him to Clemson and became an All-ACC defensive back and later a very successful coach at Furman and Vanderbilt.] One day at practice, John Henry was helping us put on plays as a junior varsity back. There was a very big varsity tackle about 6 ft 8 inches, 250 pounds who liked to hit backs late after a play was over. I knew John Henry wouldn't put up with that, so he attacked the big lineman. Coach calls the team up in a circle to finish the fight. The lineman knew all about John Henry, and told Coach, "No way" and walked away.

When I attended my first spring practice, I was surprised to hear profanity all over the field. It bothered me every day. I was now a Clemson Tiger and wanted us to be the best we could be. I prayed about it, and then it really began to bother me. I finally got up enough nerve to go to Coach Howard. It was in the summer before fall practice began, and he was at his beautiful home near the "Clemson House," sitting in his swing outside. When he saw me, he told me to come over and sit down and asked what was on my mind.

I stammered around for a minute and finally said, "Coach, you know we have a great program here. Our players are performing well in their classes, they are graduating, and they are getting good jobs. They are growing as fine young men, but they don't have a chance to grow spiritually."

Coach Howard was a long-time member of Central Methodist Church. He said, "Well, what do you recommend?"

I told him about the great work the Fellowship of Christian Athletes was doing all over the country. [As I noted in Chapter 6, I first became involved with FCA while I was at Eau Claire High School and started a chapter there.] He then asked me if that was the group some leading coaches in America (he listed several names) were in. I told him, "Yes."

He said, "Well, I go to our National Coaches Conventions and I see their actions there." [In those days, not many wives accompanied their husbands to the conventions, so some coaches, shall I say, took advantage of the situation. Today, most coaches do carry their wives, who comprise a very strong group.] Coach Howard continued, "I'll tell you one thing: they [the coaches] are not Christians. They are phonies and I don't like phonies." But he said, "If you think the FCA can help us, go ahead and organize it. Just don't include me."

I was elated and began to have meetings. The group was very small in the beginning with just 15 to 20, but they grew. We met once a week and were allowed to meet before each game. It's been a great thrill to watch this group grow through the years. Others have taken over the reins since I left. Today, Clemson has the largest FCA group in America; it meets every week with 3000+ attending. Is that not awesome?

Later in the season we were playing Duke, and Coach Howard was making his usual pre-game comments. He said, "You know boys, that FFA thing is not too bad." [FFA stands for "Future Farmers of America," a very large group in South Carolina, but everybody knew he meant FCA.] He continued, "Last week we were playing Maryland and leading 14-10 and they had the ball driving on us late in the game. We tried every blitz and safety blitz, and nothing seemed to slow them down. I finally took my hat off and said, 'Lord, help us out'. I'll be [expletive deleted] if they didn't fumble on the next play." I'm not sure that's exactly what FCA's purpose is, but I was glad Coach finally "came around."

Some Job Offers

After my second year at Clemson, I felt I had done okay. I was very fortunate to have been offered several jobs. The Orangeburg High School superintendent called to see if I would consider going to Orangeburg as athletic director and head football coach. I told him I was happy to be coaching in college, but I would highly recommend Dick Sheridan, who got the job and led them to two state championship games. Newberry College offered me their head coaching job to replace retiring Harvey Kirkland, my long-time friend and mentor. Western Carolina offered me their head coaching job, as did Spartanburg High School. These were all good jobs and I was flattered; however, I was locked into the Clemson Tigers.

Additionally, on at least three occasions while I was at Clemson, I was offered jobs at USC, once by Coach Marvin Bass and twice by Coach Paul Dietzel. Coach Bass offered me the quarterback coaching job after my first year at Clemson. Because I had been at Eau Claire High in Columbia just four or five miles from the university for five years and they hadn't shown any interest in me, I felt I would not leave Coach Howard and Clemson after just one year there.

The next time was several years later when Coach Dietzel offered me the offensive coordinator's job along with a raise. Edie and I went down there, and he showed me "my" office in the new "Round House." He took us to his home for ribs and all the extras. During dessert, Tom Price, the USC sports information director, arrived at Coach Dietzel's house with a photographer. Coach Dietzel said, "Come on, we're going to have our picture made together in front of this Gamecock picture." I asked what was the occasion, and he said, "This will be in "The State" newspaper in the morning announcing you as the new offensive coordinator." I almost fainted! I wasn't ready to make up my mind and simply refused to take the job at that time.

Edie and I drove back to Clemson, and I talked to Coach Howard, who encouraged me to stay at Clemson. "Captain Jervey" was the No. 1 Tiger on the Board and was involved in all major decisions involving Clemson athletics. He told me that I had a great future at Clemson and would be considered as head coach if and when Coach Howard stepped down. Also, Dr. Edwards, the Clemson president, told me, "Art, when Frank steps down, you will be one of the first people we will consider." Based on these conversations and my loyalty to Clemson, I declined the USC job. I later would remember that these promises made would not be honored, but I was, and still am, convinced that the Lord had a plan for my life and being head coach at Clemson was not in the plan.

When Coach Howard did step down after the 1969 football season, it was a time when he and the president were not on the best of terms. We assistant coaches were asked to continue to recruit; I actually signed Mark Fellers from Charlotte, who later became the starting Clemson quarterback. I kept thinking each weekend I came home from recruiting that Dr. Edwards would call. He never did. I saw in the papers where they were interviewing other coaches for the Clemson job. I finally went to Dr. Edwards' home on a Sunday afternoon and asked him whether I was a candidate for the job. He said, "Art, since you and Whitey Jordan have both expressed an interest in the job, we've decided to go outside the staff to hire a head coach."

Eventually, Cecil "Hootie" Ingram, an assistant coach at Georgia, was hired as the Clemson head coach. He sent word that he wanted me to attend his press conference announcing his being named coach. After the conference, he pulled me aside and asked me to stay on his staff. I told him I would like to be the offensive coordinator, and he told me he was not going to have a coordinator. I told him I would continue to recruit and let him know.

In the meantime, my friend Dick Weldon called from USC to say they had a quarterback coaching job open and Coach Dietzel wanted me to call. It was Sunday, and I missed Sunday School to call him. He finally told me to come to work at USC the next morning. I went to church and slipped Edie a note saying we were going to coach at USC, and I was going to work there the next morning. After church I met Hootie at the office and told him I had decided to go to USC. I was shocked when he became angry and said I could go anywhere except USC; he would not release me from my contract with Clemson to go to USC. He said he was going to talk to Dr. Edwards. Edie and I had spent a lot of time in prayer about what we should do. When I got home, the children went out to play, and Edie had egg salad sandwiches for lunch, since we didn't feel like going out for lunch.

I felt I was in a three-way dilemma. Should I stay at Clemson even though they had not kept their promises to me? Or, should I go to USC and break my contract with Clemson, causing many hard feelings? Or, should I look for a new job? The good Lord had a plan. While we were munching halfheartedly on our sandwiches, the phone rang. I answered, and it was Jim Carlen, a long-time FCA friend, who was the new head football coach at Texas Tech University in Lubbock, Texas. Edie had suggested several days earlier that I call Jim because he had once told her that he was going to hire me someday. He offered me the quarterback/running back job and said I could take several days to decide. I looked over at Edie, and she already had a map out trying to find Lubbock on it. I asked Jim if I could accept the job over the phone, he said sure, and I accepted, "sight unseen."

I called Coach Dietzel to tell him I would not be there the next morning. He was mad and told me I would have to call Herman Helms, the sports director at "The State" newspaper and tell him I wasn't coming because he (Dietzel) had already released a story that I was coming. I called Herman and told him I wasn't coming to USC and he wanted to know where I was going. He asked, "Are you going to Texas Tech?"

I said, "I can't say."

The next day's paper said I was going to Texas Tech. Jim Carlen got mad at me because he hadn't even talked to the old staff at Texas Tech, but I explained what had happened and he was okay.

Then I had to call Hootie and tell him I was going to Texas Tech. He was agreeable, since I wasn't going to USC. I guess I was somewhat relieved that I wouldn't leave Clemson making people mad, but I was also somewhat disappointed that I wouldn't be going to USC to coach with my friend Dick Weldon. Ever since I had been in coaching, I had secretly hoped deep down that someday I could coach at USC. But at the same time, Edie and I, for some strange reason, were excited about moving to Lubbock and working with a group of coaches and people for whom I had great respect. It was also exciting for me that I would be coaching in the Southwest Conference against such teams as Texas, Texas A&M, Arkansas, Southern Methodist, Texas Christian, and Baylor.

Visiting Washington

Before moving to the final stage of our time at Clemson, I want to tell about a wonderful trip to Washington, DC. Edie and I decided to take Ryan and Curtis to Washington one summer. Being older, Artie and Kim were working at the time. As I mentioned in Chapter 2, when I was at P.C. the guy that pledged me into the Pi Kappa Alpha fraternity, Harry Dent, worked for Senator Strom Thurmond. [He later worked for President Nixon and others.] I called him at Sen. Thurmond's office and asked if we might be able to visit the Senator. A little later the Senator's Office called me and asked if we could have lunch with the Senator and his family. I told them I thought we could. What an honor and experience it was for us to have lunch in the Senate dining room with Sen. Thurmond and his wife,

Nancy, and his children. He introduced us to three or four senators who were kind enough to come over and talk to us. Being a Clemson graduate, he talked a lot about Clemson and Clemson football. He also remembered Edie's dad who represented Sumter County in the S.C. House of Representatives for many years.

At this time my brother George was a Captain in the Marines and lived at Camp David. He was in charge of the Marine White House Guards. We stayed with them. We saw the memorials—Arlington, the Grave of the Unknown Soldier, etc. George's wife, Irene, was our wonderful tour guide. Also, George and Irene took us to the Friday evening Marine Corps Parade at the Marine Corps Barracks. The Band was super with all the Sousa marches, and the Marine Corps crack drill platoon was fantastic. It made me proud of the great tradition of the Marines. It was a very memorable trip!

Preparing to Move Again

Jim Carlen had called a few days before Christmas in 1969, so I had a few days before I was due there after the first of the new year. But those days were filled with my packing enough clothes for at least a month; I knew I would have to "hit the road running" doing recruiting. I hunted ducks a few times in the Wateree Swamp with Joe Kirven, E.M. Watt, and Kirby Jackson. And, as usual, we had the "Edens Christmas" with Mr. Edens and Curt and Ruth at the big house in Dalzell. I still loved to hear Mr. Edens' stories about the old farm days, and Edie spent a lot of time cleaning up his house and kitchen. I don't know where he got his country linked sausage, but he had it every time we came. I've never found any since then that was nearly as good.

When it came time for me to leave Dalzell so I could fly out to Lubbock, Curt really got onto me hard for taking his sister and our children all the way to Texas. He said, "Baker, I don't understand you. Why would anybody leave Clemson to go anywhere, much less Texas, when you don't have to?" I didn't really have a good answer for him.

I had one final chore to do before moving. Once again, I had a house to try to sell. As before in Eau Claire, I lucked out when a friend from Sumter who taught at Clemson, Ernest Rogers, called to say he wanted to buy our house. We had paid around $22,000 for the home to be built to our (that is, Edie's) specifications, and Ernest, who was a brother to one of my childhood playmates, Luke Rogers, offered us $28,000. We accepted his offer with the understanding that Edie and the children could live there until we found a home in Lubbock.

Whereupon, we moved 1244 miles to Lubbock, Texas, which is,

believe me, starkly different from Clemson, South Carolina.

8 AT TEXAS TECH UNIVERSITY

Lubbock, a city similar in size to Columbia, is located in northwest Texas about 70 miles from the New Mexico border. The nearest city of comparable size is Amarillo, 125 miles to the north. Lubbock is a wonderful city and West Texas, a great part of America. Geologically speaking, the area is also referred to as the "High Plains." However, all of this was vastly different from what I was used to, having lived all of my life in South Carolina. The most impressive things we noticed were how flat the land is there and how dry it is. Little if anything grows without irrigation. Nevertheless, they have the nicest lawns and take great care of them. There are no tall trees—mostly just mesquite, some low cedars, and cottonwoods. It is not uncommon to see tumbleweed rolling down Main Street.

Even though it is very dry, there are huge cotton farms outside Lubbock. Because the plains are up on a cap rock at some 3300 ft above sea level, there is a large water reservoir underneath. They pump water to irrigate the crops of cotton, sorghum grain, and wheat, oats, and barley. Some farmers irrigate with huge sprinklers; others dig deep furrows around the cotton fields and fill them with water so the water will run down the cotton rows and irrigate. [Edie's dad visited us several times and, having farmed all his life, he was very impressed.] Lubbock has no drains in the streets for runoff underground. All the streets were made to drain naturally to a prepared city park where they have tanks or small ponds for water collection. Since it is so flat, the streets are laid out in squares. As you go east-west, streets are named with alphabet letters until they run out of letters. When they run out of letters, the street names are words in alphabetical order. As you go north-south, streets are numbers beginning with 1. This naming system makes navigation relatively easy. But the most impressive thing about Lubbock and West Texas is the people. They are very friendly and are good neighbors and great football fans.

Massive dust storms occur in West Texas in the spring when farmers are plowing. The fields are so huge you can't see the ends of the rows. Even the tractors that plow the rows go out of sight as you watch them. Too, the sun shines and the wind blows every day. When the farmers plow their fields, tons of dry sand are blown into the atmosphere. Often dust clouds will be blown up high into the atmosphere; then miles away the wind might stop blowing and tons of sand will simply "rain" down on whatever is below. Houses have sealed windows to try to keep out the dust, but it doesn't work entirely. After a big dust storm, the inside of the house is covered with dust. You can almost feel or hear the dust settling.

Because the High Plains area is so flat, all the roads and highways are straight as an arrow for miles and miles. Everybody waves from their cars, and slower drivers always pull over to let you by. With the land being so flat, tornadoes are frequent—especially in the spring and summer.

The High Plains area was the last place in the west for the U.S. Calvary to subdue the Apache and Comanche Indians. An often-told story said the last group of Apaches to surrender to the U.S. Calvary occurred near Lubbock. The story was that a Calvary patrol was chasing a group of Apaches who had left the reservation. Both groups were practically out of water after four or five days of chase and there was none anywhere around. Finally, the Calvary had them trapped in a small valley but could not overcome the Indians. They finally agreed to a ceasefire, and it was said that the captured Indians had to guide the Calvary back to civilization!

Our Third House

Leaving Edie and the children temporarily behind in Clemson, I flew to Lubbock on January 2, 1970, setting foot on the ground there for the first time. The football staff were housed in a local motel where we stayed only on weekends; during the week we were all "on the road" recruiting players. Toward the end of the recruiting season several weeks later, it was decided that the wives would come in for a weekend to look for houses. Except for when I was in the army in 1946 before we were married, this was the longest time Edie and I had been separated. Man, I missed her and the children, and I was so excited she was coming. The wives were to come in on Friday even though we still had recruits coming in. I was recruiting in Houston that Friday and wasn't able to leave there until late, and it was a nine-to-ten-hour drive back to Lubbock. I got back about 2:00 a.m. only to find Edie didn't make it. She missed the plane. She just did not like the idea of leaving the children and flying halfway across the country. [She said the reason she couldn't leave Clemson was because the roads were full of ice and snow; but in typical "Edieisms" she said it was the Lord's plan because she stayed till Monday and we didn't find the house we wanted until Monday.] But the next day she arrived, and we enjoyed seeing and being with each other.

We were surprised with the homes we found available in Lubbock. They were well built, really well finished with small, immaculate lawns; and almost everyone had enclosed back yards with flowers everywhere. We found a nice home we really liked. It had four bedrooms, a glassed-in garden room, a comfortable den, living room, and dining room with a mural on the wall. The back yard was enclosed with a nice, wooden fence and there were roses, wisteria, and many other flowers and shrubs. The only drawback, I soon learned after we moved in, was that the nice, thick lawn had to be cut twice a week. But we really liked the house and decided to take it. We paid about $41,000 for our new home, which was in the southwest part of town on Louisville Drive.

Edie and the children moved to Lubbock after the recruiting season ended. I drove back to South Carolina to help pack and load our furniture on a truck. I then packed up the family and drove to Sumter to say goodbye to the Edens and Bakers and to Columbia to say goodbye to Aunts Bess, Katie, and Ruth. We then headed toward Lubbock with Edie, the children, and Bonnie Blue, our beagle. We spent the first night in Monroe, Louisiana, and then drove all day the next day to Dallas and then Lubbock some 350 miles west of Dallas. While we were driving through some of the desolate country between Dallas and Lubbock, Curtis said, "Daddy, is Lubbock at the end of the world?" (A good question!) We met the moving truck the next day and eagerly moved into our new house.

Edie had always prided herself in that when the lawn needed fertilizer, she would wait until rain was predicted in order to save turning on the sprinkler. We had been living there only a short time when she saw rain forecast for the afternoon, so she went out to fertilize the grass and remained out there until dark. Four of us coaches had driven to El Paso that day to visit the coach there (Coach Dobbs, I think) about their passing game. We arrived late, got something to eat, and went over to Juarez, Mexico, where we went to a raunchy show. Meanwhile, back in Lubbock, Edie finished up with the fertilizer and fed and bathed the children in preparation for bed. Around eight or nine o'clock the biggest tornado ever to hit Lubbock rolled into town. [There was an old Indian legend that tornadoes would never hit Lubbock. So much for old Indian legends!] The tornado actually came down at our football stadium and snapped two tall, concrete light poles in halves and proceeded toward downtown. The storm was about a mile wide and stayed on the ground for eight miles, destroying virtually everything in its wake. There was a 15-story building downtown that was twisted some 10 to 15 inches on its foundation. Edie and the children saw the tornado warning on television; then the lights went out and Artie helped get all the other children in the bathtub in the middle bathroom where he put a mattress over their heads—pretty cool for a 15-year old. Edie had succeeded in getting the fertilizer out before the "rain," but it probably was all blown away. But the important thing was that our family and house were unscathed. Unfortunately, others were not so fortunate.

After coming back from Juarez, we coaches stopped at a donut shop to eat a donut and drink a cup of coffee. We had just gotten comfortable and the shop owner had his radio on. A "news flash" came on about a terrible tornado. We listened half-interestedly until the announcer said the tornado had hit Lubbock. We all jumped up at the same time and ran to the only pay phone in the room. [There were, of course, no cell phones back then.] Unbelievably, we were all able to reach our wives and determined that our families were all well and our homes, undamaged. What a blessing! As soon as we determined that everybody and everything were okay, we spent the night and got up early the next morning to drive the 375 miles back to Lubbock. There were a lot of prayers offered from us coaches that night.

The next day, as we drove to Lubbock faster than we should have, we were introduced to our first West Texas dust storm. If you've never been in a dust storm in West Texas, it's a scary experience, especially after a tornado scare. It was difficult to see very far in front of the car, and at times we had to pull off the road and wait a few minutes. But we eventually made it back to Lubbock and confirmed that our families and houses were okay, although many others in Lubbock were hurting. Incidentally, Jim Carlen, the new head football coach and my new boss at Texas Tech, and his wife Sharon were at a movie when the tornado struck. He helped a lot of people get to safety and became somewhat of a local hero.

Another happening in our house after we had been in it only a few weeks involved Artie. As I mentioned previously, windows in Lubbock were sealed to keep out dust. One night after we had gone to bed, Artie got hot in his room (Edie always kept the air at 78 or 79° no matter how hot it was or where we lived) and tried to put his bedroom window up. Of course it was sealed so he got a kitchen knife to try to force it open. He ruined the knife and damaged the window sill, and still didn't get the window opened.

We really enjoyed living in Lubbock. We made lots of new friends whom we enjoyed. They would have several "block parties" in a year. The police would put up barriers at each end of the street, and everyone would bring several dishes. There would be games for the children, and we always had lots of fun. At Christmas time, almost everyone would decorate their garages, which were generally enclosed behind partially glassed doors. Most everyone outlined their roofs in Christmas lights and put luminaries (lighted candles in brown paper sacks with sand in the bottoms to anchor them) along their walkways. The highlights of decorations each year were the main buildings on the Texas Tech campus, which were all outlined in Christmas lights on all the roofs. Lots of the roofs there were made of tile, including those at Texas Tech. Holidays were neat for us because we could celebrate with each other; we didn't have to go anywhere.

Recruiting

I feel sure most sports fans have little or no appreciation of the large amount of time spent on recruiting by collegiate coaches in all sports. You absolutely have to get out and "beat the bushes," find the best players available, and then convince them to come to your school. Many hours may be spent in cars, airports, airplanes, and hotel rooms just to get to visit one prospective ballplayer. Sometimes, undue risks are taken, such as driving too fast to get somewhere on time or taking a risky flight to get there. Probably the worst part is being away from home and family so much. But it's part of the job and can be very rewarding when you nail that top recruit. Recruiting also provides many interesting anecdotes, as follows.

As I noted earlier in this chapter, upon arriving in Lubbock, we, the staff, were all housed in a local motel where we would stay only while we were in town on weekends. Our clothes were stored while we were "on the road" recruiting during the week. After we met as a staff, Jim gave us our recruiting assignments. He threw me the keys to a new Chevrolet Caprice and said, "Art, you're covering the Houston area, good luck." I thought that didn't sound too bad—until I looked at a map. Houston is 550 miles away in the same state, and my recruiting area extended 70 miles beyond Houston down to Galveston.

Another assistant coach was Jack Fligg, who was originally from Atlanta and played football with a lot of my P.C. friends and who had actually visited these friends at P.C. while I was there. Jim decided Jack would go with me since his area would include the "Golden Triangle" area east of Houston. We drove all day to get to Houston, a lot of it through rather desolate areas. John Connerly, who had been on the old Texas Tech staff and was retained by Jim, told us there would be other recruiters at a certain motel in Houston; so we checked in there. After supper we began to try and familiarize ourselves with our areas. We had a knock on the door and a young man asked if we were football recruiters from Texas Tech, so we introduced ourselves. He told us he was Freddy Akers, an assistant coach at the University of Texas. Then he went over our small list of recruits we had secured from the old Texas Tech staff. He discouraged us by saying that most of the good recruits were already committed to either Texas or Texas A&M. Freddy later became the head coach at Texas.

After that first visit to Houston, Jack and I often traveled there together—either driving or flying and renting a car. Sometimes a Texas Tech alumnus (an "ex") would assist us and also let us use his car. My ex was Bill Jeter who always let me use his Jaguar. I had never been in one, much less driven one, but I learned quickly how to drive it. I really impressed the prospects I was recruiting in "my car." Bill became one of my best friends in Texas.

Sometimes we couldn't make it all the way home and we would stop somewhere along the road at a motel. We would get up early the next morning in order to get back for recruits visiting the campus on Saturday morning. One time while driving somewhere near Austin, there were deer eating along the side of the road. I think a truck driver blew his horn, and a deer jumped right into the front of my car. The car drove okay to Lubbock, but $1500 damage was done to it. Jack and I had fireplaces in our homes, but there were no trees growing in the area; so on some trips we would fill up our trunk and back seat with fire wood. In Lubbock we would have had to pay $100 a cord. In the Houston area or between Houston and San Antonio, we could buy a cord for $40. Jack and I both liked to save a dollar whenever we could, and we were able to afford a fire with the wood we hauled.

Jack and I worked hard that first year, but I signed only one running back who was marginal and Jack signed two average prospects. But I laid a good groundwork by getting to know high school coaches well and doing my best to sell Red Raiders football. I found out who the good juniors were and started calling and writing them. We as a staff did pretty well overall out in west Texas and around Dallas. Jim was really good. We actually signed the top two quarterbacks in Texas, Jimmy Carmichael from Brownsville and Joe Barnes from Big Spring. In our second year my groundwork the first year paid off for me. I was able to sign five of the top sixteen players in the state, and each one of them became outstanding starters for us.

Jack and I became close friends. We shared an office and we bought homes about a block apart so we took turns driving to work. Our children were near the same age and we both joined the Methodist Church and attended together. We were both in the same Sunday School class and often had socials on Wednesdays and Saturdays at the church. Once our class sponsored an "all-men wedding." Jack was the "bride" (6 ft 2 inches), and I was the "groom" (5 ft 8 inches). We got a new preacher while we were there. The first Sunday, he told how glad he was to be our preacher, and then he explained to the congregation what his and the church's schedule would be. Then he said, "I might as well tell you now that on

Saturdays I go quail hunting during the season, so I won't be here on Saturdays." Then he hesitated a moment or two and said, "That's just the way it is." [This phrase became one of Jack's favorite sayings.] Nobody argued.

On another occasion when I was recruiting in Houston, Jesse Stiles, our freshman coach, was helping me recruit there. We drove all the way back on Friday, and the weather got bad as we got to West Texas. Rain and snow had turned to ice on the bridges. Jesse was driving about 80 going over a bridge before he knew the ice was there. We began to slide and slide. I was praying; he was talking to himself. He finally got the car under control. That was one time the good Lord allowed us another day. I didn't have my seat belt on, as I had been asleep when we began to slide. Jesse also helped me acquire a taste for oysters on the half shell. He, Jack, and I were starving after we left practice one day and flew to Houston. When we got there, Jesse took us to a seafood restaurant and ordered a dozen oysters on the half shell. He offered me and Jack some; I was so hungry I could have eaten the shells. He told us to get a soda cracker and put some catsup on it. We did and ever since, oysters are one of my favorite foods.

The Lord spared me on another recruiting trip when Coach Bob Brown and I were flying in to Love Field in Dallas. As we touched down on the runway, all of a sudden the pilot gunned all engines and we "took off." We later learned there was another plane crossing the runway we were landing on.

In an unusual twist, I went back to South Carolina and recruited a player from Eau Claire High School. He was an outstanding fullback named Sammy Green. He was about 6 ft 1 inch, 215 lb and had excellent speed. He signed with us and played on the freshman team. He averaged over 100 yards rushing for the five-game schedule and made All SWL freshman team. After football season, I was out of town recruiting most of the time. In early February, I came into the office and at a staff meeting, Jim said, "Art, get Sammy a bus ticket back to South Carolina." I said, "Why?" He said, "He hasn't attended a class this semester." This was a good lesson for the rest of the team and for me.

Coaching and recruiting at Texas Tech was tough. Several of us would leave practice early on Thursdays, catch a plane to our recruiting areas (Houston, for me), get there late, eat supper, have a Texas Tech "ex" meet me at the airport. He would already have game films he had collected from high school coaches, and I would start looking at them. I would get up early and visit as many coaches and prospects as I could after 10:00 on Friday morning. Then I would catch the first half of one high school game and the second half of another. Then I would catch the last plane to Dallas where Jack Flagg would pick me up. We would spend the night in Dallas, get up early Saturday, and either fly or drive to our game site that day. On one occasion, Lubbock was fogged in and we had to fly to Amarillo, which is about 125 miles from Lubbock. We grabbed a rental car, and Tom Wilson, who was with us this day along with Jack and Dale Evans, drove from Amarillo to Lubbock in a little over an hour, driving 100 mph all the way. I was in no condition to coach as we hurriedly changed into coaching gear and ran on the field for the game against Texas Christian University with little time to spare. [As I mentioned before, all roads in West Texas are straight and flat for miles, so driving 100 mph was not quite as bad as it might seem. In fact, most people in that part of Texas drive quite fast, though maybe not 100 mph—at least not all of them!]

Football Talk

Jim Carlen was hired as the head football coach at Texas Tech University after the 1969 football season; he had been the head coach at West Virginia University. After flying to Lubbock on January 2, 1970, along with all the new staff, the Red Raider fans met us and really made us feel welcome. A Mr. Charlie Verner, who was the president of a local bank and was originally from Belton, South Carolina, took me especially under his wing, probably because I was the only new coach from South Carolina. Later, he and his wife became our good friends, and he introduced Edie to a new system of banking unbeknown to us before. He claimed Edie could never overdraft in his bank and, thank goodness, we never did.

I was initially introduced to the "winter workout" program. Jim and his staff had used it at West Virginia before coming to Texas Tech. I had learned how it worked from other coaches and clinics. It's designed to teach players to learn all the agilities used in football. It is done at a high intensity level, mostly insides. The workouts are executed on mattes or whatever is available. There are lots of yelling, encouraging coaches, and players cheering for players really going hard. Winter workout also involves running and weight lifting. Competition is encouraged between individuals and groups. The program was excellent for morale and team building. I loved it. Texas tech had excellent facilities and great areas to conduct the drills.

The first spring practice was very special for me. I had been a high school coach and an assistant coach at Clemson and was now joining a new staff where I was one of a few new ones to join the staff. I had to learn a new offense, a new numbering system and terminology, but I had an ol' friend who proved to be a big help. One thing I loved was that Jim and staff wanted to run the option play as part of our offense. This was right down my line, for I had come to love the possibilities of the option attack.

Our first spring practice was most impressive. I was a new coach to the staff. Jim Carlen had kept John Connerly (defensive line), Tom Wilson, and Jesse Stiles from the old staff. Richard Bell was named the defensive coordinator; Dale Evans, secondary; and Marshall Taylor, receivers. On offense I was more or less the running-game coordinator; and Tom Wilson was the passing-game coordinator. Jack Fligg was the offensive-line coach. That arrangement worked out really well. Working with Jim Carlen, I had a lot more to learn about coaching. When I was head coach in high school, I used to keep players out on the practice field 2½ to three hours; and since I didn't get any complaints from parents and we were winning, I thought that was okay. Now that some of my former high school players are not afraid of me, they tell me we used to wear them out. Then when I went to Clemson, Coach Howard quite often kept players out on the practice field three hours. I know for a fact that one year our players' legs were all gone—worn out on the practice field. Jim had a policy that we would be on the practice field 1½ hours. At the beginning I had a hard time getting all my drills and teaching into 1½ hours, but I soon learned to be more efficient and fit everything into that time frame. I liked it and tried to remember that lesson for my 14 years as a head coach. Also, for the first time Coach Carlen and his staff introduced me to weight training, and running and agility drills.

After spring practice, which was a very good one, we went about keeping up with our players and looking at films—ours and the next season's opponents'. In those days you could "scout" your opponents in their spring games, so Dale Evans and I were assigned to the University of Utah's spring game in Salt Lake City. We flew there in a small, private plane. When the pilot realized we were seeing some of that territory for the first time, he flew us over the "Bad Lands" and we saw many mountain scenes, actually spotting sheep, elk, moose, deer, and bear. In Salt Lake City we visited the Mormon Museum and listened to the Mormon Tabernacle Choir practice. It was a great experience. And, we did scout Utah's spring game.

Texas Tech and Lubbock had already accepted the opportunity to host the College All-Star East-West game the first summer we were there. Because of the tornado, however, things were in a mess: houses were missing, underpasses were filled with water barely revealing cars and trucks, tractor-trailer trucks had been thrown several blocks. Some 100 people were killed, many injured, and trees were uprooted. Pieces of houses, roofs, cars, and animals were scattered all over the place. The city of Lubbock did a tremendous job of clearing up all the debris left by the tornado.

Lubbock and Texas Tech also did a miraculous job of cleaning up the city and university and had the stadium and hotels ready for the Coaches All-Star game. Since we were all staff at Texas Tech, we were assigned duties to the staff of coaches coaching the game and we were invited to all the functions. The players were mostly All-American players who were high draft choices in the NFL. One in particular was Charlie Waters whom I had recruited and coached at Clemson as a wide receiver; but the Cowboys had drafted him as a strong or free safety, so he played that position in the game. He was an All-Pro several times with the Cowboys. There were many star players there who would later be stars in the pros.

One of the social events was an evening barbeque for the two teams. West Texas barbeque was quite different from South Carolina barbeque. West Texas barbeque is always beef, whereas South Carolina barbeque is mostly pork. You couldn't find pork barbeque in West Texas. The event was on a nearby ranch where they barbequed a couple halves of beef. You went up and sliced off what you wanted. The sides were baked beans, slaw, and sour-dough bread. O.J. Simpson, the Heisman Trophy winner in 1970 from Southern California, was a player at the game and sat at a table with me and Edie.

Our first season at Texas Tech was really exciting. Jim Carlen had brought a new kind of football program to the Red Raiders. Jim's concept of a college football program was somewhat unique out there. He emphasized Christianity in our program. He did not allow the use of alcohol, smoking, profanity, or drugs, and all players were required to attend all their classes. The players really took to him and his staff. The city and all of West Texas were all excited.

Fall practice got off to a great start. We practiced in the stadium when our next game was on Astroturf, and as I've said our practices were highly organized and limited in time to at most 1¾ hours. It took a lot of planning, but I found it refreshing after the three-hour practices at Clemson.

Jim ran well-organized meetings, and he liked to get them over in a short time unless one coach had questions. We all knew one of our coaches loved to ask questions, and often his questions would prolong a meeting for 30 minutes. We had a lot of work to do before practice, so we all tried to get him to save his questions. Jim was very short and to the point. We knew not to bring up controversial subjects, for he was going to solve them quickly. For instance, the same coach recruited in south Texas, the doorsteps to Texas A&M and the Texas Long Horns. He believed they were outside the recruiting rules and made the mistake to say that at a staff meeting one morning. Jim said very curtly, "Who is cheating? What's his name? Get him on the phone! We are going to report it!" Most of what the coach had said was hearsay, so he backed down quickly. He seemed never to get our message though, and continued to ask questions.

I usually, along with other coaches, took my sons to practices at times. Ryan seemed to want to go more than the other boys. He was about the same age as Jim's youngest son, Jamie. One day we were finishing up practice and I heard Ryan's voice yelling. Finally, I located him on top of the press box, some 100 feet or more above the stadium where we were practicing. There was only a railing along the roof of the press box. I can still see him and Jamie leaning over that railing, yelling to us that they caught the elevator up and couldn't get down. With my heart in my throat, I yelled for them to back down from the edge while I came up. I had never run so fast or prayed so hard. When I got there, they thought it was fun to be up there. I tried not to show how scared I was, but I made sure they never pulled that stunt again.

We had a good quarterback, Charlie Napper and some very good running backs in Doug McCutchen, Miles Langehennig, Larry Hargrave, and others. I really enjoyed working with the quarterbacks and running backs. We finished our first season at 8-3 and accepted a bid to the "Sun Bowl" in El Paso, Texas. What a thrill it was for me to coach in my first bowl game! We played Georgia Tech and lost a tough game 17-9. The wives went on our bowl trip, and Edie had a good time. We had a sitter in Lubbock to keep the kids.

I was surprised when the next season rolled around to find that our quarterback had not worked out during the summer and was not physically or mentally prepared for the 1971 season. We had two excellent sophomore quarterbacks, Joe Barnes and Jimmy Carmichael, who could play for the first time (freshmen could not play on the varsity team at that time). Joe was an option quarterback who could pass; Jimmy was strictly a drop-back passer with average running skills. Jimmy was from Brownfield where he had played for the legendary Coach Gordon Blackwell. After losing several early season games to Tulane, New Mexico, and Mississippi State with the senior at quarterback, we went with Joe and Jimmy the rest of the way. We still ended the season 4-7, a very disappointing one for us. Never again did I take for granted that players would improve because they were seniors.

After our bad second year, we decided we had great, tough running backs, but for football in the Southwest Conference we needed speed. Finding no prospect with speed nearby, Jim sent me to California junior colleges to find one. I found what we were looking for in Los Angeles City College, a junior college that had a great "speed merchant" named George Smith. He was a very impressive young man, about 5 ft, 11 inches, 175 pounds. He had a huge Afro and a mustache, and was well dressed and businesslike. He agreed to a visit. When he arrived, I was out of the office, so he walked into our office and Jack Fligg looked at him and asked if he could help him. He pointed to a picture of me, and said, "Dat's the Dude I'm looking for."

George signed with us and was married to a nice young lady. I told him I would help him find a job for her; she was a telephone operator. I arranged for an interview for her, and the company called to say she didn't show for the interview. I ran George down and asked him where she was.

He said, "Coach, she's sick."

I said, "George, I saw her earlier today and she looked well."

He said, "Yeah Coach, she looked good to me too."

She got the job and George became one of our stars.

In a game against Texas A&M at College Station in my third year at Texas Tech, it was back and forth in a real physical game. In the fourth quarter, we were behind, but a touchdown for us would win. At that time the entire corps of cadets stood around their goal line and up both sidelines to "protect" their goal. We were moving the ball towards that protected goal. George Smith took a pitchout and was running well until being knocked out of bounds and into the corps of cadets. Jack Fligg sent Doug McCutchen into the game; he was a thick 5-ft, 11-inch, 210-pound runner and it never got too tough for him. He later became a very successful high school coach in Texas. I asked Jack why George didn't go back in, and he said George wasn't going back. He said when George was knocked into those soldiers, they told him if he came back into them they were going to use their swords on him. Anyway, Doug ran well and we moved to the A&M 20-yard line. I called a trap play up the middle and to my horror they moved into a split-four defense with two defensive guards and two linebackers in the middle—the worst call I could have made. But I forgot Doug McCutchen was the ball carrier. He ran over one linebacker, leaving A&M's All-America linebacker between him and the goal line. He ran over him into the end zone and then ran ten deep into the A&M cadets behind the back of the end zone. That's my kind of runner!

Later that year, we were playing Baylor in Lubbock for the right to be invited back to the Sun Bowl. We were down to the fourth quarter driving for what could be a winning or losing season for us. We were at the Baylor 45-yard line with fourth and three. We didn't consider punting; there was not enough time left. Jim got on the phone with me upstairs. "Alright, what are we going to run?"

Like Coach Kirkland taught me, I'm going to run it behind our best blockers with my best back, Doug McCutchen. I called the "outside veer" (off tackle).

Jim must have been on that phone three more times saying, "Are you sure that's what we need to call? Do you need to change it?"

I said, "No, this is the play."

Jim said, "Okay 'Bake', this is for the Sun Bowl."

The play made 34 yards, and then Doug ran the remaining 11 for the game-winning touchdown.

Hence, we rebounded from the previous year and had an 8-3 season that fall. And again, we were invited to play in the Sun Bowl, this time against North Carolina. We lost this game 32-28.

Jim Carlen usually let the offensive staff develop the "game plan" and during games to call plays. One week we had played poorly on offense but still won the game. He was upset with the offensive staff because there were certain things he liked that we weren't planning to use in the next game. During Tuesday practice he came into our offensive staff meeting and asked us to show him the game plan. He didn't like it and was ticked off about something else, so all of a sudden he said, "I'll run the offense this week." He began to put a lot of "motion" in "his" offense. We complained that we couldn't put in a new offense in a week, but he was stubborn. Practice that week was terrible, but he was like a "mule."

We played the game against Arizona on Saturday and luckily won it 7-3 on a punt return by Mark Dove (who later coached on Coach Carlen's staff at South Carolina). The offense, however, did absolutely nothing—less than 100 yards rushing, less than 100 yards passing, and an embarrassingly few first downs. Afterwards, Jim never admitted he had "messed up," but he never again entered our offensive game planning sessions. We offensive coaches never dared to smile, but we did "high five" each other when he wasn't around.

There were many exciting things about being a coach at Texas Tech. It's a great part of the country with great people in general and football fans in particular. They were the "Red Raiders," so a student dressed like Zorro rode a huge black horse on the field. When they put in Astroturf, they found the horse could not run on it, so they put a rubber track around the field. When Texas Tech came onto the field or scored, the Red Raider would circle the track. One night we were playing Arkansas in our stadium. As the two teams ran out onto the field to begin the game, the Red Raider came charging full speed, barely missing a collision with Arkansas Coach Frank Broyles. That horse could run!

A story about the Red Raiders that past coaches and fans often told referred back several years when the Red Raiders were playing Mississippi State. Texas Tech had a great running back, Donny Anderson, who was starring for the Green Bay Packers while I was at Texas Tech. Texas Tech, driving close to the Mississippi goal line, was on the eight-yard line with fourth down and three yards to go for a first down. They gave the ball to Anderson who dived over a line to the four-yard line. Apparently thinking the five-yard line was the goal line, one of the side judges threw up his arms signaling a touchdown. The cannons went off, and the Red Raider charged around the field. However, Anderson did not score a touchdown but did make a "first and goal." The referee came over to the Texas Tech Coach King and patiently explained the "mistake." After explaining it to Coach King a couple times, Coach King said, "I understand the play; you don't have to explain it again!"

The referee said, "Coach, I just want you to have enough time to reload the cannons and remount the horse."

Travel

During the summer, we had some time off to be with our families. We felt we would not be in Texas for too long before there would be an opening back in South Carolina, North Carolina, or Georgia; so we decided to travel and see some of the western part of the United States while we were living there. We traveled to Houston, San Antonio, Austin, Galveston, Amarillo, Dallas, Pala Duro Canyon, and Mustang Island State Park in Texas. And, we went into Mexico a few times at Laredo and El Paso. We tried to get the children to see a bull fight but they didn't want to go. We did see a number of rodeos. On another occasion, we took a long trip, visiting California, Arizona, New Mexico, and Nevada. Those states are not as big as Texas, but they are big enough to require significant travel time between points of interest.

We all had good doctors in Lubbock. In 1971 Edie's doctor determined she needed a female operation which would help her avoid cancer. She had the surgery and it was a great success. Her doctor was so impressed with her that he offered his condo in Red River, New Mexico, after her complete recovery. We took him up on the offer and took the opportunity to visit Taos and Santa Fe in New Mexico. This was an example of the kind of people in Lubbock.

Then every summer, we would take the family back to South Carolina for two weeks. On one occasion, we flew the entire family—all six of us— back and forth, flying out of Dallas. When we drove back and forth, we would take different routes. One time we went north to Amarillo and picked up I-40, on which we drove 1229 miles east to Asheville, North Carolina. From there, it was a relatively short, straight shot down I-26 to Columbia. Another time we drove the 350 miles to Dallas and picked up I-20, which would take us 996 miles east all the way to Columbia. Probably our favorite trip, however, was to drive to Houston and pick up I-10, take it to Jacksonville, Florida, then I-95 into South Carolina, where we would pick up I-26 to Columbia. This trip totaled about 1700 miles. These were long, hard trips, but they gave the children the opportunity to see a lot of the country. Each time it was great to get back to South Carolina and see our loved ones and friends. We would spend most of the two weeks at Edie's dad's beach house.

But about those years, Artie and Kim were teenagers, and Artie had a girlfriend, Jeanie Hobbs, and he couldn't wait to get back to Lubbock. We liked Jeanie and she spent a lot of time at our house. Kim was dating too, but not serious about anyone. Her best girlfriend was Terri "Stick" Turner, who delighted in pulling all kinds of tricks on me. Once she took a picture of me asleep on the couch in my underwear. We still keep up with Terri and saw her a few years ago when Edie and I returned to Lubbock.

Hunting

The second Christmas we were there, we didn't go to a Bowl game, so I had some free time to hunt. One of the most memorable hunts we went on was to the ranch of one of our player's dad. Paul Page was his name, and his dad had played for Southern Methodist University in the famous backfield with All-American Doak Walker. Coach Jim Ragland, Marshall Taylor, and I were invited, and I was allowed to bring my son Artie, who was about 16 then. We were put in an aluminum-wrap-around blind on the ground in some cedars during the dark early morning. Paul was with us. Around daylight, a big, eight-point buck came across the pasture about 250 yards away. Paul said, "Coach, it's your shot."

I had never shot a high-powered rifle at anything except targets in the army. I took the rifle, sighted through the scope, put the crosshair on the chest, and squeezed the trigger at the trotting buck.

I couldn't see him through the scope after I shot; but as we ran toward him, Paul said, "Coach, I believe you got him." I really thought I had missed him. When we arrived at the spot where I thought he was when I shot, there was no deer in sight. But, after closer inspection, we found him—dead—about 30 yards from where he was shot. Paul loaded the deer on his truck and left Artie and me in the blind. He said he would come back for us for some lunch.

Artie and I saw several more deer but they were does. Then about 11:00 we looked out to see 15 to 20 wild turkeys coming straight for our blind. Having never hunted turkeys before, we didn't know how to distinguish gobblers from hens. I knew we were not supposed to shoot hens. We sat very still and soon all the turkeys were walking around the blind. So we guessed, and Artie shot the biggest turkey. The rest got away, but thank goodness the turkey he shot turned out to be a gobbler.

We went into a Mexican tenant house where a nice "senorita" had prepared an authentic Mexican meal for us; it was great, but mighty "hot."

After lunch Artie and I returned to our blind and Marshall and Jim, to theirs. Artie and I were hardly settled before we looked up on the hill to see another line of turkeys marching single-file toward our blind. This time we picked out two with "beards" and shot them for Thanksgiving and Christmas meals.

It was a warm and sunny afternoon and before too much time had passed, Artie fell asleep. About 30 minutes later, I was watching and a pretty, little doe came right in front of our blind. Then, suddenly, there was a beautiful eight-point buck. I tried to wake Artie to shoot the buck, but in those days he was not easy to wake up. Finally, I said, "Artie, do you want to shoot a buck?"

Still half-asleep, he said, "I guess so; where is he?"

I whispered, "Right in front of you."

He said, "Where? I don't see him."

I took the rifle and pointed it right at the buck. Artie's eyes got "as big as saucers" as he took the rifle, aimed carefully, and shot our second eight-point buck of the day. I think he was actually sorry he had shot the deer. I learned later that Artie liked to hunt but not kill.

Marshall and Jim did not have the luck we had had. They got no turkeys, and their only shot at a deer came when a buck had mounted a doe just in front of their blind and they refused to "shoot a buck when he was performing such a chore."

My first year after recruiting ended, we were back in the office preparing for spring drills. There was a guy who would come by to speak who looked like the guy in the Marlboro ads. I asked somebody who he was. They said his name was Jack Kirkpatrick and he had formerly played quarterback for Texas Tech. He lived on his ranch in Post, Texas, a small town about 30 miles southeast of Lubbock. I asked what he did for a living; they said he was a rancher who had rotating crops, cattle, and oil wells. He and I became friends. He married "Miss Lubbock" and like me had married way over his head. They had five sons; four of them like their dad loved calf roping and other rodeo events. Jack had great hunting on his ranch and took me hunting often. He had an abundance of quail, ducks, and deer. He had both quail and Bob Whites like we have in South Carolina as well as "blue quails." The latter have a topknot on their heads and are gray like a dove but speckled like a Bob White. They are a little larger that Bob Whites and sometimes come in coveys of 75 to 100. They rather run than fly. We usually hunted them in a pickup. We would run them up and watch for them as there are no trees and everything is flat. They fly to cover. Single hunting was great. We had to look out for rattlers on sunny days. Jack and his family were so nice to us. It was by far the best of the hunting and fellowship we had while we were in Texas. We still keep in touch.

One weekend when we had recruits in for a visit, Jack Fligg and I were working on a great offensive lineman from Victoria, Texas. He loved to hunt so when he came to Lubbock for his weekend visit, we promised him a hunt. Jimmy Ragland and I took him to Post to hunt on Jack Kirkpatrick's ranch because we knew he would see plenty of game. Each time a bird would get up, either Jimmy or I would usually shoot the bird and when Kim Burgner, the prospect, fired, we said, "Great shot!" I think he picked up 20 birds and was so proud of everything. He signed with us and was All-Conference. Texas A&M, who thought they would get him, turned me in for entertaining a prospect more than the limit of 30 miles from your campus. They couldn't prove the exact mileage, and anyway we were within the limits. Whatever, Aggies! This was the only time in my 43 years of coaching I was accused of a violation.

Another bonus in West Texas was that because water is scarce, every rancher had to push up a dam wherever they could to catch water for the cattle; they called them "tanks." The weather was so clear that ducks loved to feed in the grain fields during the night and sit on the tanks during the day. We would drive the pickup below the dam, get out and walk to the top, and shoot ducks as they got up. We didn't need a retriever because the wind blew all the time and we could come back later and the wind would have blown them ashore.

In addition to hunting, I also loved tennis. Jim Carlen loved to play tennis too. The coaches were given memberships in the Lubbock Country Club, so Jim and I both began to play tennis there. Jim usually beat me in singles, but I really worked hard on my game and finally beat him one day. I knew I best not brag about it around the office, but one of our coaches, Dale Evans, was there and saw it all so I didn't have to say a word. Dale did. Jim and I continued our tennis for years after we left Texas for South Carolina and later when he was living at Hilton Head in South Carolina. He loved to "drop shot" me and rub it in when I couldn't get there, but finally his knees gave out and he could only play doubles.

Family Matters

Artie played football from the first year at Monterey High School in Lubbock. The second year his coaches made him run track. He remembers that he didn't like it, but they taught him how to run. In his junior year in 1972, Monterey had a good team and went all the way to the quarter finals, playing Midlands High School in Jones Stadium (Texas Tech's stadium). It was a great game before 34,000 fans. They won and subsequently flew to El Paso for their next game in the Sun Bowl. The cheerleaders put each player's number in his yard. The mothers took a bus to each game. Often I was in Houston when he played, but I looked at his film.

Kim was not into sports, though she could have been. I do, however, remember fondly her first dance rehearsal. The girls just swirled around, but it was funny. From my viewpoint, it seemed she was the only one in the show. I found my eyes tearing up. Daddies have a special spot for daughters. Otherwise, Kim chose to work and had a good job at the "Grid Iron," the best steak house in Lubbock, owned and operated by a former Red Raider. She was a special waitress who took around freshly baked blue berry muffins to her customers. She dated a football player.

Curtis had to have hernia surgery when he was in the first grade. We felt so bad for him but he did well. He and Ryan played sports in Lubbock; we watched them play as often as we could. Ryan was on a basketball team. We went to one game he didn't start but sat on the bench next to his coach, who was our dentist. We noticed he would pull his coach's sleeve during the game. When we got home, I told him not to bother the coach—that he would put him in when he was ready. Before the next game I felt compelled to tell him his team dribbled too much; they should pass the ball more. At the game we saw him pulling the coach's sleeve again. After the game, I said "Ryan, I thought I told you not to bother the coach about playing." He said, "Dad, I wasn't asking him to play; I told him you said we dribbled too much." I dreaded going back to the dentist after that.

Cowboys were a big part of West Texas. Every man wore a ten-gallon hat, soiled Levis, and cowboy boots. They were real. Roundups, rodeos, and rattlesnake roundups were big events there. Texas Tech had a rodeo team.

Jack Kirkpatrick invited me to bring my family to his ranch for roundup every spring where he and neighbors would brand, give shots, and "fix" the male calves. My boys loved it; I did too. It was like watching a John Wayne movie. Jack let the boys "help out" sometimes. An unusual part of the roundup is after cutting the young bulls, they keep the testicles and at any function, social, or banquet they serve "Calf Fries," a delicacy in West Texas.

If there is one thing West Texas has a great supply of, it's rattlesnakes. Every small town has a rodeo arena. We found out that Sweetwater, Texas, had a "Rattlesnake Roundup" every spring in their rodeo arena. So I gathered our family and we decided to go. Rattlers stay in their dens during cold weather. The hunters go out loaded with a tank of natural gas attached to a long pipe, a large trash can, and a gadget with a means to catch the snake just below his head. They go around until they find a hole. Often when the sun is out, the snake will be out of his hole sunning. If not, they put the pipe into the snake den and turn on the gas. He will come out and they put the catcher on him, take the top off the garbage can, and dump him in. Inside the arena they have a pig-pen looking apparatus—a plastic circular pen about five feet tall. The participants dump their snakes into the pen. They have a larger penned-off area that keeps the people safe. Inside there are several experts with high snake boots on. They catch a snake holding him just behind the head and milk venom from him. They then hand the snake to another person who kills the snake and cuts the edible meat off to sell. They have prizes for the most snakes caught, the largest pound-wise, the longest, and so on.

When we first entered the arena, there was a food stand in one corner where some Mexicans were cooking something that smelled good. Edie and Ryan will try anything, so they went over and learned they were cooking rattlesnakes. Edie and Ryan bought some and ate it. All in all, it was a good show.

Back to South Carolina

In my first year at Texas Tech, at the end of the football season, the head football coaching job at Wofford College in Spartanburg, South Carolina, became open. They contacted me to come for an interview, which I did. Part of the interview was to sit down with Jerry Richardson and Charlie Bradshaw—two former Wofford All-Americans. Jerry is the current owner of the Carolina Panthers. They offered me the job, and it was a wonderful opportunity to be a head college coach and to get back to South Carolina. It was tempting, but Edie and I realized that Jim Carlen and Texas Tech had spent a lot of money moving us to Texas and we had not been there a year, so I turned them down.

In my third year at Texas Tech, I learned of a job opening as head football coach at Furman University in Greenville, South Carolina. I got in touch with Lyles Alley and John West, the athletic director and associate athletic director at Furman, respectively, to let them know I was interested. Subsequently, I had several calls to and from Furman friends. Eventually, they called and invited me to be interviewed for their head coaching job. I talked to Jim about it, and we felt after the Baylor game would be the best time for me to go. He gave me a manager and a car to drive me to Dallas to catch a plane to Greenville-Spartanburg. I missed my connecting flight in Atlanta and arrived in Greenville after the board had met, so I met with Dr. Blackwell, the president, and Dr. Bonner, the provost.

I returned to Lubbock and finished the season and had heard nothing from Furman. I was recruiting in Houston when I finally got a call from Dr. Blackwell. He said, "Art, we are offering you the job of head coach at a salary of $15,000 non-negotiable." I was making $20,000 at Texas Tech and with a (bowl) bonus and raise, I would be making $22,000. Once again, I had the chance both to become a head coach and to return to South Carolina. I talked to Edie and the children, and we decided to take the financial loss and move back to South Carolina—and to become a head college football coach. Unlike before when I was offered the job at Wofford after one year at Texas Tech, I felt after three years I had fulfilled my commitment and obligation to Jim Carlen and Texas Tech.

We enjoyed and learned a lot from our three years in Texas. The people there were really good people. But we were thrilled to be relocating to our beloved South Carolina and for me to become a collegiate head football coach for the first time.

9 AT FURMAN UNIVERSITY

Furman University is located in Greenville, South Carolina, a medium-sized city in northwestern South Carolina, an area known as the "Upstate." It is 33 miles east of Clemson and about 100 miles northwest of Columbia.

Building My First Collegiate Staff

I arrived at Furman in late November, 1972, for the press conference announcing my appointment as head football coach of the Furman Paladins. I arrived late and checked into a local motel. The press conference was set for 11:00 a.m. the next day. I had already contacted my old Eau Claire crew—Jimmy Satterfield, who was currently at Irmo High School in Irmo, South Carolina; Dick Sheridan, who was at Airport High School in West Columbia, South Carolina; and Steve Robertson, who was at Newberry College—about joining me at Furman. They were all happy and successful in their jobs, but they eagerly agreed to join me anyway, even though they were taking salary cuts like me. God really blessed me with great assistants—men of character and men who could coach, and as I soon found out, men who could recruit!

About 10:00 that night, I received a call from Hootie Ingram, the head coach at Clemson, telling me he was leaving Clemson and if I was interested in that job, I should go after it. I told him I had already told Furman I was going there. In another hour or so, I received a call from the athletic director at Clemson, Bill McLellan, calling to say the job at Clemson was open; and if I was interested, I would be one of the top three he would interview. However, he could not promise me that I would get the job. I told Bill I had given my word to Dr. Blackwell, the president of Furman, that I was going to Furman. While I was appreciative and probably would have walked to Clemson in order to get the job, I simply could not go back on my commitment. [Jimmy "Red" Parker subsequently got the job at Clemson.]

The press conference at Furman went off without a hitch. However, I thought it was strange that on the day I accepted the job at Furman, the faculty senate also met and voted to recommend that the President and Board of Trustees drop football and apply the monies spent on football toward faculty salary increases. Think I wasn't nervous? But things worked out okay.

One of the hardest jobs I had was to tell the existing staff that I could not keep them. I did, however, keep one graduate assistant. Steve Robertson recommended that I hire Harold Wheeler from Newberry as our secondary coach, which I did. I was also able to hire as graduate assistants several outstanding young coaches who were just out of playing college football—Rick Gilstrap, Billy Ware, Eddie Williamson, Ken Pettus, and Eric Hyman. They were the best bargains I ever negotiated, as all these young men became excellent coaches.

I had hired all except Eric, who had been an all-ACC tackle at North Carolina and was drafted by the NFL but failed his physical. His Wife, Pauline, had been a cheerleader at UNC and was (and still is) a beautiful blond. She had been hired as the Dean of Women at nearby North Greenville Junior College. The president of the College called me to say that Pauline had a "big-ol', football-looking husband" and wanted to know if I would be interested in him as a coach. I didn't have any salary money left, but I invited him for an interview. I always liked to interview the wives with the prospective coaches so they would know what to expect in terms of our coaching habits, such as not always being home for supper at 5:00. I had never met either of them. They came in and Eric was a fine-looking 6 ft, 4 inches, 250 lb prospect who no longer had playing eligibility. But when they walked into my office and I met Pauline for the first time and determined that Eric could coach a little bit, he had a job. [Eric subsequently served as athletic director at Virginia Military Institute, Miami University (Ohio), Texas Christian University, the University of South Carolina, and Texas A&M University.] I often teased him about whether it was he or Pauline who got that first job with me.

John West was the associate athletic director when I arrived at Furman. The legendary Lyles Alley was the athletic director, but John soon took over after Coach Alley retired. John was another one of those characters I worked with through the years. He had been an outstanding sprinter in track and an outstanding track coach at USC. Working with him was an adventure each day. While he didn't know a lot about coaching football, he wanted to help us as much as he could. He was a very popular speaker; and because of some of his "pranks," the coaches did not always understand him.

That First Winter, Spring and Summer

When we arrived at Furman, the dressing rooms were in pretty good shape because the Atlanta Falcons used the facilities for pre-season training camp, and they made sure the dressing rooms were up to their standards. The training room was pretty good also, but for a weight room we had to beg and borrow what equipment we could and make weight stations under the stairway and in the landing below the stairs in the athletic field house. Our two side-by-side fields were in good shape and well kept. The coaches' dressing room was roomy with nearby showers.

Inasmuch as the previous two years' football records were 1-9 and 2-9 and there were few returning players, our most pressing immediate need was new and good football players; hence, we had to hit the road recruiting. I had Dick Sheridan, Steve Robertson, and the other coaches, none of whom except Steve had ever recruited before. Somehow, those guys were naturals. We faced many obstacles at that time trying to recruit football players to Furman, including: stringent entrance requirements, never having graduated a black player, a faculty that wanted to drop football, very little coverage in the news media, and an old stadium shared with the two local high schools located downtown away from the new Furman campus. As in many situations like this in life, we had to find the positive things about coming to Furman—the quality of academics, the records of graduates in their chosen fields, and the most beautiful campus in the country—and accentuate them as we tried to recruit players.

With a rookie head coach and a rookie staff, and with 50 scholarships (most other Southern Conference schools had 95) and a very small recruiting budget, we hit the road recruiting. We had only four or five cars we could use, so not everybody could recruit at the same time. But we persisted and the results were perhaps the No. 1 recruiting job by any school in America. We brought in the nucleus of the future of Furman football. David Whitehurst (who went on to play for the Green Bay Packers), Tommy Southard (St. Louis Cardinals), Jeff Holcomb, Vince Perone, Larry Robinson, Steve Wilson, Tommy Marshall, Frank Moses, Tony Cox, Ike Simpson, Brette Simmons, Robbie Caldwell, Dan Utley, and others were all super players and leaders. All of them graduated from Furman and are a credit to the school, and they laid the groundwork for the many championship Furman teams that followed. The staff were uncanny in finding players who could get into Furman and graduate, and also play football at the Southern Conference level.

Furman had never graduated a black player in 1973, and the university was seeking qualified black students. Dick Sheridan worked real hard on recruiting. He developed a good relationship with Charlie Brock, director of admissions, and Charlie allowed us to bring in six or seven black athletes who might not normally have been admitted but had excellent transcripts in GPA but low scores for Furman. I must add that many of these athletes made all-conference and/or all-state, and every one of them graduated from Furman in four years. All in all, we recruited an outstanding group of freshmen—maybe the largest number of leaders we ever had on one team.

After recruiting season, we conducted a winter workout program, patterned after what I had first learned at Texas Tech. When we looked for places to have our workouts, we found none. I found I had hired the right people, however, as we went about finding a room for workouts upstairs in the athletics offices building where visiting sports teams stayed. When they stayed upstairs, we moved the beds back in; when they left, we moved them out. We did not inherit a great group of athletes and after two bad, losing seasons they needed some faith in themselves and some hope for the future. So mostly we worked on making our players believe in themselves and in what we were going to do on offense, defense, and kicking. We really tried to "sell" the winter workout program, and the players "bought into it." Our biggest problem in the spring was lack of speed and quickness, so we worked hard on these areas as well as strength. Harold Wheeler and Steve Robertson handled the strength program, but we all worked in all areas. We did not have a strength coach per se, as did most schools.

Because we needed to improve our speed, during winter workouts Steve, unbeknown to us, laid off 40 yards in the parking lot with the running lanes going downhill. The players were actually improving on their 40-yard runs. Then we found he had purposely measured off 37 yards, so the times should have been good! Every Friday, we tested every player in sprints, agility, and strength to let them see their improvement. They actually did improve. They had a great attitude and wanted to be good.

We all got our families moved in either during spring practice or just afterwards. We were excited to move into our new home on Grandview Circle. Like the name, we had a "grand view" of both Paris Mountain and the Blue Ridge Mountains from our front yard. We had great neighbors, including John West, who lived just down the hill from us.

Every day at lunch time, we coaches would usually go to "Shaws" for lunch (meat and three veggies). We would come back and play three-on-three basketball in the practice gym just outside our offices. Usually Dick Sheridan, Jimmy Satterfield, and I would be one team and play three of the younger coaches. They would rotate after each "21" game. I don't know how, but the "oldies" usually won. Maybe it had something to do with the fact that since I was the head coach, I was the self-declared referee—well, somebody had to do it. These games were very physical and very competitive, with lots of pushing, shoving, holding, and trash talking. Several times, a play ended with two of us on the floor, but everybody knew we were there to have fun as well as to provide a break in our long work days. [It was more fun when the old guys won, however.] Quite often we would have collisions, resulting in bruises and sometimes cuts. We had a rule that we had to play man-to-man defense and you drove the basket at your own risk.

Eddie liked to guard me, and he thought if he ran hard the whole game he could "wear me out." He came close, but I can't ever remember him succeeding. One day he was running me more than usual and while chasing him I ran into Eric's elbow. He (Eric) caught me just above my eyebrow and split my forehead wide open. The trainer, Jay Shoop (who later served at Georgia Tech and with the Atlanta Falcons), came out and looked at it. Blood was everywhere, so he took me into the training room, laid me down on a training table, and called the emergency room to tell them I was coming in for stitches. He asked everyone not to tell me how bad it looked—about a six-inch slit in my forehead. He was afraid I might go into shock. About that time Steve Robertson came in (he never played basketball with us) and came over to me, and he picked up the ice compress and said, "God Almighty, what a hole!" So much for shock.

They took me to the emergency room, but Dick had had a bad experience with stitches and told Jay not to let an intern or even an emergency-room doctor sew me up. Jay called Dr. Dayton Riddle, our team orthopedic physician, and told him. He said, "Don't let them sew him up; bring him to my office." His office was nearby, and he looked and said, "Art, I've never done any plastic surgery before, but you need it. I can call a couple of my doctor friends over and you can be my first attempt if you're agreeable." He also said the cut was not straight or smooth, and would have to be trimmed before suturing. He did the job in his office with four or five doctors helping or at least observing. He did a great job and today, unless you look mighty close, you can't see the scar.

We had a good summer, but only a handful of our players were around for the summer session. We had no budget for summer school and Furman was so expensive that most players could not afford to attend. We were allowed to watch the Atlanta Falcons practice every day during their pre-season training camp. This was a big plus for us. They invited us to all their meetings and socials. Tommy Nobis, the great Texas linebacker, was a big country-music fan, and he always got his country-music buddies to come in for one big, "closed" performance and invited us. Johnny Paycheck and many other top entertainers also performed. We began our fall practice before the Falcons left camp, so often we would be working out on one field while the Falcons were on the other. This helped our players and coaches too. The Falcon kickers actually worked at times with our kickers. The Falcon coaches and players were impressed with our freshman quarterback, David Whitehurst. When the Falcons left, they gave us a large amount of used shoes, balls, and pads.

Prior to the season opener, we had "Meet the Paladins" for students and alumni. We had a good crowd and I introduced every player by name, hometown, class, and some tidbit about him. I felt it was important to know each player on our team and care about him as I would like a coach to care about my sons. We did this every year at Furman.

My First Season as a Head Coach

The 1973 season was a most exciting time of my life—my first head coaching job in college. Edie and the children gave me a Golden Shamrock for good luck. We, the coaches, felt we had had a great beginning—good winter workouts, a good spring practice, and a great recruiting coup. We felt fortunate to have had the Atlanta Falcons practice on our fields, and that "fired" us up for our coming season. My staff molded together, and we made an unusually good coaching team.

Our first game was against my alma mater, Presbyterian College. Their coach was Cally Gault, my ol' friend from P.C. and my coaching opponent when he was at North Augusta High and I was at Eau Claire High. I knew he was a good coach and had a good team. Being all new at Furman, we had very little scouting information on P.C. Nevertheless, we really had a very good preparation for our opener. We had two pretty good upperclassmen quarterbacks in Charlie Elvington (later a very successful high school coach at Mullins High School) and Mike Shelton, who had started games as a sophomore and junior, plus our new recruits. The game was scheduled at P.C. We had decided to start as many of our seniors against P.C. as we could and actually played pretty well, but found ourselves behind 7-6 at the end of the first half. The second half we decided to put David Whitehurst in as quarterback. He was a freshman from Atlanta, Georgia, and he made the difference in the second half, as we won our opening game in a hard-fought contest 13-6. [By this time, freshmen could play on the varsity team.]

The next week would be different though, as we were playing one of the best teams in the conference, Appalachian State, in our home opener. We prepared well and at least had a film or two to review. They had soundly defeated Furman the year before, and they were heavily favored this year. We played our home games in Sirrine Stadium, an old Greenville County high school stadium. The dressing rooms and other facilities at the stadium were so bad that we dressed in all but shoulder pads and helmets in our dressing room on campus and rode on our purple-and-white school bus seven or eight miles to the stadium—not "big time" by any means! On our way to the stadium, the bus broke down about a half mile from the stadium, and coaches and players alike had to take our gear and walk to the stadium. Some caught rides with fans. I thought, "What a way to begin my first home game before our hometown fans, walking to the stadium."

Appalachian State was very well coached by another friend, Jim Brakefield. It might be noted that he had several young coaches on his staff who would later be elevated to head coaching jobs—Mack Brown, Buddy Sasser, and Sparky Woods. We had decided to feature the option and the sweep for this game. Our fullback, Ike Sampson's (who was partially deaf) blocking assignment on the sweep was to block the Appalachian strong safety. We ran the play 27 times in the game, and he knocked the strong safety down 26 times, a rather remarkable feat. Needless to say, with Ike blocking like that, our tailbacks, Larry Robinson and Donny Griffin, had a great game, and we won the game 17-0 for a most impressive home-opening win.

Richmond was the best team in the conference in 1973. Frank Jones was the coach and they were undefeated. They had a fullback named Barty Smith, about 6 ft 3 inches, 250 lb, who would later play for the Green Bay Packers. Nobody had been able to stop him. We were 3-0 and suddenly people were beginning to pay attention to the Paladins. The game was in Greenville, and we had a large crowd. We had prepared well, and our players played well. We controlled Barty pretty well; our senior tackles Dan Utley and Stan Walker played exceptionally well. During the game we had a humorous incident that still stands out in my mind. We had a particular play where we would put our tailback in motion to either side and throw him a sort of screen pass with lead blockers. The only thing was that we put Larry Robinson in motion and threw him a screen pass; the play was not working as it should. During the half when we were going over with the team the things that needed improving, Larry held up his hand and said to Coach Satterfield, "Coach, you know when I go in motion on that screen pass, there "bees" too many men out there." That was Larry's way of expressing himself in a tight situation. He graduated from Furman in four years and went on to become a high officer as a chaplain in the U.S. Army. Richmond finally won a hard-hitting game 20-17. Even though we lost, we played well.

Pat Dye was the coach of East Carolina, and they were really beating up on teams. They had several all-star players, but Furman had for several years played well against them despite their records. We knew East Carolina would be better than we were, and we knew we had to rely on some trickery. We had an outstanding place kicker—maybe the best in the conference—so we planned that one time during the game we would have a chance to kick a field goal and with a good kicker they would expect us to kick; hence, we would try a fake field goal. The game was close, due mainly to our defense. Steve Robertson was a very good defensive coordinator and could really motivate his players. Harold Wheeler was a hard task master with the secondary; his players played well. They had a great game plan, and in the fourth quarter we drove down to the East Carolina 18-yard line and had fourth down and four yards to go for a first down. The score was 14-3 with 10 or 11 minutes left to go—time for the fake field goal. We had worked on one during practice where we had our extra point team on the field, with 11 men on the field. Andy Goss, a straight-A student who played halfback was, after we lined up, to yell, "We've got too many men on the field; get off Andy!" He was then to run toward our bench as if to run off field, and then to turn and head downfield for a pass as the ball was being snapped. All week in practice, we had him running off the field to our right, assuming he would know to run toward our bench. In the game, Andy got excited and ran off the field toward East Carolina's bench, to our horror. But you know what, he turned up field and nobody covered him. We completed a pass to him at the one-yard line, but out of bounds. We as young coaches learned a valuable lesson that night. Never assume a player will do what you think he will. Make sure you coach the play to cover every situation. Incidentally, we lost the game 14-3.

We finished our regular season at seven wins and three losses, and John West, our athletic director, asked me if we would agree to play the University of Louisville to close the season in order to get a healthy check (payoff). We agreed because I was told that the university was having to pay $150,000 per year in order to field a football team. Louisville was a big-time program that was down some at the time. We figured we might put in some tricks and not be too conservative against them. David Whitehurst had a very good game and we moved the ball well, but we just had a hard time stopping them. They had a really good running back named Peacock, and he had a great day. The score was 35-14 in their favor, leaving us with an overall record of 7-4-0. Some of our coaches were a little upset over our having to add a loss to our record to get a big check.

In 1973 we had one of those unusual teams—not a lot of great players but a lot of players who played as well as they could on every play. We had some of the most outstanding leaders I had ever seen—Vince Perone, Dan Utley, Steve Wilson, Larry Robinson, Larry Anderson, Tommy Marshall, Robbie Caldwell, David Whitehurst, Charlie Elvington, Mike Shelton—all good men. Our team was honored by the National Dunkel Service as the most improved team in America, something we were really proud of. The team and coaches with their 7-4 record enabled me to be named the "National Churchman Coach of the Year," the "Southern Conference Coach of the Year" (shared with Pat Dye), and the "South Carolina College Coach of the Year" (shared with Willie Jeffries). It was a very good beginning for my head coaching career. A number of our players received honors also. My staff was truly great! And our players really reacted to our coaching and motivation. Actually, we lost a couple games we could have won.

After our first successful season, things perked up around Furman and Greenville. Some faculty members even "came out of the closet" and became football fans. The Furman students became football fans and actually became a great help in our recruiting efforts. The coaches sat in one dining room where everybody ate, and we began to "scout out" the girls as to who would be willing to help recruit when we brought prospects on campus. We also began to try and improve our facilities and did well with limited funds.

During our first year at Furman, Artie was a rising high-school senior, and through Dr. Blackwell's son-in-law (who was the coach) he received a scholarship to Christ School, which was the No. 1 private school in the Upstate. Artie was sick to be moving to South Carolina, being in love with Jeanie Hobbs back in Lubbock. He went back in the summer to work out in Texas. Her parents seriously considering moving to Greenville and beginning a Cardigan water business there. Kim went to Christ School to begin with, but after a short spring semester she decided to go to Travelers Rest High School her final year. Ryan and Curtis got into Travelers Rest Elementary School, and Ryan played Little League baseball and played well. Both he and Curtis were frequent visitors to our spring practice drills.

We joined Travelers Rest Methodist Church and began a five-year further spiritual growth in our family and lives. [Travelers Rest is a small town just north of Greenville, not far from Furman.] We loved our new home; the only drawback was that it was on 2½ lots so it was a lot of grass to cut. Edie and I had been married some 22 years at the time and would celebrate our 25th anniversary while there. I thought (and still do) she was perfect. She was upset with her spiritual life, however. The Lord allowed her to meet a pastor's wife, Libby Hanford, who led her to become a great Christian.

The Remaining Four Seasons

The next year, we had a pretty good recruiting year and a very good winter workout and strength program. The 1974 season began with a loss to VMI followed by a win over P.C. Next, we had William and Mary, a power in the Southern Conference. We had recruited a wide receiver from Charleston who had previously committed to The Citadel but signed with us from Burke High School. He could fly, but he was undisciplined and lacking in fundamentals. David Whitehurst hit him on a couple deep touchdown passes and really outplayed their outstanding quarterback in a great win for us. The bad thing, however, was that after throwing a long touchdown pass into the end zone, we encouraged the offense to all go down and celebrate together. You might know a second-string fullback jumped up and came down on David's ankle, and he was out for three or four weeks. Fortunately, we had Charlie Elvington, who was a good quarterback in his own, and he came in as quarterback and played well. We won 10-0.

Subsequently, we beat Richmond at Richmond while Charlie was quarterback. David came back, and we had some upset players and parents when we put David back as our starter. We lost to The Citadel in Greenville when one of our punt returners let the bouncing ball brush his leg. They recovered the ball and beat us in a hard-fought game for the second loss in a row to The Citadel.

We played Lenoir-Rhyne, a smaller school, but they had a great big running back (a transfer from Georgia). We did not play well, probably all of us thinking we should win, and found ourselves leading just 14-10 in the waning moments of the game. They had a fourth and three at our three-yard line in the last few seconds. One thing we always did well was to study in great detail the opponent's tendencies; in other words what play would they likely call in a particular situation? I just knew they were going to run the "toss sweep" to their great tailback to their right. I grabbed Tommy Marshall, a 5 ft 11 inch, 185 lb defensive end transfer from Georgia and said, "Tommy, they are going to run the sweep at you; you've got to beat the tight end's block, get up field and force the play deep, and Mark Gordon will make the tackle." He was a very excitable player; his eyes were big as saucers as he assured me he would stop him. I said, "Go in for Dolphus Carter." He went in, they ran the sweep, and he beat the tight end's block and made the tackle himself for a four-yard loss. We ran the clock out and won the game 14-10. When Tommy came out, I grabbed him and we both jumped up and down hugging each other. I grabbed his helmet, looked him in the eye, and said, "Tommy, that was a great play; you played it just like we taught you; that was super." He grabbed me and said, "Coach, I can't take all the credit. Dolphus didn't come out!" Usually, I was more than honest, but I didn't feel inclined to tell the refs we had 12 men on the field.

We finished the 1974 season with a 5-6-0 record.

By the time of our third season (1975), we were pretty well organized and were getting great work out of our young coaches. They each were assigned important duties. One night we were playing Wofford at Spartanburg. Probably one of the greatest players I had anywhere to coach was Vince Perone. He was our free safety, and Harold Wheeler said Vince was never beaten on a deep pass. He was also our kick-off return player. In the beginning of the second half of the Wofford game, we received the kickoff and Vince ran it back for a touchdown. The team celebrated by piling on him in the end zone. An official flew a penalty flag on the pile of players. I motioned that I wanted to talk to the head official. He came over and I demanded, "What was that penalty for?"

He said, "Coach, you had a coach in that pile of players."

We covered in all our coaching staff meetings that no one could ever leave our bench area. I said, "There's no way we had a coach in the end zone!"

About that time Coach Billy Ware came up to me like a puppy and said, "Yes we did, Coach, I got carried away." (My apologies to the referee!)

In 1975, our record was 5-5-1, with the tie being against Wofford.

Our first year at Furman was a good one, but 1976 was better, even though the record was 6-4-1 compared to 7-4-0 in 1973. We started the season playing North Carolina State University in Raleigh. This was "Bo" Rein's first season as head coach, replacing Lou Holtz, who left "State" to coach the New York Jets. [Lou was asked before his first season as the Jet's coach what the main difference was between coaching with the Jets or at N.C. State. Lou, never bashful at a microphone, quipped, "We don't have any Furmans on our schedule."] We had a good team and kept the score close till the fourth quarter when State scored with five minutes to go and went ahead 12-10. Their ensuing kickoff went out of the end zone, so we started on our own 20. We came up with a "third and fifteen," and David Whitehurst hit Tommy Southard with a bootleg pass for 18 yards. We ran Harry King seven or eight times on the sweep and scored with a little over a minute left. Two plays later we intercepted a Johnny Evans pass and killed the clock for the 17-12 win. It would be hard to explain how exhilarated I was; it was the greatest thrill. Our fans were "out of sight." David Whitehurst's mother broke her ankle jumping down from the stands to hug her son.

The following Monday at the Greenville Touchdown Club's meeting, I was recognized and applauded for the win. That one game marked the direction Furman football would go for the next 25 years and beyond. To add to my pride, Artie was named the high school player of the week the same week. He played fullback and linebacker and was truly an outstanding two-way player at Christ School. After our win over N.C. State, I had mentioned how I felt my faith and the players' faith were a strong point in our play. Several days later I received a nice letter from Rev. Billy Graham congratulating me on our win and encouraging my continued growth in my faith in God. Cliff Barrows, the music and program director for the Billy Graham Evangelic Association, lived near Furman; we sometimes played tennis together. I suspect he might have prompted Dr. Graham's letter.

It did not take me long to "get down from cloud nine." As I left home Monday morning practically walking on air, Edie said, "Don't forget to empty the trash." I got to thinking of a way to get her out of town and away from being swarmed with well-wishers wherever we went. So, we went to a small movie house near Easley. I paid for two tickets and we entered the theater where the lights were on before the movie began. As we entered, the people began to applaud. I acknowledged the applause with a big grin and sat down. I leaned over to the man sitting next to me and said, "I guess you all heard about our big game Saturday."

He said, "No, the movie manager said he would only show the movie if he had 15 people. We had only 13; you two got us to 15."

My big grin suddenly disappeared.

We lost to The Citadel in a hard-fought game that was decided by a questionable call. We also lost a game to VMI. We just played poorly and they were always tough under Bob Thalman. Later we had East Carolina playing at our home. They were very good and had beaten UNC pretty badly and had lost only one game. Pat Dye's Pirates were heading for a bowl game. They had a great defensive end, Cary Godette, who literally played one side of their shade defense. We decided we would run at him most of the game, hoping to tire him out by the fourth quarter. We played great defense that year against the Pirates and were tied with them going into the fourth quarter. During a timeout David Whitehurst told me, "Coach, I think our strategy is working; Godette's blowing like a train." With three or four minutes left, we checked to a sweep when we recognized the blitz coming, and David did a great job pitching to Larry Robinson. Our line, backs, and receivers all made good blocks, and Larry ran 70 yards for the winning touchdown. We won 17-10 in one of our best games ever.

The 1976 team was probably the best one we had during my five years at Furman. I truly believe that year should go down as the year Furman football grew up and realized they could play with any team in the country and hold their own against many top 1-A teams. From 1976 Furman's football fortunes began to climb, and they have continued to do so. The class of 1976, the coaches, administration, teachers, and students deserve the credit. We all worked hard to reach this point. [I might note that the seniors on this team were the players my staff and I recruited in our rookie year.]

In 1977 we began our first year without David Whitehurst; he joined the Green Bay Packers and remained a quarterback there for seven years. We had recruited well though and were prepared to go at quarterback with Jimmy Kiser, a great athlete and winner wherever he played. This season was a tough transition for us to start over with new players. We had good players but did not play as well as we could and should have. Probably our low point was losing to Wofford. We were playing them at Wofford and leading 15-13 in the fourth quarter. We attempted a throw-back pass, which they intercepted and ran back for a game-winning touchdown. Dr. Blackwell, Furman's president, had worked many years at UNC and while he was a Furman graduate, he disliked losing, especially to Wofford. I learned later that when the UNC chancellor called Dr. Blackwell for a recommendation, he said, "Art's a good coach, but he lost to Wofford!" It's amazing how small things can help you or hurt you.

We still had good players—just not "a Whitehurst" at quarterback. Jimmy Kiser was a wonderful athlete who played tail back, wide receiver, and quarterback; he was around 5 ft 9 inches, 170 lb. Probably our greatest win of the season was at Chattanooga, where Coach Joe Morrison had an outstanding team. Between Jimmy Kiser's play at quarterback and Bobby Church's play at nose guard, we kept them in the hole just enough for a close victory.

On the last game of the season, we lost a game against The Citadel 10-3. Although I didn't know it at the time, this loss against Furman's instate rival plus the losses to them in each of our first four years at Furman constituted my greatest disappointment while at Furman. Citadel Coach Bobby Ross was very good; we did a good job of coaching against him, but never good enough. [Every year in the summer, the Southern Conference had a "Rouser" at Appalachian State where all the football coaches met the press and played golf and tennis and "wined and dined" the press. Every year, Bobby and I played tennis, and we would eventually get into the finals of the tournament. In 1974 we played three hours and 15 minutes on hard courts. Neither of us would give an inch. I regret to say I lost the match, and I was the better player. How? I don't know till this day. I still think about that loss but there would be other chances!]

After the season ended with a 4-5-2 record, we were all disappointed but knew we could have and should have done better. Being determined to rebuild our program based on the excellent group of talented players we already had, we began a determined effort to work harder than ever at recruiting new players for the next year's team. At this time I thought I would spend the rest of my coaching career at Furman; but the Good Lord had other plans for me.

An important and necessary aspect of all sports competition is the officiating. In one game Steve Robertson had complained the whole game to the official on our sideline about the opposition holding his defensive linemen. They carried on the conversation back and forth until late in the third quarter. Finally, the official, whom most of us knew somewhat, asked Coach Robertson what were the bugs that were biting so much. [Sirrine Stadium was located in a low place where in the fall deer flies were prevalent, and they bite.] The next time he came near our bench, Coach Robertson told him they were "ZoZo" flies.

A little later the official came by and said, "What's a ZoZo fly?"

Coach Robertson, with a straight face, said, "They are flies that hang around a horse's rear end."

The official turned on Coach Robertson while reaching for his penalty flag and said, "Are you calling me a horse's rear end?"

Coach replied in a serious manner, "Oh no, but it's hard to fool a ZoZo fly!"

Fortunately, the official took it in good stride.

Another funny officiating story happened to me. We were playing East Carolina at home in Greenville, South Carolina (East Carolina is located in Greenville, North Carolina!), and leading in the fourth quarter. We had worked hard on a play to use when we got near their goal line. We would pitch the ball to Andy Goss on a sweep and our tight end Steve Hall would run at the defensive back as if to block him but before any contact was made he was to slip off to the corner of the end zone for a pass We ran the play in the game, and it worked to perfection for a touchdown. But, the official watching the play develop thought the tight end made contact with the defensive back and called a penalty based on what he thought happened (or what he anticipated happening) instead of what actually happened. Hence, the touchdown was called back. [If the end makes contact with a defensive back, the end is no longer eligible to catch a pass; it's a hard call to make.] I complained bitterly to the referee (the head official), who was also an NFL referee on Sundays. After a bit, he said, "Art, I believe you are right, but we will not change the call. I'll give you two minutes to wave your arms and stomp your feet; your fans will be disappointed, but they will still love you for fussing." (Thanks, ref!)

Reflections on My Time at Furman

As I think back now some 40 years later to my time at Furman, I am again amazed by the number and quality of outstanding football players we, a rookie coach and a rookie staff, managed to recruit to Furman is spite of various obstacles. Furman was a private, Baptist school and the cost to go there in 1973 was $15,000, a sizable amount at that time (today the cost is $40,000). [Some other schools in our conference were state supported, with considerably less cost to attend.] Many potential students, perhaps particularly student athletics, simply could not afford it. To overcome this obstacle, we had to provide football students with scholarships. Here again, we were at a disadvantage. We had 50 scholarships available and were competing in the Southern Conference where most schools had 95. We had to compete in recruiting with these schools, so we had to break up our scholarships into parts in order to recruit some 80 players on 50 scholarships. Often, we would be able to offer a half scholarship to a good player while The Citadel, Appalachian State, Marshall, and others could offer the same player a full scholarship. Students from South Carolina could get S.C. grants of about $2500, and Pell Grants amounted to around $1000. Occasionally, needy students would also qualify for further aid. You can bet we utilized everything we could.

Furman had never graduated a black player in 1973; hence, many outstanding football players were being missed. As I mentioned previously, Dick Sheridan worked very hard on recruiting black students, with the result that six or seven minority athletes, who might not normally have been admitted, were admitted the first year; and they all graduated in four years

Not only were the entrance requirements to Furman very strict, the academic programs were rigorous. There were no "easy" majors or classes student athletes could take to get or remain eligible. [I'm not complaining about this—just telling how it was then and there.] We certainly could not rely on these young men to keep their grades up on their own. Coach Sheridan, an engineering graduate from USC, was our academic advisor as well as coach; he did a great job in that capacity in guiding our players and keeping them on track with their studies. [Most schools had a separate person who did this duty.] Further, we documented classroom attendance and demanded total concentration for athletes in their classes. We also arranged volunteer tutors from faculty and students. Violations, such as skipping class, were not tolerated. I always felt that if we recruited young men to play football for us, it was our responsibility to see that they graduated and were not exploited for athletic purposes.

Sirrine Stadium was certainly not a positive for Furman. This 40-year-old stadium we played our home games in was the Greenville County high school stadium where Greenville High School played cross-town rival, Parker High School, on Thanksgiving Day before 15,000+ fans. The dressing rooms were not really dressing rooms, but just small huts for the visitors and the home team. They were so bad you could see through slits in the walls and floors. There were no showers, no heat, and minimal rest room facilities. The visiting team had to dress in the nearby motel where they stayed and had to walk a couple blocks to the stadium; we dressed at our own dressing room on campus and had to ride seven or eight miles to the stadium. Parking was very limited. The surrounding area was a rather bad part of town. Some people found their cars broken into or their hubcaps stolen when they returned to their cars after the game. The playing field was adequate. Despite the poor conditions, however, the Furman students and loyal fans came to the games and really supported the team.

Actually, the overall location of a new stadium had already been designated on campus, and we had long pointed out to recruits its location and future construction. As fate would have it, a new stadium was built not too long after I left. Paladin Stadium is a beautiful facility with a scenic view of Paris Mountain. How I wish it had been there when I was there!

On the other hand, there were many positives to enticing young men to come to Furman. Furman was in 1973 and continues today to be the most beautiful campus in the world. The "new campus" was built from scratch in the late 1950s. [The old campus had been downtown near Sirrine Stadium.] I sat with the design engineer at a dinner for the 25th anniversary of the "new campus." He told me he had actually planned where every plant, tree, and flower were to be planted. Students used to say Furman was the only school in the nation where plants were fed better than students.

A degree from Furman was as prestigious as one from an Ivy League school. Furman students rarely had problems being accepted to law and medical schools, or to leading graduate schools. Most other graduates were hired for top jobs before graduating.

The community of Greenville became one of our strongest supporters. Vince Perone owned the premiere restaurant in Greenville; he put on our Monday press conferences at "the Forum," which helped us a great deal with public relations. There were other long-time loyal Furman fans who were strong supporters of our program. We coaches worked real hard to gain the confidence of local and South Carolina, North Carolina, and Georgia high school coaches.

The biggest plus and advantage we enjoyed were our coaching staff. They were by far the difference in our success at Furman. Dedicated, loyal, knowledgeable, and motivators, they loved our players and the players knew that and responded. Six of them would go on to become college head coaches, one was the athletic director of the year in the nation, and three would be named national "coaches of the year" at the American Football Coaches Association convention. Yes, I'm very proud of each of them.

Family Matters

The years at Furman were fun years. I liked being a head coach and also liked the role I had of being a Christian coach. I spoke quite a bit at high school athletic banquets and at churches. I always included either my testimony or a message I hoped would lead young people to Jesus Christ. We loved our church, Travelers Rest Methodist, and Edie and I were both active in several areas of church life. Our athletic director, John West, and I were very active in the Fellowship of Christian Athletes; our chapter met each week at John's home, which you may remember was a stone's throw from my house. His wife Charlotte and Edie and others usually baked cakes or cookies for the meetings. We had 40 to 50 attend. Amy Grant, a student, came often and sang for us. Beth Daniel and Betsy King, LPGA golfers, were also at Furman those years and attended FCA meetings. We had some good times and many of us grew in the Lord.

Artie graduated from Christ School and was an outstanding athlete. He was all-state in football at fullback and linebacker. He also made all-state in track, winning the state title in the 100-yard dash, shot put, and discus and also ran on a winning relay team. [Texas had been a great boost for him. Almost every high school had winter workouts and weight training, and every school had an obstacle course which was really tough and which they had to run every day during fifth or sixth period at school.] Artie truly was an outstanding athlete. I wanted him to come to Furman; the coaches did too. In later years, he told me he regretted not playing for Furman. He told others he didn't because he was close friends with David Whitehurst, Beech Foster, and several other players, and he smoked cigarettes and did not want to make his daddy look bad.

Ryan and Curtis were beginning to play team basketball and baseball. Ryan also had promise as a future football player; he was always a little big for his age. In fact, there were several occasions where he played in a league where they had to weigh under a certain amount. Often, he would have to not eat before a game and run some to get below the required weight. Ryan had talent and loved to play. Curtis was not a great athlete, but he was a competitor and played hard.

Kim did not participate in sports. I've often said she is and was our toughest child; she chose to work and save her money for clothes and college.

As a family we continued trying to "eat out" every Wednesday. We had several favorite places, including "The Peddler," a great steak house with a terrific salad bar and "The Pizza Hut," which the boys really liked. Often, we would go to Table Rock State Park and eat at a great restaurant there. They served "family style" and had great fried chicken and catfish (finger small); we got our money's worth. Edie and I continued our long habit of taking our family to Ocean Drive Beach in the summer where we felt like it was our second home.

Head Coach Perks

During our five years at Furman, my first job as a head coach, Edie and I were invited to the "Tournament of Champions," sponsored by the Citrus Bowl in Orlando, as were all the other head coaches in the country. We were put up in one of the nicest hotels in Orlando each year, usually a different one each year. The host bowl would have a golf tournament and tennis tournament each year. We would play tennis in the mornings and we had tickets to Disney World, Epcot, and MGM for the afternoons. Then at night we had a nice banquet dinner.

While in Orlando the five years I was at Furman, I won the tennis tournament twice. Besides a nice crystal ice bucket, we also won a trip for two to St. Thomas Island for a week. Included on that trip were scuba lessons in a pool near our hotel. The instructor told us to put on our scuba gear and put our heads under the water to get used to the gear and water. Now Edie was not sure about putting her head under water, but she did put the gear on. Then the instructor told us to swim or dogpaddle across the pool. There were 10 or 12 of us in the class. We all swam or paddled across the pool. When we got to the other side and I was still looking under water, I looked back across the pool and saw a pair of legs still standing at the spot we had left from. I recognized the legs immediately as Edie's. She refused to put her head under water or swim; we all about died laughing.

The Dallas Cowboys and Dr. Pepper put on a similar "outing" along with the Cotton Bowl. It was held in Dallas, and the format was usually about the same as Orlando. Again, I was fortunate enough to win the tennis tournament a couple times. Once I won a pair of "Tony Lama" western boots. [When at Texas Tech and playing in the Sun Bowl, Tony Lama made each of the coaches a pair of black western boots with a red "T" cut on the front.] On another occasion, I won a trip for two to New York with some Broadway shows included. It was a prize from Braniff Airlines, and before we could use the trip (because of the football season), Braniff went out of business and we lost the trip! On another occasion I won a tennis tournament at Orlando with the prize being a trip to the Bahamas. We departed from Ft. Lauderdale and landed in Freeport. To travel to the main part of Freeport, we had to catch a water taxi that ran back and forth every hour. There were some nice sights in Freeport and there were some sorry ones.

Part of our trip to the Bahamas included a boat ride out to the reefs to see the underwater life by scuba. There were about 15 others on the boat, and we were instructed to "pair up" and make sure we stayed together on and off the boat. When we got on the boat, we saw our first "thong" bikini bathing suit on a very attractive lady on the boat. All the men including me were keeping up with her every move. Going out, the water was rough, and it didn't take much for me to get seasick. But I wanted to scuba some, and Edie and I got in the water and were rewarded with some wonderful aquatic life. But the water was still rough and I got sicker. I went back to the boat, climbed up the ladder, and went over to a group of three or four men who were in the same condition I was. I thought Edie knew I was going back but she didn't. After a while she missed me and just knew I was off looking at "Miss Thong." She eventually began to panic and asked if a man who looked like me was on the boat. Everybody including me were too sick to answer. She went to the boat captain after looking for me underwater and finally found a very seasick husband who at the time couldn't care less about thong bikinis.

As we shopped around Freeport, we noticed a certain "dish" was advertised in several places—boiled codfish with onions for breakfast. It did not appeal to me, but Edie will try any exotic food. She had eaten frog legs, rattle snake, and chitterlings in her life, and sure enough she tried the boiled codfish with onions. She liked it!

Enter Fate!

During the January following our 1977 season (my fifth), I was in Moncks Corner, South Carolina, located about 30 miles from the beach near Charleston, on a combined recruiting and hunting trip. I usually stayed at Berkeley Motel there; they had great breakfast—my favorite meal. After hunting one day, I had a call from Edie saying that the athletic director at the University of North Carolina, Bill Cobey, had called to say they had been so impressed by our wins over N.C. State and East Carolina in 1976 that they wanted me to come to Chapel Hill to interview for the position of head football coach. I hadn't given any thought to leaving Furman, but I returned Bill's call and could hardly contain myself when he invited me to come for the interview. I drove directly the 240 miles from Moncks Corner to Chapel Hill for the interview. He warned me that I should not get too excited, for I was to be one of several candidates and probably being invited to be one of the "minor candidates." Even so, I was very excited driving to Chapel Hill; I worried that I didn't have my best wardrobe but did the best I could.

When I arrived, the committee was in the process of interviewing several candidates, and they were surprised to see me there. Coach Jim Donnan, who later became the head coach at Georgia, was on the staff of the outgoing coach, Bill Dooley, and he had already been interviewed. We had known each other through some meetings at Ocean Drive Beach while we were on vacation together at the same time. He, Bill Parcells (later the head coach for the New York Giants, New England Patriots, New York Jets, and Dallas Cowboys), and I would get together several days at their cottage to "talk football." Coach Donnan more or less told me he didn't think I would be one of their top candidates. Thus, I felt I could go into the interview feeling I could "be myself" without a lot of pressure. The committee consisted of 15 or so professors, administrators, and booster members. My interview went really well, I thought.

I left Chapel Hill and drove back to Travelers Rest, and Edie and the family were all excited with me over this unexpected opportunity. I did not hear anything for several days and attended the last days of the AFCA meeting in Atlanta, Georgia. I always enjoyed these meetings, and I still attend when I can to see old friends and keep up with football. I have served on a number of committees, chairing the "Summer Manual" committee. While I was checking out of the hotel after the meeting, I received a page and answered it. John West was calling to tell me the athletic director from Wake Forest, Gene Hooks, had called him to get permission to talk to me about the open Wake Forest head coaching job. He gave me a number at a nearby motel, and I called Gene Hooks. He asked me to come over and have supper with him in his room. My interview that night went well, and we arranged a meeting for the next Wednesday at Wake to meet with the committee and the Wake team. I could not believe that in a matter of one week, I was being interviewed by two ACC schools!

On the following Monday, I met with my staff and told them what had transpired; they were as excited as I was. Later the same day, Bill Cobey from UNC, called to say the committee had been impressed and wanted me to come back and bring my wife to meet with the chancellor and the chairman of the Board of Trustees. They were aware that Wake Forest had called me and asked that I meet with them on Wednesday morning. Edie and I couldn't help but be excited to be asked back. The interviews all went well; I was even interviewed by Dean Smith, the head basketball coach, whom I knew from FCA. When we were leaving, Bill walked out to the car with us. It was raining and he came close to Edie's window under his umbrella and talked to Edie. I'll never forget his words. He said, "Edie, it looks very much like your husband is going to be our football coach."

We drove directly from there to Winston-Salem for our meeting with Wake "on a cloud" following our positive experience at UNC and really a lot less interested in the Wake job under the circumstances. The interview there went well, but Gene had warned me that the committee had several liberal professors. Some of them questioned my rather strict rules. I then met with the team. They were not nearly as impressive as our own Furman team. There was lots of long hair, beards, and beads. I told them if I were their coach, they would have to cut their hair and shave their beards among other things but that these things would prove beneficial to our team. We left Winston-Salem and drove back to Travelers Rest that night. The next day, the Durham newspaper ran an account of everything I had done at UNC. I still think some of the powers-that-be thought I had spilled the beans, which I had not.

The next day nothing happened. Two days later Bill called from North Carolina to say the committee had voted and tied between me and Jim Donnan, then voted again with the same result. But nothing yet had happened. Then Gene Hooks from Wake Forest called to ask if I would reconsider my rule on long hair and beards. I told him I had always felt you have to pay a price to be winners, and I would not abandon this rule, effectively removing me from further consideration. Then Bill from North

Carolina called to say the committee had decided to reopen the interviews and they eventually hired Dick Crum from Miami of Ohio. Thus two potential opportunities were suddenly gone. But, do not despair!

Some years earlier, I had been at a Southern Conference meeting, and Eddie Teague, the athletic director at The Citadel, and I were talking, I told him how much I admired the job they did at The Citadel. He confided that when he had hired Bobby Ross as head coach he had thought hard about offering the job to me. I told him it would have been an honor.

After missing out on the UNC and Wake Forest jobs, neither of which I had sought, I got a call a week or so later from none other than Eddie Teague saying Bobby Ross was leaving The Citadel to coach for the Kansas City Chiefs. I guess I had prepared myself to possibly leave Furman with the UNC and Wake Forest interviews, so I agreed to meet with Coach Teague and the search committee. No one had mentioned my name for The Citadel job. I talked to Edie about it and as with all the other jobs we considered, we prayed that God would give us wisdom in this opportunity.

I went to Charleston to meet with The Citadel people not really expecting to take the job. There were, I found, some advantages to coaching at The Citadel over Furman. There were the problems I have previously discussed about being at Furman—strict entrance requirements, lack of adequate scholarships, rigorous academic programs, the poor location and condition of the "home stadium," etc. At The Citadel I would get a salary of about $30,000, compared to the $22,000 I was making at Furman; and at The Citadel, I would be provided a four-bedroom townhouse on campus facing the Ashley River. I would only have to pay for utilities, and I could walk to work. The Citadel had a nice training table and an on-campus stadium and in those days averaged 12,000 to 17,000 for home games (compared to 8,000 to 10,000 at Furman). I currently had five full-time coaches; at The Citadel, I would have seven, with small salary increases for the assistant coaches. One more thing: when I coached at Clemson, Coach Howard had impressed on me the value of the State Retirement System. At The Citadel, I would add to my 17 years of state retirement. [Although at Furman they matched up to 15% of my salary for any moneys I put into TIAA-Cref, to be honest those five years at Furman have subsequently proved to be a valuable retirement benefit in addition to my state retirement benefits.] One drawback at The Citadel, however, was that I knew recruiting would be more difficult there because all students had to be in the cadet corps. [As I learned later, players being in the cadet corps also limited football practice time somewhat.]

I went to talk to Dr. John Johns, the then-president of Furman, and we had a wonderful talk. He assured me that my stay at Furman was secure. I asked about any possible salary increases for my coaches and me and most importantly about any possibility of a new on-campus stadium. I knew that if Furman could ever build an on-campus stadium, it would be the choice spot in the Southern Conference. I told Dr. Johns this and assured him that with a new stadium, I would never leave Furman on my own. He told me he realized that, but that Furman was already making a substantial contribution to athletics in order to keep football, and he was afraid I would be retired before Furman ever had a new on-campus stadium.

After Dr. Johns told me no significant raises for coaches, no increase in scholarships, and no new stadium any time soon, I began to explore more closely the pros and cons of The Citadel offer. First, I realized that to leave Furman on my own and go to Furman's No. 1 rival in state was not going to be very popular, and I enjoyed great relations with Furman supporters. Second, John West was telling me that Furman would probably replace me with Dal Shealy, who was coaching at Auburn and Baylor. I was pushing Dick Sheridan on my staff to replace me.

After considering all the pros and cons and all our prayers, Edie and I decided to go to The Citadel. I met right away with Dick, Jimmy Satterfield, and Steve Robertson—all from my old Eau Claire staff—and strongly suggested they support one of themselves rather than all three go after the job. Jimmy and Steve supported Dick. I next went to the team and told them if they felt like me and the other coaches about Coach Sheridan, they should form a committee and go to the president, athletic director, and search committee and tell them they wanted Coach Sheridan. They did and I believe their action helped Dick get the job eventually. This was probably not very smart on my part because if Dick did not get the Furman job, he, Jimmy, and Steve and others would probably have gone with me to The Citadel, though I have to admit they were not as excited about it as I was. If he did get the job, I suspected they would stay with him at Furman. I wanted him to get the job, but I selfishly wanted all of them to come with me.

I don't know how, but the news of my going to The Citadel was kept a pretty good secret. They flew me to Charleston for the press conference to announce me as the new head football coach. They made the announcement during the noon meal in the mess hall. Afterwards, I met my (new) players for the first time where I spoke to each one of them. I remembered some advice Coach Howard had given me at Clemson when I was going out for my first recruiting trip. He said, "Art, if you can look 'em in the eye, they are too little [short] to play." As I spoke to each Citadel player, it seemed I was looking too many of them "in the eye."

When I came out from meeting with the players, Eddie Teague said to me, "I've got good news and bad news for you. Dick Sheridan was just named the head coach at Furman." Dick, Jimmy, Steve, and I were strongly like family. I was very pleased for him but realized that each coach knew what I could pay them at The Citadel. Well, Dick didn't "come over on the turnip boat," and he wanted the coaches to stay with him at Furman. He shared with Dr. Johns what I could offer them at The Citadel, and Dr. Johns suddenly came up with more money for them at Furman; thus, Jimmy, Steve, and several graduate assistants chose to stay there. So it was indeed good news and bad news. I was happy Dick would now be a head coach, something he had earned and richly deserved, but I regretted the other guys would be remaining behind, and I would now have to hire a new staff "from scratch."

Another House to Sell

Once again I had a house to sell. We had a great home in Travelers Rest and had just built a tennis court on the 2½ lots our house was on. At the time the interest rate on home loans had soared from 5% to 13%, so it was not a good time to be trying to sell a house. Unlike previous times when we were moving and buyers had called unsolicited to say they wanted to buy my house, this time It took over a year to sell it, although we did lease it for a while to the (new) Furman athletic director, Dutch Bachman.

Thus the Baker Furman era ended. As usual, we enjoyed our years there but looked forward to the future at The Citadel in Charleston.

10 AT THE CITADEL

The Citadel (full name: The Citadel, The Military College of South Carolina) is located in the beautiful and quaint city of Charleston, which is located on the coast of South Carolina. It is around 110 miles southeast of Columbia. Founded in 1670, Charleston has a long and rich history.

Building My Second Collegiate Staff

I moved to Charleston as head football coach at The Citadel in 1978 without a family and without a staff. My children were still in school in Greenville, and my staff were still employed at Furman. They put me up in the Mark Clark Hall (like a little hotel) on campus. I don't ever remember being so lonely. Each morning I was awakened at 5:00 a.m. with the bugle at Reveille. I must admit I suffered through some second thoughts about making the move, but not for long. Thinking about all the work I had ahead of me, I put aside my melancholy and went to work.

Bobby Ross had a good staff at The Citadel; I had been impressed with them while coaching and recruiting against them while I was at Furman. I wisely asked Frank Beamer to remain as my defensive coordinator, Ralph Friedgen as offensive line coach, Charlie Rizzo as defensive line coach, and Cal McCombs as secondary coach. Some of the Citadel people were upset with me because I didn't keep some of the other coaches already there, but I went outside and asked Rick Gilstrap to come (from Furman) and coach quarterbacks, Mike O'Cain to work with running backs, Ricky Diggs with receivers, Wilbur Grooms with defensive ends, and Ellis Johnson as defensive coach. Actually, I put together an outstanding staff rather quickly. Tom Park was on campus to be interviewed by Bobby

Ross and Eddie asked me to consider him. I hired him; he could recruit in Pennsylvania and New Jersey. After spring practice, I met Brad Scott and asked him to join my staff as a graduate assistant. Along with Steve Patton who joined my staff later, nine of my Citadel staff eventually became outstanding head football coaches. God seemed to bless me with the ability to choose and hire outstanding men and coaches to be a part of my staff.

I had really been pent-up about the fact that none of my Furman staff (except for Rick Gilstrap) came with me to The Citadel, though when I first told them I was going none of them indicated they really wanted to coach at The Citadel. The first time I went back to Furman, I asked Dick to let me meet him, Jimmy, and Steve since we were the original Eau Claire staff. I very emotionally told them how disappointed I was that they didn't want to come. They were very respectful and listened to me pour out all my frustrations. This probably did us all some good. The respect, concern, and love for each other never lessened, but we never worked together again.

Besides building my staff, one of the first things I had to do was look at the athletes (former) Coach Ross and his staff had already recruited. One such player was Cedric "Get Down" Brown from near Atlanta, Georgia. He was a big, defensive tackle—275 lb—and was very talented as well as an outstanding student. I immediately made an appointment to visit him and his family. The visit was going well when Cedric said, "Uh Coach, everything sounds great but what about what Coach Ross promised me?"

I thought to myself, "Oh no, what did Bobby promise him?" I knew Bobby would never break a recruiting rule, but I was afraid Cedric might have misunderstood something Bobby might have said.

He said, "Coach Ross promised me I could wear white shoes."

With a big sigh of relief, I said, "Cedric, you can surely wear white shoes and I will buy you two pairs."

I still keep in touch with Cedric, who wore his white shoes and played exceptionally well. He had a great singing voice and sang at Coach Diggs's wedding.

Another recruiting story: Jim Ettari was one of several excellent players located by Coach Ralph Friedgen in the New York City area. Ralph's dad was a high school coach in the area, so Ralph knew many of the coaches in the area through his dad. When I visited Jim at Brentwood High School, it was cold and everyone was wearing cold-weather clothes, sweatshirts, and coats. Later, when he visited Charleston and The Citadel, it was 80° in the Port City, and Jim was wearing a short-sleeve tee shirt. It was then that I noticed he had tattoos on both biceps. One said "Saturday Night's All Right For Fighting"; the other said "Death Before Dishonor." I knew we had the right guy, and he lived up to all his promise, becoming an All-America defensive lineman.

When I arrived at The Citadel, the football offices were in the old field house. There was no area for winter workouts. The school would not alter any existing area to fit our needs. There was old Thompson Hall unused for a long time and used then as a storage area. My coaches and I cleaned up the building and borrowed mats and used it for our winter workout program. Then we had to adjust to practice fields that were often underwater on one end that bordered the Ashley River, especially at high spring tides.

Then the new staff and I had to learn to dress appropriately to combat the sand gnats, vicious insects that will crawl down your collar and up your sleeve then into your mouth nose and ears. Their "bite" leaves a painful, often burning, sensation, which may result in a lesion. The experienced players taught us to "cover up." This meant tape our ears, wear shirts with long sleeves and high necks, and stockings. We all learned the value of Avon's "Skin so Soft," which we applied liberally to keep the bugs off. We had to overcome quite a few obstacles before we had been through our "Plebe year." Our coaches all worked hard to provide our players with facilities and means to properly prepare our players strength- and agility-wise. We had to do most of the work, or it would not get done.

Moving to Charleston

As I mentioned previously, it took over a year to sell our house in Greenville, but thankfully as part of my agreement to accept the Citadel job, we were given "Quarters" on the Citadel campus and had only to pay utilities. They took a while to prepare it for us. Edie chose colors for the rooms and bought some new furniture, rugs, etc. The unit was excellent; it had a nice, big, dining room and four bedrooms. I could walk to work each day. Tennis courts were across the street, and the tennis coach, Don Bunch, lived several doors down the street. The President's house was 50 yards or so away. We finally sold our house in Travelers Rest in about 13 months and decided to take the equity and begin buying a beach cottage on the Isle of Palms ("Wild Dunes") near Charleston. We kept it for some 24 years and sold it to Walter Cox, Jr. It was the best investment we ever made. Kim and Curtis lived in it for a while.

When we finally moved to Charleston, Artie had already gone to Mars Hill College, Greenville Tech, and North Greenville, and he decided to stay in Greenville to work awhile. He lived in a small house George (my brother) and I bought and rented to Artie and a bunch of Furman players. Kim transferred from Furman to the College of Charleston from which she later graduated. Ryan went to Bishop England High School and played tight end on their championship football team. He caught a touchdown pass in one of the playoff games. Curtis went to First Baptist High School and loved it; he ran track there and later graduated.

We really enjoyed living and working on campus. Edie and I began walking every evening and would go by the barracks and enjoyed getting to know a lot of the cadets. They were a great bunch. And Charleston was a great city to live in.

Artie came down the first summer and worked on the campus at the Gate.

The First Four Years

When I began winter workouts and spring practice, I learned many things about being a head coach at a military school. Football is actually an outlet for the players. The military regime they are required to follow takes precedence over all their daily life. You don't get to see them as often as you really need to. When we began spring drills, I had a very impressive thing happen. A walk-on was knocked out in a drill and scared me to death. I thought, "Here lies a man who could die and I don't even know his name or anything about his home or family." He was okay, but you can bet your life I got to know and love every one of them after that.

Our first season went pretty well. The new staff did very well; our team was well coached. We probably won the games we should have and lost games we could have won. Our biggest win was against Delaware. We were tied in the fourth quarter, and Delaware lined up for a field goal attempt from our 25-yard line. We had a very quick defensive player we called "Slam Bam Cunningham," who was good at blocking kicks, and he blocked Delaware's attempt. Mike Adams was a small but very tough defensive end. He picked up the ball and was a little confused as to which way Delaware's goal line was but got some yelled "advice" from a few teammates and easily outran the Delaware field-goal team for a very exciting win against a very good Delaware team.

When we played Georgia Tech in Atlanta that year, Pepper Rogers was the Tech coach. He and I were talking before the game, and he mentioned how he had been getting some criticism from some Tech fans. He wore a little golf hat. He said ever since he had an assistant coach about the same size he was, he made the assistant wear a hat just like his. Then if some fan got too excited and decided to shoot him, there was a 50% chance he would shoot the wrong guy!

The biggest disappointment of the first season was the game against rival Furman in Greenville. It came down to the end with a score of Furman 17 – Citadel 13. Furman committed pass interference on the last play in the end zone, giving us one play from the one-yard line after the clock had run out. Our regular quarterback, Tim Russell, had a bad ankle and couldn't play. A senior, Marty Crosby, had played well; he was big and an excellent passer but slow afoot. We had Stump Mitchell at tailback. Everybody in the stadium thought we would surely run Stump. I told Marty I wanted him to fake an isolation play to Stump and run a bootleg around the end. He said to me, "Oh no, you're not putting this game on my shoulders."

I was really upset but did not have another quarterback to play. So we ran Stump who was to dive over the line of scrimmage. The field was wet from having been underwater the day before. Stump slipped on his dive, and the officials made a very close call of "no touchdown." Thus we lost the game and ended the season with a 5-6 record.

Each year, the week after the end of the season the Charleston Touchdown Club had Dick Sheridan from Furman and me from The Citadel to speak and explain the Furman-Citadel game. I sure hated to have to explain our tough loss.

Our recruiting that year was really pretty good. We recruited several outstanding players from the Lehigh Valley region in Pennsylvania—Mike Knox, an All-Star quarterback and punter (who actually played more baseball at shortstop than football); and Rich Sniscak, who was outstanding as a defensive back. We recruited three outstanding players from New York—Jim Ettari, an All-American nose guard; John Gamby, an offensive guard; and Joe Pipczynski, an All-Conference offensive tackle. We also recruited two young men from Darlington, South Carolina—Gerald Toney and Prince Collins. Gerald became our quarterback later and subsequently worked with Sunoco as their No. 1 general manager.

Our second year at The Citadel was a 6-5 season; we played some good games and some bad games. We played Navy at Annapolis, Maryland, in the second game of the season. U.S. Senator Ernest Hollings, a Citadel graduate, invited the players and coaches to have dinner with him in the Senate dining room. As we pulled up to the parking place in the team bus area, Jim Ettari's family was waiting to see him. I had been in their home and knew what a great family they were. Jim came up to me in the front of the bus and asked if he could go out and speak to his family. I said sure. Now Jim was one of the toughest players I ever coached and was intimidating as a defensive lineman, but he walked out in full view of his team and hugged and kissed his dad, his mom, and each of his sisters. That was a great example of what should be so important in our lives. We lost the game to Navy 26-7.

Our third game of the season was against Vanderbilt. We had lost our first two games to Presbyterian and Navy, and Vanderbilt was playing Alabama the next week. Under these circumstances, they did not respect our team. We got to Nashville Friday evening and relaxed at a park across from our motel. When the game began, we had Tim Russell at quarterback and Stump Mitchell at tailback. Tim was an excellent option quarterback and Stump was an excellent runner. They ran the option and sweep to perfection and Vanderbilt couldn't stop us. We were leading 20-0 at halftime. I went into the locker room to find the players celebrating. I said, "Wait a minute; this game is just half over."

They said, "Yeah coach, but we haven't been ahead at the half before!"

I told the team that if we were not careful and did not go out and play the second half like we did the first half, we could be beaten.

Sure enough, Vanderbilt came out and quickly scored twice making the score 20-14. Rick Gilstrap called down from the press box and said, "Coach, they are overplaying the sweep. I believe the reverse to Mark Slawson would be a good play." I thought about the play and remembered how the play worked. Tim would pitch the ball to Stump who would run to his right and then hand the ball to Mark going the other way. Then I remembered what Tim's assignment was after pitching the ball; he had to go the other way and block their right tackle. I looked out on the field and their right tackle, No. 77, was a 6 ft 5 inch, 330 lb giant. Tim was 5 ft, 11 inches, 155 lb. I remembered after every games Tim's mother saying to me, "Coach, I'm depending on you to watch out for my son."

Before we could run the play, Vandy called time out. I called Tim over to the sideline and told him the reverse seemed like a good play and asked what he thought of it. I reminded him he would have to block No. 77.

He said, "Run it, coach; I'll kill him!"

I wasn't so sure myself. But we ran the play and it worked like a charm. Tim sneaked up on their giant tackle, cutting his shins making the tackle cut a flip. Mark scored a 60-yard touchdown.

After the play, I looked back on the field to see what had happened to Tim. That big tackle had Tim lifted up to his face and was shaking him.

When Tim came to the sidelines, I said, "Tim, what was that guy saying to you?"

He said, "If you ever do that again, I'm going to chew you up and swallow you whole."

I said, "What did you say?"

Tim said, "I got in his face and said if you do, you'll have more brains in your stomach that in your head!"

Tim was a tough little fellow!" We beat Vanderbilt 27-14 that day for a great victory.

Once again, our last game of the season against our rival Furman was a heartbreaker. We scored on the last play of the game to make the score 45-44 in their favor. I decided to go for two points for a win rather than one point for a tie. Tim Russell, our quarterback, was not a good passer but was a great option quarterback. He threw for 400 yards passing that day but barely missed hitting Brian Walker for the winning two-point play. Hence, we lost the game 45-44, and I had to face the Charleston Touchdown Club with Dick Sheridan again!

The third year at The Citadel went 7-4. One game was perhaps more memorable for what happened after the game than during the game. We played USC in Columbia. They had George Rogers, the eventual Heisman Award winner, and we had Stump Mitchell, who finished second in the nation in rushing behind George Rogers. They had a bowl team and we had a pretty good team too (7-4). We got off to a good start recovering a fumble on the opening kickoff and scoring. USC eventually won 43-34. George had 170 yards rushing and Stump had 156.

During the game some of our fans were sitting with some of the USC fans. Two of them were Renken brothers who built "Renken boats" in Charleston. The Citadel fans found out that the USC Renken brother was giving USC Coach Jim Carlen a Renken boat. Since The Citadel played well against USC, the Citadel fans began to tease the Citadel Renken brother that he should give the Citadel coach (me) a boat if they could give the USC coach one. You know what? The next week the Renken brothers gave me a "lease boat." I kept it at the Citadel Marina on the Ashley River and on campus. Quite often on Sunday afternoons, we would go for rides on the Ashley River and into the Charleston Harbor. One Sunday we went out and the wind was really blowing, causing white caps in the harbor. I really knew very little about handling boats, especially in rough waves. We hit a big wave and I almost capsized the boat. We didn't go out any more on windy, rough waters.

The fourth year at The Citadel went 7-3-1, which gave us one of the very few teams at The Citadel to have three winning seasons in a row.

The Fifth and Fateful Year

In August every year after two-a-day practices began, the Brigadier Club would have a huge "shrimp boil" at the Citadel's Beach House. At this event, they had an "open bar" so by the time I arrived with my captains (an annual occurrence), several of the "Citadel men" would already be "feeling good."

My captains for 1982, my fifth year, were Jim Ettari, Joe Pipczynski, and Gerald Toney, the first black quarterback to play at The Citadel. They were truly three outstanding men who were not only outstanding players and cadets, but also outstanding human beings.

Before I was asked to introduce the captains, one of the prominent members of the Citadel Board of Visitors, who like everyone else there was a bit "feeling good," came up to me and, as we discussed the upcoming season, he nodded his head at Gerald who was standing nearby and asked me, "You're not going to play that N------ at quarterback, are you?"

First of all, I never liked being told whom to play or not to play; my staff and I made those decisions. Second, Gerald was one of the finest young men I ever coached anywhere and was an excellent quarterback. I don't normally have a "short fuse," but when somebody insults one of my family, and I included my players as part of my family, I react strongly. I looked this "prominent board member" in the eye up close and said, "Let me tell you one thing. Gerald Toney is one fine, young man who happens to be our best quarterback; and like every other player on the team, if he has won the job on the field, then yes he will be our quarterback. If you have a problem with that, you need to get you another head coach."

He got in my face and said, "Well, I can do that too, you know!"

I stayed close to his face and said, "Well, you do that because I don't want to work for someone like you!" The program went on, and I introduced the captains, told about the coming season, and we left. I don't know whether anyone actually heard that conversation.

Our two-a-day practices continued and 1982 proved to be the worst two-a-day preparations in my entire career. We were following two seven-win seasons in a row and three winning seasons in a row and losing Stump Mitchell. We had Stump's backup, Eric Manson, and two promising freshmen, Marty Long and Mike Lewis, who would later prove to be very good. In our first scrimmage I decided to have a short-yardage-and-goal-line scrimmage, so we would have less chance of injury. Unbelievably, all three of these young men were injured (knee injuries), keeping them from playing in 1982. At The Citadel you were fortunate if you could get 11 good players on offense and 11 on defense, with a few adequate subs. Thus, to lose all three of our tailbacks in one early scrimmage was devastating. A few days later, we lost Mike Rosenburg, our first-string fullback, for the season with a broken arm. Hence, we had to go way down on the depth chart to fill in for these positions or move players from other positions to running backs. But you know what? Our players and coaches responded in a great way and with Gerald Toney at quarterback we won five games, beating the Southern Conference leader, Western Carolina on their field.

As the season began, several strange things began to happen. First it took me a while to notice that each time the Citadel Board met, some of them would come out to watch practice. They usually met on the third Monday of each month and because of lab schedules, we would practice on Monday nights. I didn't notice them that much. Even though they were "the brass," I didn't stop practice to go over and recognize them. We had our share of problems trying to find running backs.

One memorable game that year occurred against East Tennessee State.

We were playing in Charleston and had a score of 0-0 with a minute to go, and we had the ball on our own 40-yard line. We had a freshman quarterback whose forte was passing. We put him in to throw a "Hail Mary" pass; we had practiced it every week for just such a situation. We sent all receivers straight to the end zone and hoped the ball would be tipped and we could get it. For some reason I'll never understand, our quarterback had a high-school friend who was a linebacker on the other team. As the play began the linebacker yelled our quarterback's name and he threw the ball to his linebacker friend who ran it back to our 20, where they kicked a field goal to win 3-0.

As the season progressed, rumors began to surface that the "in crowd" of Citadel men were becoming disenchanted with my methods of coaching. With about three weeks left in the season, Eddie Teague asked me to come into his office. He closed the door. Eddie was a good person and athletic director, though a little tight with the money. He never was a talker, but a little careful with his words. I could tell he was nervous.

He said, "Art, the General [the Citadel President] has asked me to tell you he wants you to let three of your coaches go after the season is over."

I said, "Eddie, what did these guys do? Did they steal something, or were they arrested, or get a DUI?"

He said, "Art, you know they didn't; I'm just delivering the General's message."

I said, "Eddie, you know we lost some key players before the season even began, and actually if anything the staff has done a better job of coaching than last year when we won seven games."

Eddie said, "Well, what should I say to the General?"

I said, "You tell him he was on the committee that hired me when I was told I would be allowed to hire and fire my own staff. You can say that I am considering changing some coaching assignments—some offensive coaches switched to defense, for example—but that I do not plan to fire any of my coaches."

Eddie said, "Are you sure that's what you want me to say to the General?"

I said, "Eddie, I know you're just the messenger, and I appreciate all your support, but that's my answer!"

The last week of the season and afterwards, all "the talk" was that I would be replaced. Former Citadel Coach Red Parker came to Charleston to speak to the Charleston Touchdown Club, and some individuals said he was invited because some Citadel people wanted him to come back as the coach. My main concern was that this kind of talk was hurting our preparation for our final game and our recruiting efforts.

We lost the final game against Furman and the Tuesday after the game (after the cadets had gone home for Thanksgiving), I had a meeting with

Eddie Teague and the General. This was a regular meeting we had at the end of each season. After we sat down the General asked me right off the bat if I was going to make any changes in my staff—in other words, was I going to fire any of my coaches? I said no but I was considering some staff swaps from offense to defense. Then he went into a 20-minute oration about how much he appreciated what I had done for the football program at The Citadel but he was beginning to see warning flags that our football program was heading in the wrong direction. He ended by saying, "I have decided that I am going to relieve you and your coaches of your jobs."

During his talk, I could see what was coming, so I was somewhat prepared when the "blow" came. I told him that I had two questions. (1) I still had one year left on my contract, and I wanted to know how they intended to settle my contract. (2) I wanted my assistant coaches taken care of until April, or until they got other jobs. Eddie and I had already agreed on this.

I had never been fired from any job and deep down I knew I should not have been fired from The Citadel because of my record or anything I had done wrong. [My winning percentage those five years was the best of any Citadel coach in 40 years at that time (and was the best for the next 30+ years).] Despite being fired, I did and still do admire The Citadel and what they stand for and would love for my two younger grandsons to attend there. I was fortunate to have made many friends while working there whom I still see.

They had a press conference at noon the same day and announced my firing. The television cameras were at my home at 11:15 p.m. as were sports writers and television and radio people. The press was upset to say the least and generally took my side in the firing. At the time I did not know all the information stated above, and I really respected The Citadel a great deal and didn't want to embarrass the football program in any way. The next day we attended the P.C.-Newberry game—P.C. being my alma mater—and it seemed all the press from the upper part of the state wanted to get in on the act. All that was sort of rewarding for my hurt feelings.

As the days passed I realized that while I had no job but did have a year's salary, my coaches also didn't have jobs, so I concentrated on helping them get jobs. Ricky Diggs got on at USC; Cal McCombs and Tom Miller went to Air Force. I was offered the head coaching job at Mars Hill but talked the committee into hiring Rick Gilstrap. Steve Shankweiler was rehired by Tom Moore, my replacement at The Citadel. Tom Park went into private business. Steve Patton went to Gardner-Webb, and Ellis Johnson, to Alabama. As I have said before, they were a great staff; I regretted that we would never work together again.

Looking for a Job

I began a slow process of looking for a job; I knew I couldn't do without coaching. The Citadel allowed us to live in our Quarters until March 1. We had the cottage at Wild Dunes. Curtis was a senior at First Baptist and we wanted him to finish there, so Edie moved out to Wild Dunes with Curtis and Ryan.

My first opportunity came when Buddy Sasser, my former assistant coach at Eau Claire and then head coach at East Tennessee, offered me the job of offensive coordinator. We visited and really liked the idea of working with Buddy again, but we really did not want to live in the mountains of Tennessee. Then Gene Corrigan, the athletic director at Notre Dame, called to say they had an offensive coordinator's job open there; they had offered the job to someone else, but if he didn't take it, they wanted me to come for the interview. The guy took the job! Then Dal Shealy, the head coach at Richmond, called and offered me the job of offensive coordinator there. I visited there and really liked Dal and Richmond but delayed any decision until after the American Football Association meeting in Los Angeles. At that meeting, I ran into the new head coach at Memphis, Rex Dockery, and we talked briefly about what he had at Memphis. He asked that I call him if I was interested.

When I got home, an ol' friend Larry Beckish called to say he was leaving East Carolina as offensive coordinator to go to the pros, and if I was interested the Head Coach Ed Emory would call me. My staff and I had visited East Carolina the previous spring and I knew they had some good players. I was interested! Edie and I visited and while the salary wasn't very good, I was still getting money from The Citadel, so we felt we could afford to take the job. Which I did!

A Memorable Traveling Incident

I mentioned in the previous section that I visited Dal Shealy at Richmond and attended the American Football Association meeting in Los Angeles. Ricky Diggs and I planned to attend the AFA meeting, but because we were no longer employed at The Citadel we had to pay our own way. Ricky found a bargain $98 round trip air fare to Los Angeles. The only problem was that the fare was from New York City to Los Angeles, and we were in South Carolina! Dal had offered me a job, and I wanted to visit him in Richmond to discuss the job. So the University of Richmond flew me to Richmond where I met with Dal. In the meantime Ricky drove my car to Richmond and picked me up. Then we drove to New York and spent the night with my cousin Evelyn and her family.

The next day her husband Emmett drove us to La Guardia where we got on a plane to Detroit. [Yes, it was not a direct flight from New York to Los Angeles.] I sat in a nonsmoking area; Ricky smoked so he sat in the back. In Detroit six beautiful young ladies came on board, and their seats were next to me. They all had roses and were obviously together. During the flight, I asked the beautiful lady sitting next to me if she worked in Detroit. She said she did, so I asked her what they all did.

She said, "We just show up; we work for 'Play Boy'." She said she had been the cover girl for December. [I didn't remember seeing her!]

I asked her what her folks thought about her working for Play Boy; she said they didn't like it to begin with. She said she had a brother who was in the Navy whose ship had selected her "mate" of the year.

When we landed in Los Angeles, she asked if I had a ride to the hotel. I said that I didn't but I had another coach in the smoking section. She said she would give him a ride too. One piece of my baggage had been misplaced, so I told Ricky to go with her, but she said she would wait. Ricky came to the luggage area, and his eyes got really big. She had a big limo, and she showed us around Los Angeles.

When we drove up and stopped on the curb in front of our hotel, I saw three coaches I had worked with at Texas Tech and were then at South Carolina. I told the young lady that she might not believe it, but those three guys where we pulled up were life-long friends of mine. The driver got out and put our bags on the sidewalk. Then she got out and waited until I got in front of my three friends. She came over and hugged my neck and kissed my cheek. Jack Fligg, my ol' office mate at Texas Tech, told me he wished he had had a camera so he could take a picture of me and send it to Edie. I told him I wished he had had one too, for she would never believe what happened.

A Few Parting Remarks

We really enjoyed our time living in Charleston. We were members of Central Methodist Church. We visited several churches, but Central was an old, historical, downtown church and we knew several members already there. We really enjoyed worshipping there. Phil Jones was the minister most of our time there; we really liked him. We attended a Sunday School class where the wife of a deceased Methodist minister was the teacher. It was a great class and we had great socials. One member of our class was a local "character" who had been a great college boxer and football player at The Citadel. He was a prosperous whiskey dealer in Charleston. Every Sunday Gunter would use some portion of the lesson Mrs. Clyburn would teach or some portion of the scriptures she used and disagree with her or ask a question in his best "Charleston Brogue" such as, "Now Mrs. Clyburn, you don't really expect us to believe that God made a path through that Red Sea, then let it go on the Egyptians, do you?' Gunter remained a friend for many years after we left Charleston.

After church every Sunday, we always enjoyed eating out together. At Texas Tech we ate at the training room with the players and other coaches' families, at Furman we ate at a cafeteria in Travelers Rest, and in Charleston we enjoyed eating at "Gourmet Tisserie," which was in the "Old Market" in downtown Charleston. The place was unique in that it was a group of fast-food places where you could find barbeque, country food, pizzas, Greek food, and so on. Then they had tables in the middle. We would let the children eat whatever they wanted; we usually had barbeque. We almost always rode by the "Battery," a landmark seawall and promenade, on the way home.

While at The Citadel, I knew there were good hunting areas around Charleston and I had many hunting opportunities. A Citadel graduate, Grady Phillips, from Winnsboro, South Carolina, had some good bird dogs, and we often hunted on the Summers brothers' land in Cameron, South Carolina. We often went by Bobby Summers' home where the quail were plentiful.

On one occasion, I was speaking at a civic club lunch in Santee, South Carolina, and was to meet Grady at the Summers' home. I wore a "coat and tie" for the lunch speaking engagement and carried my hunting clothes with me. When I got to the Summers' home, Mrs. Summer showed me where I could change to my hunting clothes. I did and we had a great hunt. That night after I got home, the phone rang. Edie answered and Mrs. Summers said to Edie, "Please tell Coach Baker he left his clothes in my bedroom!"

Every year the Summers held a statewide dove shoot on their farm and invited about everybody in South Carolina, including the governor, senators, judges, and so on. After the hunt, the Summers hosted a big barbeque. And every year Mrs. Summers told the story of how I left my clothes in her bedroom!

On another hunt at the Summers', I had decided to take Edie on a dove shoot. They had big tractors pulling flatbed trailers that we rode on to the hunting fields. I had carried buckets for us to sit on. Edie was posted in the next "blind" from me about 40 yards away from me. We settled down, sitting on our buckets. In a little bit, she called me and I could tell she was desperate. She had stepped into a bed of fire ants and they were all over her legs. [If you've never encountered fire ants, be advised that their bite, or sting, is very painful.] In order to get the ants off her legs, we struggled to pull down her hunting pants. Finally, we got the pants down and got the ants off her legs, and moved to another spot (where there were no ants).

I did not realize that my friend Grady was also on the hunt and was on a nearby blind. He had witnessed Edie's plight but at such a distance that he did not recognize who we were. As we were riding the trailer back to the house, he told me of watching what had happened and said he thought to himself, "Look at that old man taking advantage of that young lady!" Edie holds Grady in high esteem.

As I mentioned previously, Edie loved to walk in the evening and her path took her by the student barracks. She met many students who were not sports players. At the end of the semester, we always invited the graduating seniors to our home for a dinner. These cadets had completed all work for graduation and would "open up" as to how they had "beaten the system." After dinner we would sit around and enjoy each story. For example, there was a tunnel out from the campus, and at low tide you could walk its entire distance to an "outlet"; many told of doing that. Others told of repelling out of second- and third-story windows, since repelling was something all cadets had done. One group told of repelling out a second-floor window and then after a beer party being unable to pull themselves back up. They had to be pulled up with a rope tied around their cheeks! They knew we wouldn't share their secrets—until now, that is, but we're not naming names!

I was a history major and have always loved and still do love history. Charleston is simply a preserved history museum. You can walk down the streets and every home or building has a history, some dating back 300 years or more. We lived in Charleston five years and did not get to see half the historical sites. While working at The Citadel, I had a friend who was a civil war buff. Almost every week he would visit the battle sites out toward Morris Island where the confederates held out for quite a while from trenches and "sand forts." Wally took me a time or two to look for "Minie balls" (ammunition from Civil War rifles) and for shells stored in small caves. The only thing was that they were unexploded shells and still quite dangerous. When they were found, they had to be dealt with very carefully by an expert in explosives. I didn't find any and was a little afraid I might. I did see some of Wally's, however; he had a good collection.

One of my former football players at Eau Claire High School, Jake Halford, who had earned a Ph.D. at Duke, was working for the Citadel President developing an engineering program for non-cadets while I was coach there. He lived on campus with his family, and we played a lot of tennis. One day I discovered a little four-year old fellow in the elevator of the athletic building (Dees Hall); he was punching buttons and riding up and down the elevator, having a wonderful time. I recognized him as "Spencer," Jake's boy. I called them and ended their panic as they were frantically looking all over campus for him. Jake's twin brother, Jack, who also played for me at Eau Claire, refereed Southern Conference basketball games and always did several games each year at The Citadel. Jack was very tall and most of the players had to look up at him. He always joked around with me and Jake and Citadel Coach Les Robinson before the game. Jake and I also spent many relaxing spring evenings watching Citadel baseball games. One last thing: Jake and his sons would often ride their bicycles around the campus and would always stop by the football field and watch our football practice. There were often fathers of players standing around watching the practice. Jake said that one of the fathers told him the only reason he sent his son to The Citadel was because he could play football for Art Baker. I was humbled but did appreciate his remark.

Marion Thomas, a Citadel booster, told us early on that we would have access each summer to his Pawleys Island "Liberty Lodge," a 250-year-old beach house that was supposedly "haunted." We spent a wonderful week there each summer for five years. We seined for shrimp, had crab traps, and had Aunts Katie and Ruth come down for a few days, which was special. Cally Gault (my ol' friend from P.C. and coaching opponent when he was a North Augusta High School and I was at Eau Claire High School and again when he was at P.C. and I was at Furman) and his wife, Joy, were usually down that weekend and we would get together with them. My teammate at P.C., Wade Camlin, lived at Georgetown and had a beach cottage; we often got together with them. I played tennis at Litchfield several times during the week. Our friends Kirby and Patricia Jackson also spent a week with us at the beach each summer (as they did for some 20 years or more).

During our years at The Citadel, Edie and I continued to enjoy each summer the Citrus Bowl summer outings in Orlando and the College Football Association meetings in Dallas at the Cotton Bowl. The Cowboys always had a big party out at the stadium where they put a picture of each coach and his wife along with a message on the big scoreboard. It was exciting to see our picture and message saying, "The Dallas Cowboys Welcome Art and Edie Baker from The Citadel." We always enjoyed being with old friends and also being back in Texas again.

The Citadel is a special place and we really enjoyed our time there. Citadel people are very special, our neighbors were nice people, and we had special relationships with many people in the Charleston community. I especially enjoyed going to the "Brigadier Club" (the boosters) meetings with basketball coach Les Robinson (we have remained close friends), baseball coach Chad Port (who was really funny), and Les McElwee, who was the director of the Club (later Stan Hurteau). These were all good people.

Most of all, I remember the Citadel players—they were special. Often I have realized not many football players would go through the military and Spartan life required of every cadet at The Citadel. It was the only place I coached where the players looked forward to practice to "get away." We had unusually good luck winning at home. With each home win, the Corps was awarded free "overnight" beginning after the game. Hence, they were really motivated in their vocal support.

I cannot end this story without praising my staff during the Citadel years. While the head coach gets most of the praise (and the criticism), no coach will get a lot of praise without an excellent staff backing him up. I am still amazed that nine of my staff went on to become collegiate head coaches—Frank Beamer (VPI), Ralph Friedgen (Maryland), Mike O'Cain (N.C. State), Rick Gilstrap (Wofford), Cal McCombs (VMI), Ricky Diggs (Morgan State), Ellis Johnson (Gardner-Webb and The Citadel), Steve Patton (Gardner-Webb), and Brad Scott (South Carolina). Additionally, Steve Shankweiler subsequently became the offensive coordinator at East Carolina et al; Bruce Johnson, the defensive coordinator at Air Force et al; and Charlie Rizzo, the defensive coordinator at Rice et al.

I finish this chapter with a tribute to Coach Cal McCombs. When we had prospects come for a visit with their families, we usually entertained them and fed them at Maurice's Barbeque on James Island. Getting there we would pass some low places in the marshes where the tides would raise and lower the water level. Each coach would have a prospect and his family in his car coming to and going from the restaurant.

One night as we were all leaving at different times, Coach McCombs was taking his group back to the motel. When he crossed a small bridge, the tide was high and he noticed a car about 40 to 50 yards out from the bank with the tail lights just showing above the water. Several people who had escaped the car were being attended. Cal asked if everything was okay. A lady standing on the bank said there was a young lady still in the car. Cal immediately swam to the car, looked in, and saw a teenager in the car. He got her out and to the shore. Upon getting the young lady safely on the bank, he searched for the lady who had told him there was someone in the car. He never found her. The girl's family begged her to call them so they could properly thank her. Television and newspapers sought her, but she never came forward. Till this day, we all believe the mysterious lady was an angel sent by the Lord. Do you believe in angels? We all sure do!

We all were so proud of Cal, a former Citadel cadet and athlete, who later was an assistant coach at the Air Force Academy and head coach at VMI. He was later recognized by the Coast Guard and the city for his heroism.

11 AT EAST CAROLINA UNIVERSITY

East Carolina University (ECU) is located in Greenville, North Carolina. Having previously coached at Furman University in Greenville, South Carolina, I wonder how many people have coached football at universities in two different cities with the same name. I heard a story of a professor who was traveling to attend a meeting at ECU. He deplaned in Greenville and asked about local transportation to East Carolina University. He was told it would be a trip of 350 or so miles eastward. He had gone to the wrong Greenville—probably not the only time that has happened. Greenville, North Carolina, is about 85 miles east of Raleigh and about the same distance from Morehead City on the North Carolina Coast.

Moving Again

When I went to ECU, I once again had to leave family behind and live alone for six months or so. Edie stayed in Charleston (Isle of Palms) to allow Curtis to graduate from high school with his class there. I stayed in a Ramada Inn in Greenville along with three or four other coaches who were in a similar situation. During this time, I went back to Charleston as often as I could, and Edie came to Greenville some to look for a place to live. We got a local real estate man to help us; he promised to give us back what we paid for a house if I were to get another head coaching job. We finally decided on a townhouse being built in a development called "Quail Ridge," located several miles from my office.

Each weekend I could get away, we borrowed a pickup and took some of our furniture to Greenville. I was never a good packer, and we looked like the "Beverly Hillbillies." One time we were riding at night and lost some of Edie's curtains. Amazingly, on a later trip we found most of them.

On one trip I drove the pickup and it was just about out of oil. I barely stopped just in time to save the engine. East Carolina was paying for the move, but having handled budgets at Furman and The Citadel, I always wanted to save as much as I could.

Edie finally moved to Greenville in midsummer and we moved into our little townhouse. We had very nice neighbors. Curtis was enrolled at Presbyterian College (I finally got one of my children to go to my alma mater). Kim was married to Gil Kirkman and living in Mt. Pleasant, South Carolina. Ryan was going to Nilsen Electronics School in Charleston. And Artie was living in Dalzell, South Carolina, with his friend Mark "Aluba" Clifford and was dating Sherri Tickel, a divorced second-grade teacher. He was teaching and was the offensive coordinator at Hillcrest High School (Edie's alma mater). For the first time in 30 years, Edie and I were "empty nesters"; it was strange but also rather nice. Edie never had a problem adjusting to anywhere we moved; people always loved her. So she sunbathed at the neighborhood pool, became active in our church, and played some bridge. She always seemed to find several elderly citizens to look after. Greenville was no different.

The Spring and Summer

The six months before Edie moved to Greenville were very lonely for me. To help thwart the loneliness, I threw myself into my new job. I watched a lot of game films, and I studied hard. I had been a head coach for ten years and was now going back to being a position coach (quarterback) in addition to being offensive coordinator and assistant head coach. I was motivated and determined to prove to The Citadel that they had made a mistake in firing me. I drove myself hard to be the best offensive coordinator in the country.

Ed Emory was one of those unusual and talented head coaches I worked with. He had great organizational skills and was one of the best recruiters I ever knew. And he was sometimes "funny as all get out." Our staff meetings, like Coach Howard's, were "a hoot." I always sat beside my friend Phil Elmassian, who coached our defensive backs. He had a breathing problem and his nose was usually stopped up. He and the other coaches liked to drink beer and stay up late. Ed would get to expounding on some subject, and Phil would become frustrated and "whisper" to me that he wished that fat so-and-so would hush up. More times than not, Ed could hear him.

Our coaches' dressing room was very small, with three or four shower heads and the dressing area just outside the shower. One day Phil and I came in early and did not know Ed was already in the shower. Phil complained to me in his usual loud voice that he was really disappointed with his defensive backs and that he actually had better ones at Ferrum Junior College. About that time Ed came running out of the shower with soap all over him from head to toe. He had a way of pointing his index and little finger at you, and did so at Phil, saying, "You little shrimp, if you had such good defensive backs at Ferrum, then go back and coach them!" Thereafter, Phil and I always checked out the shower before we discussed any subjects that might upset big Ed.

One of the first staff meetings I attended was before spring practice at a nearby lake house for me to be oriented to ECU football. Larry Beckish, whom I succeeded at ECU, had installed his version of the "freeze option" in 1982. I had always been an option-oriented coach and had installed some of the freeze into our offense at The Citadel, so I was familiar with it. I needed fine tuning, for I didn't want to change a lot of things just to suit me. I did want to add the sweep, which had been very good for us at Furman and The Citadel. I disagreed with some of Larry's coaching points and installed my own. Since we ran the veer option and outside veer at Furman and The Citadel and we had visited ECU the spring before, I really liked what Larry was doing with the option. At the same time, Georgia Southern under Erk Russell was adding some new aspects to the freeze that I especially liked. I was going over the details of the sweep and Coach Emory said, "Well, why don't we call somebody who's an expert on the sweep?" and he asked the staff who they would recommend.

Phil Elmassian said, "Hell, Ed, we've got the best sweep expert right here in this room—Art Baker." (Good for my ego!)

We had a very good spring practice. Our offense was almost exclusively from the "I" formation and was mostly pure freeze option with a sprinkling of several basic passing routes. We had good kicking; Jeff Heath, our place kicker, is still an all-time leader in field goals and points after touchdowns. Our punting was adequate; and our defense, coached by Tom Throckmorton, was very good.

Ed Emory and his staff had recruited very well, and we had the best group of players I had ever coached. Kevin Ingram was a quarterback with great skills; he had great feet and a great understanding of the skills to run the option; and he was a good passer and he was tough. Kevin was a transfer from Villanova when they disbanded the program.

One of our most consistent running backs was Earnest Byner who came from Georgia Military. A great runner and receiver, he went on to play in the NFL for Cleveland, Washington, and Baltimore. He subsequently coached for five NFL teams. Regrettably, he is perhaps most remembered for his crucial fumble at the end of the 1987 AFC Championship Game between Cleveland and Denver.

Another outstanding player was an Eau Claire High School graduate—

Terry Long. When he graduated from Eau Claire, he was 5 ft, 10 inches, 185 pounds. He joined the army and was stationed at Fort Bragg, North Carolina. He became a dedicated weight lifter and became the third-ranking person in the world in the three power lifts. When he came to ECU, he was 5 ft, 11 inches, 280 pounds, but he could run a 40-yard dash in 4.6 seconds. And he could dunk a basketball with either hand. He was so powerful. He was an All-America guard who went on to play for the Pittsburg Steelers. On one occasion, a small church in the boondocks of eastern North Carolina invited Terry and me to speak at a Saturday evening service. We arrived to a packed church—most there to see and hear Terry Long. We were seated behind the preacher where the choir usually sat. The preacher got up and made some opening comments. Before we realized what was happening, he pulled from underneath the pulpit a rattlesnake and began shaking the snake as he preached. Terry punched me in the ribs, his eyes big as saucers, and said to me as he looked all around, "Coach, where is the back door?"

I said, "Terry, they don't have a back door."

He responded, "Where do you think they would like for me to make one?"

There were many other outstanding players on that 1983 team—the Adams brothers, receivers; Reggie Branch, fullback; Henry Williams, wide receiver (no telling how fast he was as a breakaway receiver and kick returner); Norwood Vann, tight end who later played for the Los Angeles Rams and Raiders. It was fun coaching them; they were a great group to be around. I knew we were very good and should have an outstanding season in the fall. I also highly respected the coaches I worked with.

During the spring and summer, we had staff meetings every day. I found with the other coaches what it was like working with Ed Emory. He was definitely a character. He had married his sweetheart from his playing days at ECU; they had two children, a daughter and a son. Both lived in Greenville. They eventually divorced and he married a nice looking blond lady he met while coaching at Georgia Tech.

Nancy was his new wife from Atlanta, and she got deeply involved in the ECU football program. She actually was an excellent recruiter; she was very good with the mothers of prospects and with entertaining prospects and players in her home. She and Ed had a nice game room in their home. They had every kind of entertainment machine. The players used it a lot. She sat in on all our recruiting meetings, and she was good.

Nancy was also determined to make Ed lose weight and she had put him on the "Cambridge diet." She would bring his salad and mail to our morning meetings. We hated this because we had to sit there and watch Ed eat his salad and open his mail. While Ed was on the "strict diet" he would often curse the diet when Nancy wasn't there and brag however on how much weight he was losing and how good he was staying on the diet. One night I was at the office late watching film, and Ed was in his office (he loved to call his ol' cronies from all over the country at night). Anyway, I finished and as usual went by to speak to him before I left. His door was ajar so I knocked as I entered, just in time to see him stuffing a large pizza in his desk drawer. He had pizza all over his face and mouth. I managed not to smile as I waved good night to him. So much for Nancy's Cambridge diet!

Early one day in August I was at the office and one of our junior college transfers from California came in to see Coach Emory to tell him his grandmother had passed away and he had to go home for the funeral. Ed said, "That's okay; go ahead."

The player said, "Coach, I don't have the money to fly home."

Ed said, "Well, how much is a roundtrip ticket?" The player gave him the price—several hundred dollars. Ed reached into his pocket and gave the player the money.

I waited until the player had left and Ed was in his office, and went in and said, "Ed, we can't give players expenses for trips; it's against the rules."

He pointed his famous index/little finger at me and said, "Art, you coach the offense; I'll take care of my players."

When I went home for supper that night, Edie was unpacking boxes and getting our new home in shape. I said, "Edie, based on what I saw at the office today, don't unpack any more boxes; we will be leaving in January."

The 1983 Season

Florida State was our opening-day opponent for 1983; they had beaten ECU 66-7 the year before. I learned that Chuck Amato and Jack Stanley, defensive coaches at Florida State, were speaking on the Florida State defense in August at the North Carolina Coaches Clinic to be held in Greensboro. I decided to go there for their lectures, and for some reason I wrote down every word they said and for some reason they held nothing back. It turned out to be a rare occasion where we were able to develop an offensive game plan that fit perfectly into their style of defense. During the game we had an answer for everything they did and scored 46 points. The only problem was that they scored 47 points. The game ended on a sour note, though. Our quarterback, Kevin Ingram, kept the ball on a freeze option inside their defensive tackle for a 40-yard run to their 20-yard line in the last minute of the game. He was very quick and with time running out, he jumped up and dropped the ball on the turf. The official didn't see the play as it occurred and called it a fumble. Even the Florida State fans admitted it was a blown call. Nevertheless, we lost the game 47-46.

On Friday before the Florida State game, we were riding on the team bus for our usual light Friday workout. All the years I had coached, I never allowed my teams to "cut up" once we were into Friday preparation; I felt it was time to get serious. Our wide receiver, Henry "Flipp" Williams, was a 5-ft 5-inch speedster who, upon scoring, always cut a flip after crossing the goal line. I sat on the front, right, bus seat and listened in horror as Henry entertained the team. He was loud and funny and had our tight end, Norwood Vann, as his "straight man." Norwood would ask Henry a leading question, and Henry would give some absurd but hilarious story. He had the entire team rolling in the aisles of the bus. I thought, "Oh no, this is no way to get in the right frame of mind." The next night our team surrounded the Seminole logo at midfield at Campbell Stadium (in Tallahassee) and wouldn't let the Indian with his lance on his paint horse get to the logo. They were jumping up and down and vertical jumping about 35 inches. And Henry scored two touchdowns on a punt return and a kickoff return. So much for my "get serious on Friday" policy. [I even laughed at their antics.]

Even though we lost our opening game to Florida State, I thought, "My gosh, we're going to be pretty good." And we were, ending the season with an 8-3 record. We beat N.C. State in Raleigh in a well-played game. We beat Missouri 13-7 in Columbia, Missouri, after being a big underdog. And, we beat Southern Mississippi in the worst rain storm I ever coached in. There was lightning and thunder.

All three of our losses, including the aforementioned one against Florida State, were to teams in Florida. One loss was to Florida after we had an interception called back. Again, we should have won. The last game of the season, we played Miami in Miami. They were ranked No. 1 in the nation. We led them 7-6 for 59 minutes; then they scored with 59 seconds remaining, to go ahead 12-7. We came back and on the last play of the game we had the ball with seconds to go. Ingram threw a perfect pass to Stefon Adams (who later played for the Los Angeles Raiders.). For some reason the Miami defenders left him wide open in the end zone. The ball was perfectly thrown. Just at the last second, Norwood Vann, our tight end, veered over into Stefan—both going after the ball—and knocked the ball out of Stefon's hands. Our three losses against the Florida teams were by a combined total of 13 points.

With an 8-3 record and a No. 20 ranking in the Associated Press's final national poll, we thought for sure we were headed for a bowl game, but it was not to be.

Florida State Comes a Calling

About the middle of the season, Bobby Bowden, the Florida State head coach, called me "out of the blue" to say he was going to hire a quarterback coach and he wanted me to know that until I refused the job, the job was mine. He said he would not call me back until after the season was over. Obviously, I was very excited. It was several weeks after the season was over before Bobby called back. I had almost convinced myself it was all just a dream. Finally, he did call back and asked me to bring Edie to Tallahassee for an interview. Curtis was off from P.C. and wanted to go with us.

When we arrived at Florida State, Coach Bowden had someone show us around and then took us into his office. When Edie and Curtis left, Coach Bowden said, "You know, I've been thinking about it and I think you have too much experience to just offer you the quarterback job so I'm offering you the quarterback, offensive coordinator, and assistant head coach jobs. I've never had an assistant head coach before." I was making $30,000 at ECU; he offered me $50,000, and I would have to recruit quarterbacks only.

As I met Edie and Curtis afterward, Curtis said to me, "Dad, if you don't take this job, you're crazy."

I agreed. Curtis also announced that he wanted to transfer to Florida State, which he did, getting his degree in criminal justice in 1985.

I went back to Greenville and told the athletic director and Coach Emory I was leaving. The chairman of the Board, Tom Bennett, called and set up a meeting with me. He wanted to know various things about the East Carolina program. I felt a loyalty to Ed Emory who had given me a job when I didn't have one, and I left saying nothing but praise for the Pirate program.

Hence, one year after joining the staff at East Carolina, I moved to Tallahassee, Florida, to join the staff at Florida State. The thought never crossed my mind that I would be returning to East Carolina one year later!

Before leaving the East Carolina chapter, I do want to note that the East Carolina FCA group was one of the most active I was ever associated with. They were very strong Christian young men and women. Often, they had very good, well thought-out skits. Many of the members were often asked to speak at area schools.

ARTHUR W. BAKER and JACK B. EVETT

12 AT FLORIDA STATE UNIVERSITY

Florida State University is located in Tallahassee, the capital of Florida. It is in the very northern part of Florida less than 20 miles south of the Florida-Georgia border and about midway between Jacksonville on the east and Pensacola on the west.

When we moved to Tallahassee, Edie and I were fortunate to find a nice townhouse on the Killearn Golf Course; we were right on the ninth fairway—not far from the clubhouse. We could easily walk there. The "soft" tennis courts were there along with a pool and workout area. A lot of the other coaches, including Bobby Bowden, lived in our neighborhood. Mickey Andrews, the defensive coordinator, lived nearby and we took turns driving to work. Those rides were interesting. Each day we would share the things that bothered us most. Usually, defensive coaches don't like to share their secrets with offensive coaches and vice versa, but Mickey and I really helped each other. These rides provided probably the best "clinic" I ever attended.

My Responsibilities at Florida State

I reported to Florida State in January and began my career with the Seminoles. The first thing I found out was that Bobby Bowden is a great person to work for. He lets you coach and make decisions. When Bobby told me I would install the offense we had used at East Carolina and that I would install the freeze option, he forgot to tell me that Wayne McDuffie was also the offensive coordinator. Wayne was a very good offensive line coach and resented my coming into his territory; but he did understand that I would install "my" offense though he didn't necessarily like it. We often disagreed and argued but formed a strange friendship that lasted till his

173

suicide death. He once told a group of coaches in Charlotte for the Shrine Bowl game that I was the best quarterback coach in the country. It was a compliment that I cherished because Wayne didn't hand out many compliments.

At Florida State I had the responsibility of developing the game plan each week. Obviously, the other offensive coaches were all involved in the plan, but since Coach Bowden had asked me to install my offense, the freeze option, I was responsible. I can honestly say I worked as hard as I had ever worked because Bobby Bowden had placed his confidence in me and my offense. Every Friday evening our team was together at a motel, home or away. After the Friday meal, movie, and team meeting, Bobby had me go to his room for a "game plan review." All the coaches called it Coach Bowden's "iffy" meeting. He would strip down to his undershorts, get a cigar unlit in his mouth, and say, "Okay, tell me about the game plan." As I explained about the game plan, he would occasionally interrupt and ask what if they do this, what are you going to do? Thus the "iffy" part of the meeting. You can bet your life I was prepared for every possible iffy, and I must say I cannot remember a single time when I was not up to every question. I was proud of these test results and proud of my preparation. One thing Bobby liked was Friday night fights on television. When the flight went the distance, we had to wait to begin our iffy meeting.

The 1984 Season

We had mostly a good season, considering that our quarterback, Eric Thomas, was not an option quarterback but was a very courageous young man who played beyond his limits. When he missed several games with injuries, we had Danny McManus and our third-string quarterback Kirk Coker, a walk-on, as backups.

We lost a heartbreaker to South Carolina 38-26 in Columbia when they ran the second-half kickoff back for a touchdown after the runner's knee was down on the catch and the officials missed calling it. Our quarterback, Eric Thomas, had not thrown an interception all year but suddenly threw three. He reinjured his knee in the first half. Danny McManus almost bailed us out with some great fourth-quarter passing and had he had a little more time, I think he would have pulled the game out. He was a nice-looking young man who won many games in later years.

We lost our last regular-season game to Florida in Tallahassee in a downpour. It rained so hard that there was so much water on the sidelines that our coolers were floating around like little boats. We had to play most of the game with Kirk Coker, our walk-on, at quarterback. Rain is not the best friend of the freeze option, and we fumbled once inside the ten-year line.

During the game, we had run Coach Bowden's favorite pass option, which he called "Cadillac." His favorite route off the regular route was called "Cadillac Y drag," where the "Y" or tight end would drag (run laterally) across the formation to the opposite flat (opposite side of the field). I was calling plays and each time he asked over the phone for me to call "Y drag," I said Bobby it's not there.

I had watched their off side (opposite side) defensive end on that particular route drop off the line, and he was exactly where we would throw the ball to "Y," thus making an interception more likely than a completion. Later in the fourth quarter, Bobby again wanted me to call Cadillac Y drag. I said, "Bobby, you're the boss and we will call it, but you're not going to like it."

He said, "Run it anyway."

I did and the Florida defensive end intercepted the pass. Bobby got on the phone and said, "Now I see what you're talking about." We lost the game 27-17.

One of our strongest rivals in Florida was Miami, which had been recent national champions. As I've mentioned, each morning riding with Mickey Andrews, the defensive coordinator, we would exchange ideas. So I asked Mickey before the Miami game what pass was the toughest to cover because Miami's defense was very similar to ours. He drew up a crossing deep route; we installed it and completed it three times in crucial situations.

Early in the game, we were backed up in a close game. After a ten-yard penalty, we had a "third and 18." I called a draw (fake a pass and give a delayed ball to a half back to be safe and punt). Bobby got on the phone and said, "Art, run the reverse to Jessie Hester." I was afraid we would get thrown for a loss, but Bobby was firm. We ran it and Jessie scored from 78 yards back. That's why Bobby was so good as an offensive coach. We won the game 38-3.

Probably our most exciting game was a 42-41 loss to Pat Dye's Auburn Tigers. We ran the option so well at Florida State that teams had to involve their free safety (defensive back) into covering our pitch. I had always known that in order to run the freeze option, or any other option for that matter, you had to exploit all phases of the option and what the defense did to stop what you did. Auburn had chosen to put their free safety up close to the line of scrimmage to cover our pitch. We had two excellent receivers in Jessie Hester and Hassan Jones. When we ran the option and the free safety came up to cover the pitch, we sent either Jessie or Hassan on a good blocking fake on the cornerback and then sent him downfield on a post pattern. Eric Thomas, our quarterback, was so good at making the play look like the option that he hit Jessie for three long touchdowns during the game. We scored with about two minutes left, to go ahead 41-35. They came back and had a fourth-and-ten on their own

35-yard line. They also had a good option quarterback, but our defense had handled their option pretty well all night. But they ran the option for 11 yards and a first down. They had a great tailback, Fleetwood, who was unstoppable and sure enough, they scored with 38 seconds left, to go ahead 42-41. We came back and completed three or four passes, completing the last one to the Auburn 37. We thought we had two seconds left on the clock for one last play, but the officials ruled that the game was over. After the game, I was so disgusted walking from the press box to the dressing room. I had my head down and walked into a steel beam. I spent the next hour in my locker with an ice pack on my head.

Jack Nicklaus's son Steve was on our squad as a third-string receiver. Bobby always dressed Steve and most of our scout teams for home games, as most coaches do. Anyway, here I am very disappointed over the tough loss with a knot on my head when the trainer "Rooster" sent for me to come to the training room. I got there and he told me Mr. Nicklaus wanted to see me. I went into his office and of course I was very impressed to have a one-on-one meeting with the "Golden Bear." He immediately asked why Steve did not play in the game. You can imagine my plight trying to be respectful and understanding to Mr. Nicklaus and yet explain to him why his son did not play. You can be sure I caught a lot of flak from the other coaches when they learned of my meeting with Jack Nicklaus.

This was the weekend that our daughter Kim, her husband, and our son Ryan came to the game. Curtis, of course, was already there as a criminal justice student at Florida State. We had a good weekend together despite the loss.

The Arizona State game was another great one. Eric Thomas, our quarterback, was injured and could not play, and Kirk Coker ran the offense. We seemed not to do anything wrong on offense, and our defense did a good job of stopping the Arizona State offense. Kirk and Greg Allen and Roosevelt Snipes put on an air show to lead 48-30 in the fourth quarter. We ended up beating them 52-44. They closed the gap a lot, but Kirk led a late rally for the win. It was a great game.

The one game I did not do a good job for in 1984 was the Memphis State game. For the first time, a team chose to play our wide receivers "bump and run" and then cover the pitch. That not only disrupted our option game but also our pass routes. We had not spent a lot of our preparation against two "hard corners." In addition to that, Memphis State had not had a great record, and I'm sure our players and coaches were not prepared for the changes on defense. Their defense was entirely different from what we expected. Thank goodness, our defense played well and we started a drive late in the fourth quarter behind 14-17. We finally realized that I had let the hard corners talk me out of pitching the ball. We ran the option pitch anyway with some success and found ourselves on their 30-

yard line with fourth down and not enough time to drive for a touchdown. We decided to go for a field goal. We made it and settled for the 17-17 tie (this was before overtimes).

We really had a very good season overall, especially considering that our quarterback missed several games with injuries, and we had to rely on our third-string quarterback and a walk-on quarterback. We won seven games against East Carolina, Kansas, Miami, Temple, Tulane, Arizona State, and UT-Chattanooga. Our rushing yards for the season may still be the most in the history of football there, and we did well in passing yards also. With a 7-3-1 record we were invited to play in the Citrus Bowl against Georgia.

The Bowl game was a tough game for our option attack because Georgia ran an eight-man front (on or near the line of scrimmage). Our defense played well and held them to 17 points. We were behind late in the fourth quarter 17-9 and Lenny Shavers blocked a punt and Joe Wessel picked up the loose ball and ran in for a touchdown. Being behind by two points, of course we had to go for two. Bobby asked me on the phone what I wanted to call. I knew we had two great tailbacks and I knew they would expect us to run one of them with the ball, so I said I wanted to run the reverse to Darrin Holloman, a small, wide receiver who was great in the open field. Bobby said, "Now Art, this is vital; are you sure that's what you want to run?"

I said, "Yes, sir," with my fingers crossed.

We ran the reverse and they were waiting on it, but I had picked the right guy to carry the ball. He broke several tackles and scored to tie the game. A few minutes later on the last play of the game, Georgia's field-goal kicker barely missed a 71-yard field goal (from point of kick to the goal post), and I breathed a sigh of relief as the game ended tied at 17-17 (again, this was before overtimes), giving us a 7-3-2 overall record for the season.

During this game, Georgia used a "three-deep zone defense." It is hard to throw deep against three-deep, and Bobby was persistent in wanting to throw deep. I yielded to his calls after I told him we were throwing into coverage. Georgia intercepted three deep throws that day. Knowing and loving Bobby as I did, I realized that if I stayed on as a play caller, I would have to become better in "his" passing game. I still feel, however, that "my" offense gave him something he had been missing—a running game. And we passed pretty well too. This became a "moot question," however, as I did not stay on as a play caller.

Miscellany

On one occasion, Coach Bowden had invited an ol' friend of mine, Lt. Clebe McClary from Georgetown, South Carolina, to speak to the

Seminoles football team. As a marine, he was severely wounded in Viet Nam, losing an arm and an eye, and having wounds all over his body. He has a metal right hand and a patch over his eye. Clebe speaks all over the country with his wife, Deanna, a former Miss South Carolina. He has a wonderful message for all ages.

Clebe wanted to play tennis before his speech to the team. Playing tennis with a war hero as banged up as he was, I felt sorry for him. But the first time I hit an easy shot to him, he threw his racquet down and lectured me not to play easy; he wanted to compete. He would put the racquet under his bad arm, throw the ball up for a serve, and somehow get the racquet in his good arm and make a good serve. He was a good player. Before his wounds, Clebe had been a very good runner, and he still stayed in great shape.

After two sets we had worked up a good sweat. We were changing sides and getting a drink of water. I looked at Clebe and there was something green running down his cheek below his eye patch. I was flabbergasted, not wanting to say anything but still to let him know his eye must be injured. He about died laughing when I finally got nerve enough to tell him. He had just bought a new patch and the green running down his cheek was the wet green felt spilling down. I was looking for a hole to climb into. Both of us have had many laughs when we run into each other about the green, felt, eye patch in hot weather.

On another occasion the trainer called me down to the training room soon after practice. Danny McManus was on the training table with sweats on his leg. I asked what was wrong. The trainer said, "Danny has a slightly sprained knee and needs it wrapped, but refuses to let me shave his calf."

I said, "Danny, what's going on?"

He said, "Coach Baker, my mother told me not to ever let anybody shave my beautiful, long, leg hairs." As a coach, you might hear anything!

Once we were playing Chattanooga in Tallahassee and leading 38-0. I got Bobby on the phone and said, "Bobby, I would like to play some of the backups and third-stringers."

He said, "Art, your job is to score points—no subs!"

The "freeze option" was built on the principle of holding the linebackers at home; we ran it from the "I" formation. It was vital that our fullback line up exactly five yards behind the quarterback. The quarterback would get the snap and stretch his lead step at least $3\frac{1}{2}$ yards toward the fullback, clearing the fullback's path straight up the center's rear end. The quarterback would reach as deep as he could with the ball and would freeze while he "rode" the ball in the fullback's belly. He would then count one-thousand-and-one, one-thousand-and-two, and one-thousand-and-three, then sprint to the defensive end. I had forgotten Eric Thomas was from Valdosta, Georgia, where the people speak their words a little bit slower than most of us. It was a tough job getting him to speed up his thousand-and-one, thousand-and-two, and thousand-and-three. He did and executed some truly great option plays.

One of my duties while I was the assistant head coach was to handle discipline. During our early fall practice, one of our senior tight ends had attended a fraternity party, became excited, and ran over the tops of several cars causing some slight damage. He was turned in and came to my office. I liked him; we really had a great group of young men. I had decided what I would do for his punishment, but I thought I would run it by Bobby first. I said, "Bobby, you know our tight end damaged some cars. Do you want to punish him, or do you want to tell me what you would do?"

He said, "Art, punish him whatever you want to. Just remember that I'm the only one who kicks anybody off the team."

Shortly after moving to Tallahassee, we joined nearby Killearn Methodist Church. It was the first Methodist church we had ever joined where the members dressed very casually—no coats and ties. We had a good preacher and, as always, took part in church activities.

ECU Comes a Calling

In the time between our last game and our Bowl practice, I was in Atlanta recruiting when I got a phone call from the athletic director at James Madison University in Harrisonburg, Virginia, to talk about me becoming their head coach. I met the athletic director and the president, and they offered me the job contingent on my flying to Virginia over the weekend to see the university and their facilities.

The next morning I got a call from the chairman of the Board at East Carolina, Tom Bennett. He and I had gotten to be good friends while I was at ECU, and he had been designated to contact me. My ol' boss Ed Emory was still the head coach, but the school was just being placed on NCAA probation for some 18 violations. Tom said that they wanted to know if I would be interested in coming back to ECU as head coach. I said, "Tom, you've got a head coach. I'm not interested in someone else's job."

He said, "We have decided to relieve Ed of the head-coaching job."

I told him that if that happened, I would be interested when the job was open. Tom knew I would be in Charlotte to watch the South Carolina-North Carolina Shrine Bowl practice, and he asked me to meet him at the airport there. He arrived in a small plane and we talked several hours. In our talk I agreed to take the job if it became open. Ed was fired shortly, and I formally accepted the job.

Having accepted the job at ECU, I still had to prepare for the Georgia Bowl game. I had notified Coach Bowden of my decision to go to East Carolina and agreed to stay on to coach Florida State for the Bowl game.

During this time I mentioned to Bobby that I wanted to offer jobs at ECU to a couple of his coaches. He said, "Sure, go ahead; you can talk to any of my coaches." I told him I could afford only the younger ones, Brad Scott and Jeff Farrington. He said to go ahead.

Brad and I talked about the job at ECU, and he agreed to go with me to ECU if he did not get moved up to a full-time job at Florida State. We discussed salary, but not having hired any coaches yet, I didn't know what I could pay him. The next day Bobby asked me who I would try to hire, and I told him Jeff and Brad. He asked what salary I had offered Brad. I told him I was trying to get $30,000. I knew if he wanted to keep Brad, he would have to make him a full-time coach and top the $30,000; otherwise, I would get him.

The next day, Bobby called me over and said, "Art, I've decided to keep Brad here as a full-time assistant at $35,000." At least I helped Brad advance his career! He later became the head football coach at the University of South Carolina. Incidentally, Brad had been on my Citadel staff, and once a week Edie and I would take him and his wife, Daryle, to dinner. We usually picked a certain Italian restaurant. In later years he would tell me how we took them to dinner and then he would say we took them there because I had a two-for-one coupon. He was probably right because Edie and I were always frugal. Brad was a great storyteller too.

Jeff Farrington was a graduate assistant at Florida State, and Bobby would have kept him in that capacity. But he had played for me at The Citadel as a defensive back who was a tough customer and I offered him a full-time coaching position, which he accepted. He was an important coach on my staff. He is now the head coach at North Greenville University and doing a good job.

I can't say that the hundreds of phone calls I received during this time were not a distraction for me, but we had plenty of time to prepare and I think I handled my preparation very well under the circumstances. I have no doubt that I earned my money during this time. Many of the calls came from coaches looking for jobs; I knew how they felt.

I thoroughly enjoyed my year at Florida State working for Bobby Bowden. As I said initially in this chapter, he is a great person to work for; he let me coach and make decisions. I learned a lot from him, and I am confident he would say I contributed a lot to his program. He is one of the most truthful, caring, knowledgeable people I have ever known. A lot of people have asked me if he is as true a Christian as he appears. If anything, he is even more so. Like me, he married over his head. His wife, Ann, is a true coach's wife and a good speaker herself. He has great children too, two of whom (Tommy and Terry) have been head football coaches at Clemson and Auburn, respectively, and one (Jeff) who was offensive coordinator at Florida State.

Some years after both Bobby and I had retired, we were attending an FCA Boys Camp at Black Mountain, North Carolina. We were eating at the "Red Rocker," a favorite eating place locally and for FCA adults. I happened to be sitting next to Bobby when he leaned over and asked me how old I was. I said, "Bobby, I'm almost one month younger than you are."

He said, "My gosh, if I'd known you were that old, I might not have hired you!"

I also enjoyed working with and learning from the assistant coaches at Florida State. I came in under a bit of a "cloud." I was not the offensive coordinator in name, but I was in fact, since I had been asked by Bobby to install "my offense." The offensive coordinator and I had some early issues, but in the end we respected and appreciated each other. All the other coaches were ol' pros; we got along well.

The coaches' wives were so nice to Edie too. They went out almost every week for "wives' night out." We had an empty nest, and as I mentioned, we lived a short walk from the club house and tennis courts.

Another thing: I asked Bobby if we could make Wednesday "family night' and have everybody bring their families. It turned out to be a great gathering. We had a great chef who could really make food taste good. I loved everything about it except the Wednesday before the Florida game; we had to eat gator meat—not so tasty!

I really hated to leave this "big-time" program, but I was really looking forward to being a head coach again.

13 AT EAST CAROLINA UNIVERSITY…..AGAIN

For the tenth time in thirty years after leaving Fort Jackson, Edie and I faced a move from one city to another. Again, I had to leave Edie behind temporarily to sell our townhouse in Tallahassee while I began the new job in Greenville. In Greenville a real estate friend I knew from my last stay there offered to find us a home with a guarantee that he would buy it if we had not sold it after 90 days upon leaving Greenville. We bought a house on Fantasia Street (neighborhood streets were named after musical terms— Cantata, Rondo, Sonata, Woodwind, and Cadenza, to name a few). It had a large living room with a big fireplace to entertain prospects on recruiting weekends. It had three bedrooms—all we needed since all the children had left. We really liked the house and the neighborhood. Edie and I walked each evening when I got home. We lived near an English professor who, like me, liked to split and cut firewood for our fireplaces. Every Saturday we would find someone who needed a tree cut and moved, so we obliged them. There were great people in Greenville and eastern North Carolina, or as they say, "Down East."

Prior to moving, as often as I could I went back to Tallahassee to see Edie and help pack up our goods for the move. On one of these trips, I was driving to East Carolina on I-95 and had been following three semi-rigs at about 75 mph. As we entered Dillon County, a highway patrolman put on his blue light and stopped me, letting the trucks go. While I admitted I was speeding, I told him I had been following three trucks and how did they escape the radar? He said I was the only one he got even though I remained behind the trucks. He gave me a ticket with a court date. I told the officer I would be in spring practice and could not make the hearing that day. He said I would have to write the magistrate, whose name was

McCutcheon. I wrote him telling him the situation and added a note that I had gone to Presbyterian College with a "Ken McCutcheon." He wrote me back and included my check, and told me to slow down. The letter was signed "Ken McCutcheon"!

My Big Booboo

As I discussed in the last chapter, I was offered and accepted the position of head football coach at East Carolina University during the time between the last regular-season game and the Citrus Bowl game while I was at Florida State. When I agreed to accept the job, I'm afraid I didn't take the time to properly think through the job. I failed to consider ECU's future schedule, where they were in recruiting as well as salary, length of contract, and so on. I still had preparations for the Georgia Bowl game, and I guess I felt I didn't have time for "negotiations." I loved Greenville and Pirate fans, and I was eager to get back to head coaching, so I accepted the job, as I had done before, "with a hand shake."

I knew about how much Ed Emory had been making, and I was doing relatively well with regard to salary at Florida State. They asked me what I thought the salary should be. For some strange reason, money had never been the most important factor in my taking a job. I was making $55,000 at Florida State, and like an idiot I said I could take the ECU job for $65,000. They further asked how many years I felt would be "right." I should have known that four years were not enough to do the mammoth turnaround job I faced. Again like an idiot, I was more concerned with my eventual retirement date than with how long the job would take. So I dumbly said four years.

About this time, coaching salaries were on the rapid increase, as agents (lawyers) were beginning to represent coaches (and others) in negotiating contracts. I had a friend Craig Kelly, a lawyer in Columbia, who had become a pro-agent and had negotiated a number of contracts for my friends, both coaches and players. He offered to do my contract for the ECU job free of charge. For some reason, which I later regretted, I didn't take him up on his offer.

Craig and I visited several times before his untimely death and he never failed to point out that he would never have agreed for my contract to be as low as $65,000 nor would he have agreed to four years. He said it should have been at least six years. I know he was right. I am sure ECU would have agreed to more money and a longer time; if they didn't, I could have stayed at Florida State where I had a good job that I really liked. But I was eager to be a head coach again, and I was always a trusting soul; and, as I said, money was not always the most important thing to me. Besides, I felt deep down that we could build a winner. I just made a big booboo all around.

Building My Third Collegiate Staff

For the third time, I had to build "my" staff. This time it was somewhat different, however. For one thing, I did not have men to bring from a previous staff. Additionally, I had been a member of the existing staff and knew them well and liked them. I knew some of them were good coaches, and the athletic director had encouraged me to keep them to save moving expenses and costs of turnovers. I asked Ken Matous, receivers coach; John Zernhelt, offensive line coach; Tom Throckmorton, defensive coordinator; Don Murray, offensive coordinator (who had replaced me one year earlier); and Mark Clifford, a graduate assistant, to continue on my staff. Rex Kipps, who later coached at LSU, was the defensive ends coach.

I hired Don Powers, who was coaching at Western Kentucky, as defensive backs coach. When I called him, he wasn't home (actually I was returning his call). His wife, Jane, answered the phone and said, "Coach Baker, if you're calling about a job, Don will take it."

Steve Shankweiler called me from Western Kentucky and said, "Coach Baker, if you'll have me, I'll come." I hired him for the second time, the first time being at The Citadel. He was and is a very good offensive line coach. He and Zernhelt are the best I've ever been around, along with Ralph Friedgen (on my staff at The Citadel) and Jeff Fila. I also hired Wally Chambers, the great pro player, as my defensive line coach and, later, Les Herron from Clemson as my defensive coordinator, replacing Tom Throckmorton. We also had an academic coordinator who would help a great deal; her name was Pam Penland.

The aforementioned coaches comprised my beginning staff.

A Program in Disarray

I began my job as East Carolina head football coach with at least a bit of trepidation. I was fully aware of a number of difficult and negative issues with the football program. First of all, the program was dealing with 18 NCAA violations, mostly related to recruiting. Additionally, the football program faced large student academic problems as well as on-campus and off-campus image problems. Also, the program was operating "in the red" financially. To deal with the financial shortcomings, ECU had scheduled "money-making" games against such teams as South Carolina, West Virginia, Florida, Florida State, Miami, Auburn, Penn State, N.C. State, Illinois, Virginia Tech, and LSU. These were high-level, talented programs, which ECU aspired to be but was certainly not there at the time. These teams were "rich" and could well afford to pay lower-tiered teams like ECU well if they would play them, with the expectation of notching another win in the win column.

On the other hand, however, if you wanted to move up to the higher tier, you had to beat teams at that level. The day I took the job, sports writers questioned me if I knew about the schedule ECU was to be playing. I did, but you know, I always felt we could coach with these teams, but I admit I didn't realize we couldn't recruit with them year-in and year-out. I must add, though, that I inherited a fine group of young men who would work hard and compete.

In addition to the difficult and negative issues just described, I had many routine things to do besides hiring a staff; I had to organize recruiting and recruit; install offense, defense, and the kicking parts of our program; speak to Pirates Club meetings; and sell our program to fans and the public. When I took the job, there were some disenchanted fans. We lost our car dealers who provided cars for staff use, so Dave Hart, the assistant athletic director, and I were on the road each week trying to get new dealers in the program so all our coaches would have a lease car. It took a long time to do it, but we got it done. Anyway, my work was cut out for me in the days ahead.

Right off the bat, I got a call from the NCAA requesting that I come to their headquarters and explain those 18 violations. I told them I was not there at the time the violations occurred, and they said I didn't have to come. I guess the athletic director dealt with those violations. Fortunately, there were no sanctions. Having checked that "problem" off my list, I moved on to the student academic problems.

We had pretty good players, but many of them were in deep academic trouble. I had promised our chancellor, Dr. Howell, that I would get the program on sound academic footing and begin to graduate our players. After a careful study of each player's academic standing with our academic counselor, we decided which players could graduate and which ones could not but could possibly play another year. I brought the ones who could not graduate in and told them I would help them transfer to another school but we would not keep them in our program.

For the players who remained, I initiated a program where I would have lunch at the training room once a week with several professors selected by our academic counselor. I wanted our teachers to know how we planned to improve the attitudes and performances of our players in their classrooms and to listen to their comments about our players. Two common complaints were that certain players were sleeping in class and they were having excessive class cuts. One professor complained that several of the players would go to sleep in class and then threaten the graduate assistants who woke them up. We had to do something to change these attitudes; so we began a system of "no class cuts." Further we demanded that players get to class early, sit on the front row, and stay awake; and attendance was mandatory at tutoring sessions in the evenings. Each day at staff meetings, we discussed how we could improve our players and program. I began to write each player a letter after he violated one of our rules, saying that he was jeopardizing his scholarship if he continued to break team rules.

Some years later I took back four players' scholarships after they had received five such letters. They challenged my taking their scholarship before the faculty committee on such matters. I learned a long time ago that there are usually four or five players on every team who cause 99% of the team's problems. These guys were those five or six, and getting rid of them would improve our team and make my coaching a lot more fun. With the faculty in possession of the letters I had sent, the chair and members of the committee supported my proposal to take the scholarships. As I suspected, my coaching became more fun, and our team improved. Too, this action sent a strong message to current and future players.

To deal with off-campus student-image problems, we had a dress code— dress neatly, no hair below the collar, no facial hair, no jewelry, "yes sir and no sir," and so on. We had classes for our players on etiquette, manners, how to be interviewed, and behavior on and off the field. We attended church services together several times during the season. I began to have one-on-one sessions with each of our players.

To deal with the last problem cited above—that is, the tough schedule—well, we just had to recruit and coach harder!

Installing the Offense

Our first spring practice went really well. The offense we installed was a great offense; it did not differ significantly from the one they had been running, including when I was coaching there a year earlier. The "freeze option" was named by the Florida State people in the 1983 47-46 game against ECU. It was a very difficult offense to defend and prepare for in a few days. At Florida State, Eric Thomas was probably not the best quarterback there, but he understood the freeze option and was very coachable. He was a great faker, took what the defense gave him, and was sold on the offense.

At East Carolina I had Ron Jones and Darrell Street, both excellent athletes and both excellent option quarterbacks who could really hurt you with their running, but neither one was a very good passer. With the schedule we were playing, we needed a complete quarterback who could run the option, run well, and throw the run-fakes as well as the passing routes we were running borrowed from Florida State. The freeze option was a great offensive attack, and to be honest I ran the offense in order to give us an edge against the overmatched opponents we faced. It is very difficult to prepare for the option in one week when you don't play against it every week.

I was able to talk Coach Darrell "Mouse" Davis, the father of the run and shoot passing game, into coming to stay with us three or four days, and I promised him a stay at the beach for him and his wife. My high school classmate and football teammate Ed Baker (no relation) was the CEO of a huge condo complex at Atlantic Beach, and he provided a condo. Mouse was the head coach at Portland State, and his team led the nation in passing and offense for several years. He started us with the basic concept of the run and shoot. I could see it would be a great marriage with the freeze option, mainly because there were five basic routes that could all be run from the same formation as the freeze.

Later I was able to bring June Jones in to help with the passing game. He had been Coach Davis's quarterback at Portland State and had set all kinds of records nationally. I had first met June when I was at Furman and the Atlanta Falcons used Furman facilities as their preseason camp. He was the backup quarterback and punter. At East Carolina he was between a stint in Canadian football and agreed to come and spend a couple weeks with us. He was our house guest and enjoyed Edie's cooking. So he added to our passing knowledge. Sometime later, we talked with June when Edie and I toured the Hawaiian Islands when he was the head coach at the University of Hawaii.

I had in the meantime watched Georgia Southern play under Coach Erk Russell. He ran a double wing and ran the "read" option out of this formation. I had met Ben Griffith who was his offensive coordinator and hired him as my offensive coordinator for about a week before he was offered the job at the University of New Mexico. He felt bad and asked me to visit him at New Mexico, which I did. He liked some of my ideas on putting together the offense. That was a nice visit and very beneficial to me. Joe Lee Dunn was the head coach then; his defenses gave people fits for many years. Joe Lee was later a very effective defensive coordinator at South Carolina.

We began to work on running the freeze option and the run and shoot pass offense from all formations and shifts so the defense could not zero in on what we might run from this or that formation. Ken Matous really did a good job with our receivers; their assignments were very tough for they had to come off the ball every time at the same speed and then release, run, pass, run a pass route. Kevin Gilbride was a great addition to our staff; he was a disciple of Mouse Davis and well versed in the "run and shoot." He was later the offensive coordinator for five NFL teams and head coach for San Diego.

Annual Spring Game Activities

Before moving to the first football season, I want to discuss what Dave Hart, the associate athletic director, and the promotions people did every year for the spring game. First, they sponsored a barbeque contest, featuring down-east barbeque with a vinegar-based sauce. People from all over North Carolina, South Carolina, and Virginia came to compete. They were each assigned an area underneath the stadium. The cookers cooked their half hogs in their own cookers using their secret salt and sauces. People walked around all night watching the meat cook. The next morning the various barbeques were judged and the winners announced. Then the meat was put together and sold to fans to help the Athletic Department.

One of the banks put up a dance floor and the "shaggers" shagged off and on during the night. East Carolina beaches Atlantic and Nags Head believe they invented the shag. Ocean Drive Beach in South Carolina believe they invented it. I worked five summers at Ocean Drive Beach and I say it's true.

Every year the Miller Life Beer distributors sponsored the ECU spring game. They had a panel of celebrities who came and spent all weekend. On Friday night, they had a banquet, and fans would bid on the "Miller Celebs" to see who would bid the highest amount for the opportunity to play with a celebrity in Saturday's golf outing. Mickey Spillane, The Babe (Mickey Spillane character), "Hacksaw" Reynolds, and "Boog" Powell were some who came. George Baker (no relation), who ran the Crab House on the coast, had his picture made with The Babe and asked her to sign it "I got my crabs at George Baker's."

During the day they set up kiddie cars, a Ferris wheel, and a ball-throwing, dunk machine where individuals took turns throwing balls to dunk me and the basketball and baseball coaches and even the chancellor.

Additionally, they had a beauty contest and a bikini contest as well as a tug of war between our biggest linemen and an elephant. The Pirates Club put out posters and pictures, and players signed autographs. It was a big event and well attended (many times having 20 to 30,000 at the spring game), with fun for all. Miller Life got plenty of publicity as did ECU.

The First Year

I found we had two option quarterbacks, but neither could pass well enough for us to be competitive against LSU, Auburn, Penn State, Miami,

USC, N.C. State, and others that were on our looming 1985 schedule. I knew we could run the freeze option and run it well, but I knew we had to have a passing attack too. We installed a "point system" for our spring scrimmages and kept points on the scoreboard. It made the players more competitive. It's hard to keep things interesting when you're practicing your first-string offense versus defense, so we figured out a way for the defense to score points that could equalize the scrimmage. It was fun. I found out that any time you can make practice fun, it makes things a lot better.

Our first game of the 1985 season was against N.C. State. Tom Reed was the head coach, and in the past he and Ed Emory had not gotten along very well. I called Tom in August and suggested we get together and exchange films for our game to be played in Raleigh in September. We agreed to meet in Wilson, a small city between Raleigh and Greenville. I liked Tom and we got along well. It was never a problem to get our players ready to play N.C. State; it was our nearest rival and the only team that would play us from the Atlantic Coast Conference. We both had predominantly eastern North Carolina players, so some players on opposing teams had played against each other in high school. We really played well in that first game, executing the option well and throwing the ball well enough. We won the game 33-14, beginning a very tough 1985 season.

The second game of the season was against Southwest Texas (President Lyndon Johnson's alma mater, now known as Texas State University) at Greenville. We won that game 27-16. With the first two games in the win column, I suppose some people were thinking maybe we are going to have a great season after all. Such thinking proved to be only "wishful thinking," as we lost the remaining nine games on the schedule.

We played parts of some games well that year but could not maintain the pace against the top teams. For instance, against Miami, which was nationally ranked, we had five sacks and five interceptions in the fourth quarter and led 15-13 with six to seven minutes to go. They threw a screen pass to their All-America full back Hightower, and he went 80 yards for the go-ahead touchdown to beat us 27-15.

At LSU we stayed close the entire game and scored with four to five minutes to go. We kicked an on-side kick and recovered it. We had an on-side kick plan that was developed by the coaches on the 1983 team. The kicker kicked the ball slowly on the ground, and we instructed the players around the kicker to charge forward in a sort of wedge around the ball while blocking all receiving players away from the ball. The kicker simply followed the ball and fell on it behind his blockers. Since then the football rules committee changed the rules to prevent this play, but it was perfectly legal back then. Anyway, after recovering the kick, we made a couple first downs but freshman quarterback Bert Holtsclaw from Valdosta, Georgia, forced a ball that was intercepted. We could have gone ahead on that drive but didn't, and eventually lost 35-15.

Another funny incident happened on the on-side kick at LSU. The kick was made and we recovered it near our hash mark. Of course we were elated, jumping up and down. The official on our side, a big guy about 6 ft 4 inches, 250 lb, was signaling that LSU had recovered the ball while our players were handing him the ball. Before I knew what I was doing, I was on the field right in front of him yelling, "Wait a minute, we recovered that ball!"

Very calmly he leaned down in my face and said, "Yes coach, it is your ball but if you don't get your ass off the field in a big hurry, you're going to get a 15-yard penalty." I don't think I ever moved so quickly!

Later that year we were playing Tulsa, which was having a good season but was really about as good as we were. We were behind 21-20 in the final minutes and got down near their 20 with just over a minute to go. We had East Carolina's record-setting place kicker, Jeff Heath, later to become a Hall of Fame member, kicking. We worked the ball in the middle of the field, and he missed a field goal about three feet to the right. We had all our timeouts remaining and managed to force them to punt. We completed several passes to the 25 again and ol' Jeff missed another field goal about two feet to the right. At least he was consistent that day, but we lost another one we certainly could have won.

When we visited Penn State, I'm sure they prepared for us, but they had a "Big 10" opponent after us and probably prepared some against the next opponent, thinking they were good enough to beat us anyway. They did win, but not before a big scare, barely winning 17-10. We spent the entire fourth quarter on their end of the field fumbling once at the two-yard line and on another occasion overthrowing a wide-open Tony Smith in the end zone by himself with time running out on the clock. The Penn State fans gave our players a standing ovation at the end of the game.

We played South Carolina well in the first half at Greenville and were two or three points behind at the half. We continued to play well in the third quarter, but then in the fourth quarter, we looked like we weren't even on the same field. They scored three or four touchdowns and what had been a good game became an embarrassment as we lost 52-10.

We even lost to a good Temple team 21-7, only to find after the season that their great running back Palmer had signed on with an agent. They forfeited the game, but unfortunately too late to help our poor record.

We also lost games to Louisiana-Lafayette, Southern Mississippi, and Auburn, giving us a 2-9 record, not counting the forfeit.

The Second Year

In 1986 our first game was again against N.C. State in Raleigh. By now my ol' friend and assistant coach Dick Sheridan (at Eau Claire High and Furman), who had replaced me as head coach at Furman, was the head coach at N.C. State. We played them in Raleigh and played pretty well for the first three quarters but got beat in the last quarter 38-10.

We played West Virginia in our second game and went into the final minute of the game leading 21-17. The West Virginia quarterback threw a pass he admitted later he was trying to throw out of bounds to stop the clock, but one of their receivers leapt up in the back of the end zone and was able to come down with the ball inches inside the end-zone. We lost 24-21.

Later in the year we played Southern Mississippi in Greenville and played the Brett Favre team well. With two minutes to go, we drove 85 yards to score and come within one point 19-20. We decided to go for two points and made it, going up 21-20. They came back in less than two minutes and drove 80 yards. They had fourth down and five to go and ran a bootleg pass. We had a safety blitz called—a perfect defensive call. Our safety was unblocked but went after the fake, and they completed the play and won the game. Seems we lost too many games like that. We would play hard against the good teams and still lose when we played Southern Mississippi, Cincinnati, and Temple. We would often be beaten up physically. Then too, Brett Favre beat a lot of good teams.

The Third Year

In 1987 we finally had two quarterbacks who could run our offense, and we played much better. Travis Hunter was a very good option quarterback and fair passer, and Charlie Libretto was a very good passer for an option quarterback; they gave us a pretty good pair. The only problem was that Travis was black and Charlie was white. When I sent one in, some of the crowd booed; when I sent the other one in, others in the crowd booed. In all my years as a coach, that was probably the time I became angriest. I looked up into the crowd to see the hecklers and realized that was the wrong thing to do. Don't let them know it bothers you. This was the only instance I was disappointed in our Pirates fans.

One of the most exciting games that year was against Georgia Southern. Erk Russell (a good friend) was the coach there, and they had a quarterback named Tracy Ham, who was absolutely the best option quarterback I had ever seen. They had won the national I-AA championship in 1986 and would beat Furman for the title in 1987. I remember the spring before, my athletic director, Ken Karr, told me he had scheduled Georgia Southern as a "breather" (i.e., a team you should beat easily). There was not a single I-A team in America that would choose Georgia Southern as a breather. Two of my linemen had gotten into a fight Wednesday night downtown, and the athletic director would not allow them to play in this game on Saturday. Going into the game, I told my defensive coordinator I didn't care what they did on defense, but I wanted us to take the quarterback-keep on the option away from Tracy Ham. We won the game 16-13. We went 87 yards late in the game, aided by a 15-yard penalty against Erk for going onto the field after an official. At the end of the game I checked the stats, and Tracy had 199 yards rushing, most all on keeps by Tracy. So much for ultimatums to defensive coordinators! [Nobody else stopped him either.]

Speaking of the Georgia Southern game and Tracy Ham, I digress a moment to talk about our strength program. We had an excellent program at East Carolina, mainly because of our strength coach Mike Gentry. [He subsequently had perhaps the best strength program in the USA at Virginia Tech for many years.] At ECU we didn't have an adequate strength room. My predecessor, Ed Emory, had built a nice strength room in an old tobacco barn turned into a skating rink. It had no air conditioning, but Mike had our players loving weights. His prize pupil was Terry Long who in 1983 was the third strongest human in the world in the power lifts. Mike also usually came up with some kind of gimmick before each game. For the Georgia Southern game, he brought a country ham and a chainsaw into the dressing room. Then he made a passionate talk and said, "Here's what we are going to do to Tracy Ham," and he cranked up the chain saw and cut the "ham" in two. The team went wild. There's no telling how many yards Tracy would have gained if we hadn't cut that ham!

This year N.C. State was to go to their second Bowl game, but not before we put a good beating on them. The freeze was working to perfection and the run and shoot came into its own and we won 32-14. Our student seats were in the end zone grass bank opposite their clubhouse and scoreboard. They had been partying all afternoon, watching the Pirates maul the Wolfpack. The public-address announcer kept making announcements all during the game for the ECU students to get back from a small, flimsy, chain-link fence between them and the playing field. As the Pirates piled up points, the announcer became more and more frustrated with the students. They knew they were "getting his goat."

When we played at N.C. State, the N.C. Highway Patrol assigned a state trooper to be on the sidelines the entire game. That night they had assigned a tall, blond lady about 6 ft 2 or 3 inches. She was good at her job and seemed to like how we were playing. With 25 seconds to go in the game and us having won the game, our students decided to kick the fence down and hundreds of them began to pour onto the field. I didn't believe what I was seeing. I could just see the officials making us forfeit the game. I ran out on the field waving my arms for the students to leave the field. Finally, I grabbed two guys who looked like freshmen and told them, "How do you think your mothers are going to feel when they see me kick your rear ends off this field on TV?"

About the time I got hold of both of them, the aforementioned trooper yelled to both boys, "And if he doesn't kick you off this field, I will!" The field was cleared and we won the game (didn't have to forfeit, thank goodness). But several days later, the N.C. State athletic director announced that because of our students' "rowdy behavior," they would cancel any further games. Many Pirate supporters thought it was because of getting beat two out of three years.

We went on to beat Temple, Cincinnati, and VPI and had a chance for a winning season in our final game at Southern Mississippi, again against Brett Favre and crew. It was a game where every little thing went against us. There was one punt that bounced into one of our players, allowing them to recover it. Then there was a punt returned by them for a touchdown when a fair catch had been made, but the officials didn't call it. We lost the game 38-34 and finished the season 5-6.

The 1987 turned out to be my best season at ECU. We had by this time developed our offense into a pretty potent attack, often having total offense in excess of 400 yards. Kevin Gilbride, our offensive coordinator, had developed a fine passing game with the run and shoot married to the rushing attack by the freeze option. Richard Bell, our defensive coordinator, was improving our defense each week, but we were still not ready for the teams we had to play in the Southeast, Atlantic Coast, and Big Ten Conferences.

The Fourth Year

Our opening game in 1988 was against Tennessee Tech in Greenville. Jimmy Ragland, my ol' friend and fellow coach at Texas Tech, was the head coach. We actually had a better team in 1988, but it seemed everybody else was better too. We could not do anything wrong and though I felt bad for Jimmy, we looked great and had well over 500 yards in offense. We won 52-13. Jimmy later passed away in Cookeville, Tennessee in 2006. Again, after winning our opening game, things were looking up—but unfortunately not for long.

We would have some good games but lose. For example, Florida State at Tallahassee was a game we really could have won. They had Deion Sanders at free safety, and he was so aggressive but almost undisciplined. We would run the option and pitch to the half back, and Deion would come up so fast he would tackle our tailback on the line of scrimmage. Our wing back was supposed to block the strong safety, but Deion would beat him to the tailback. So we let our wingback fake the block and cut up field. Then we faked running the option and threw the pass to the wingback who was deep behind the strong safety and Deion. We threw this pass three or four times, and Deion was fooled every time, but he was so fast that he recovered and caught our wingback before he could score every time (and our wingback was pretty quick). Steve Shankweiler, our offensive line coach, noticed that Florida State's two linebackers mirrored our offensive guards. We pulled our guards on almost every play on the option, so Steve came up with a scheme whereby we would pull the guard on our split end side towards the tight end, making their linebacker to his side run with him. Then we ran the option the other way with us pulling strong side guards. He worked out a scheme whereby the guards practiced pulling in opposite directions without colliding. The play on film looked like a busted play, but it worked very well because their linebackers ran into each other, the weak-side linebacker actually blocking the strong-side linebacker.

We played well that day, and with little time remaining, we were behind but had fourth down on our own 30-yard line. Instead of punting, we went for it and did not make the first down. They got the ball back with 20 seconds to play. With nine seconds left, they threw a bootleg pass for a touchdown to beat us 45-21. Because I had been Bobby Bowden's assistant head coach a few years earlier, I didn't say anything at the post-game press conference, but the next day some papers really criticized him for running the play and running up the score. I knew, however, that when I was calling plays for Bobby and we were ahead, I mentioned "calling off the dogs," and he would tell me my job was to move the ball and score touchdowns.

In another instance in the same game, we had a third and 17 on the Florida State 35. Kevin Gilbride asked me what play I wanted to run (he wanted to run a pass play). I said to run the option. He said, "Come on coach, we can't gain 17 yards against their defense by running."

I said, "Run the option." We did and gained 25 yards.

Ken Matous, the receivers coach, said, "Nice call, coach!"

I knew we had been lucky to make the play, but I also knew they would be in a "man" coverage, and it is hard to stop the option in man coverage. Kevin just laughed.

Another game that we should have won (via a documented mistake by the officials) was against Southern Mississippi and, of course, Brett Favre. They were playing well and led us 38-18 going into the fourth quarter. Charlie Libretto threw and ran the option well, Travis Hunter did his part, and we scored to go ahead 42-40 with eight seconds left. To avoid giving them a chance to set up and run our kickoff back for a touchdown, we kicked a "pooch" kick which they caught on a "fair catch." With the fair catch, no time came off the clock. Everyone in the stadium knew Brett would throw a "Hail Mary"—i.e., send all receivers deep and throw the ball as high and as far as possible, in the hope someone will catch it and score. Brett's pass was tipped two or three times and ended up being caught by a Southern Mississippi receiver who ran a bit and then apparently lateraled the ball to a teammate who was tackled at our 15-yard line. The officials threw a flag calling an illegal forward lateral and, more importantly, stopping the clock.

The referee came over to me and said, "Coach, your only choice is whether or not you want to accept the five-yard penalty."

Several Pirate players were saying, "Coach, the player was down before he lateraled."

The referee said, "No official saw that happen." [This was before we had replays and challenges.]

They kicked a field goal and won the game.

As soon as the game was over, the coaches, teams, and fans were in shock. One fan jumped over the wall of the stadium and hit an official and was arrested. It was learned that he was a Sunday School teacher from Virginia. Frankly, I felt like hitting someone myself.

Immediately following the game, a friend from the Greenville TV station came over to me with a TV guy from Raleigh. They said, "Coach, you aren't going to believe this but the replay film showed that the Southern Mississippi player had been tackled, then rolled over and lateraled the ball. He was down and the game should have been over with time having run out on the play." What could I say? The officials had already reviewed the replay and realized their mistake, and they were gone.

On Monday the Metro Conference officials called to set up a press conference in Greenville. The chief official apologized for their terrible mistake in the game. Even though the game was technically a win for us, they don't change the score in such situations. This was another big win we missed out on, but those things happen. Our players didn't deserve that loss.

At the Southern Mississippi game, Edie had been invited to sit in the Chancellor's box and invited Marilyn Bell, Coach Richard Bell's wife, to sit with her. Up in the stands at the end of the game, Edie was really upset, and Marilyn was in tears. They were seated behind the chancellor's seats and could see his actions throughout the game. At the end of the game, the chancellor came back to give Edie a hug, and she told him, "Don't come back here to hug me. I watched you during the game, and you seemed so pleased when Southern Mississippi was leading; but when we came back to go ahead at the end of the game, you looked very disappointed and sad. I can't believe a chancellor would not pull for his own team!" And she walked off.

The next morning I met with Dave Hart, the athletic director, as I usually did every Sunday after games. He said first thing, "Art, did you know Edie became upset and refused to let the chancellor hug her and accused him of pulling for Southern Mississippi?"

I said, "Dave, yes, she told me after the game what she said, and, you know, through the 36+ years I've known her, she is the most honest and kindest person I've ever known. I would bet anybody that she told it like it was!"

Our last game of the season was against Cincinnati at Cincinnati. As we arrived at the hotel, the officials for the next day's game were arriving. While the team was having our Friday night meal, one of the officials, Grady Ray, an ol' friend from Columbia, came in and said in a pretty-loud voice, "How about it, Coach Art; how much are we going to beat them tomorrow?"

I jumped up and put my index finger to my lips. Man, I was hoping nobody outside the room heard that. I knew, of course, that he was just kidding, but I feared others might think otherwise.

As we checked into the hotel, we noticed a lot of pretty-tall girls. We found out they were having a volleyball conference tournament there. We coaches, aware this was out last game of the season (and my last game at ECU), feared that some of our players might be tempted to see the girls past curfew. We decided we would check every room at curfew, rather than a spot check. We already had a curfew-violation punishment—30-minute workout with complete silence. Anyone arguing or talking during the workout would be sent back to their room and would not dress for the next day's game. Two players wanted to complain 20 minutes into their workouts; we sent them to their rooms and gave them meal tickets for they were off the team the next day.

One of those two players was a quarterback. We had traveled with only three quarterbacks. The next day one of them got hurt in the second quarter, and we had to play the rest of the game with our only remaining quarterback. However, we won the game 49-14 for a nice ending of the season (and, as it turned out, for my last game as a coach).

The ECU Ending

Everyone knew that 1988 was the last year of my contract. There was a strange feeling during the season. The staff and I felt that Dr. Eakin (chancellor) and Dave Hart (athletic director) had already made their minds up that they were not going to renew my contract but were hesitant to act. The reason for their hesitance, I believe now, was the fact that we were getting better every game, especially against the teams that were really "in our league"—Southern Mississippi, N.C. State, Temple, and Connecticut. They weren't knowledgeable enough to realize that our 1988 recruiting class was one of the top classes ever. Then too, they were getting messages from pockets of ECU supporters all over the state to renew my contract. Don Powers, Richard Bell, and Kevin Gilbride were strong in their belief that I should fight for a renewal. But my intuition told me they wanted a new coach. Then there was a solid group in Greenville, including Dr. Howell, who hired me, assuring me they wanted most of all to "clean up the program" first, while we were playing a "killer schedule" that no coach could have had a winning season. Another point was that for whatever reason, the press seemed to support my contract renewal—at least the Raleigh and Fayetteville papers.

Personally, I felt I deserved a contract renewal. [Actually, I should have gotten six years to begin with, but that was my booboo.] We had "cleaned up" our program. I am proud to say that in the four years I was at ECU, the graduation rates improved more than for any other state school in North Carolina. The off-campus student-image problems we inherited were largely eliminated as a result of our etiquette classes and my one-on-one sessions with the players. Regarding the tough schedule we inherited, I felt we had done very well under the circumstances and, as chronicled in this chapter, we truly could have won a number of games against better teams (I know, "close" only counts in horseshoes). We had an outstanding coaching staff, many of whom went on to become head coaches. Perhaps most importantly, our last recruiting class included Robert Jones, linebacker; Robert Scott, offensive tackle; John Jett, punter; James Blake, quarterback; Vincent Smith, linebacker; and Tony Baker, running back—all of whom went on to play in the NFL. I truly believe we had turned the football program around and we could have been very good. [It is worth noting too that I was now dealing with a chancellor and an athletic director, both of whom were not the ones who had hired me four years earlier.]

Dr. Howell, the retired chancellor who hired me, came to see me after the season was over and he said, "Art, you did everything I asked you to do—it was a six-year job rather than a four-year job." He was right too.

Early in the season, my friend King Dixon, who had just become South Carolina's athletic director, called me. He was aware of my contract dilemma and asked me about joining him at USC as associate athletic director. He said he had never been an athletic director and he needed somebody who could help him and somebody he could trust. I wasn't ready to quit coaching, but I loved the thought of working with King and I would be getting back into the S.C. State Retirement System. I told him I would get back with him. But it did take some pressure off.

Edie and I talked and prayed about the two choices I had: (1) Fight for a renewed contract (I didn't get any positive vibes from Dave Hart) or (2) take the job at the University of South Carolina that King Dixon had offered me. I finally decided I would resign with three games left in the season to be effective at the end of the season. I felt strongly that the questions asked each week at my press conference were a big distraction to our players. Whether this was true or not, I don't know; but I do know the players seemed more relaxed and played better those last three games.

After I resigned prior to the end of the season, I tried my best to get Dave Hart to hire Richard Bell or Kevin Gilbride as the head coach. Richard had been head coach at South Carolina, and Kevin was subsequently the head coach of the San Diego Chargers. I don't think Dave gave either of them a thought. He already knew Bill Lewis and wanted him. Bill did very well.

Over the four years I was head coach at ECU, we obviously didn't win nearly as many games as I wanted, but slowly but surely we improved all phases of the football program. Actually, our last two years, we moved the ball really well; we just couldn't stop the other team's offense. I'm pretty sure we were well over 300 yards for both seasons. Really, it was a beautiful offense, and I regret to this day that I was not able to continue either at East Carolina or some other school where we could have had equal talent with those we played.

Family Matters

While we were at East Carolina, Artie was the offensive coordinator at Hillcrest High in Dalzell. I tried to bring him to ECU as a graduate assistant, but Dr. Eakin, the chancellor, said North Carolina would not allow two staff members from the same family. Artie was still dating Sherri Tickel, who was an elementary teacher. She had been married but divorced, and she and Artie became interested. After courting for some time, Artie announced to us that they were planning to be married and were in June 1989 in the Dalzell Methodist Church where Edie and I had been married 36 years before.

Kim and Gil lived in our beach house at Wild Dunes on Isle of Palms. Gil was always into radio, and he was good. Kim used to say he would either be a millionaire or go broke. So far, he is still working on the million. Gil often did something out in left field and while living in our beach house he bought a Great Dane and locked him on the porch all day one day. He (the dog, that is) almost tore up our porch and the doors going inside.

In 1986 Curtis, our youngest son, graduated with a degree in criminal justice from Florida State.

Guilford Marshal Kirkman was born on January 15, 1985, to Kim and

Gil. Then on July 16, 1986, Taylor Lee Kirkman was born; he was a red-headed boy who was, shall I say, quite active while growing up. He was red headed and found himself in a large number of fights at school. I was talking with him one day and said, "Taylor, when I was in school and got into a fight, by the end of the day we were friends again. But today, some of the young people might go home and get a gun or a knife to settle things."

He said, "Granddad, I'm 6 and 0 in fights!"

Edie and I enjoyed the times we could go and keep these boys a few days—there was never a dull moment. One day Edie was taking them to school. She handed Taylor a small mirror and said, "Taylor, before you go to school every day you should check your face carefully."

He said, "Grandmom, you mean to check for boogers?"

Edie struggled to keep a straight face.

On another occasion, Edie was talking to Marshall over the phone when he said, "Grandmom, I went to potty."

She said, "Oh Marshall, I'm so proud of you."

Marshall was two or three years old and still in potty training. He was born and lived in Charleston where they speak differently from the rest of the state.

He said, "No, Grandmom; I went to a birthday party!"

While I was coaching at East Carolina, I found time to play my favorite pastime—tennis. I met two members of the faculty, Al ("Serve City") King, who taught physical education, and Tom Sayatta, who taught physics. Both were good players, and we played every week when I could work it in—mostly on Fridays around noon for home games. In the summer we played more often, and we played in some tournaments. We played out on the edge of town where a man had three soft courts in his back yard and had sort of a small "club." When I serve, I have always (like a lot of others) dragged my toe. So Joe, the pro, would let me play only on the loose, soft courts. The other guys soon named the court "Baker's Court." Joe was strange and very peculiar, but we enjoyed our tennis and I still play with Tom and Al when I go back to Greenville and eat oysters with Joe.

During the summers, my friend Ed Baker from Sumter who managed a large condo complex in Atlantic Beach would let us and our coaches use a condo for a week. A couple times we invited my cousin Paul "Billy" Baker, the son of our rich Uncle Ally. He has a beautiful home on the Pinehurst National Golf Course called "Baker's Acres." He and his wife Carolyn would come and spend several days.

Then we would always invite our long-time friends Kirby and Patricia Jackson to come. One summer we decided to visit along with Kirby and Patricia the Pirates hangouts—the Outer Banks, Hatteras, Ocracoke, Nags

Head, and then Bath and several other "Pirate coves." At one point we had to catch a ferry by a certain time or wait till the next day. We were late and they were about to leave, but just when it appeared we would miss it, someone on board the ferry yelled and they came back. He happened to be one of my players who was helping run the ferry as a summer job. Boy were we lucky because there were no motels within 100 miles. Sometimes I felt I led a charmed life!

On another morning when Paul and Kirby were both with us with their wives, we were having breakfast and Carolyn was reminding Paul to take his morning pills. Kirby asked what the pills were for. Paul, with a twinkle in his eye, replied that they were "sex pills." Patricia said, "Will you please lend Kirby a few?"

People in Greenville were very supportive and were good fans. Edie and I "ate out" quite a bit, and often when we finished and tried to settle our bill the cashier would say, "Someone has already taken care of your bill." We never knew who.

Miscellany

After each game or practice, I usually reminded the players to be careful and to call their parents and tell them they loved them. In 1987 I had a player who lost his father. He called to say he couldn't practice and stayed away all week, missing the next game. On Monday he came into my office and began crying. I hugged him and explained what I could spiritually and realistically. He cried even harder and said, "Coach, you were always telling us to call our parents and tell them we loved them. I didn't call my dad and now I can't." That hit me hard too; I went home and told my wife and called my children and grandchildren to tell them how much I loved them.

At ECU, I tried one secretary who knew nothing about football. For example, one day I had a friend in Columbia, Mac Rentz, who called me often and would sometimes "pick at" the secretary. Once I was in a meeting and he called me. She asked him who was calling, and he said to tell him Bear Bryant is calling. [Coach Bryant had been dead for at least ten years.] She came into the meeting room with the most serious face to inform me that Coach Bear Bryant was on the phone. You can imagine the laugh the coaches had. Probably one of my favorite secretaries was Joyce Pruitt, who replaced the former secretary. She was a jewel. She made it her business to keep up with everything about our program and did a great job of protecting me when I needed to be protected from petty phone calls or office visits.

Each Friday night we met with the team before the Saturday game. I would end the meetings by trying to get the players' attention on the game, but I also wanted them not to get ready too quick. I always believed in some humor, but after four years the players would tell me I had "used that one before."

Every coach likes for everything leading up to the game to be organized, smooth, with no surprises, whether playing at home or on the road. Of course, "home" was easier to have everything work out well. When we played Virginia Tech at Blacksburg in 1987, Henry Van Zandt set up our travel arrangements and going to Blacksburg we stayed in a hotel 20 miles from Blacksburg. It was a beautiful place located in a valley with mountains off to the west. Everything went well until we got to the time for our team meeting. The only place they had for us to meet Saturday morning for our pregame devotion was the bar, with beer and liquor bottles prevalent from the night before. We had the devotion there, but we coaches were worried it would distract our team and we would not play well. The next day, however, we played one of our best games while I was at ECU and beat Virginia Tech 32-23. So much for worrying about meeting in a bar! [Just proves the Lord is everywhere, I guess.]

Our FCA chapter at East Carolina was very strong and very active. Steve Patton, a reserve tight end became a strong leader. Almost every meeting they came up with a skit that was both entertaining and gave a great spiritual message. At practice and meetings, we constantly reminded our players of their spiritual needs; we prayed often.

I always visited players in the hospital, and Edie would go by to see them on her own. One day we had an offensive guard who was injured, requiring knee surgery. His name was Joe and he was from Chesapeake, Virginia. My wife visited him in the hospital and as she was preparing to leave, she said, "Joe, you're going to be fine, for you know who is in control."

Joe said, "Oh yes I do Mrs. Baker. I know Coach Baker is in control."

She had to laugh as she corrected him as to who was actually in control—the Lord.

One day I was playing tennis with a professor of a motorcycle-driving class. He said, "Art, I'm worried about your defensive end," and he gave me his name.

I said, "Why is that, Al?"

He said, "Today in class after they had made it around the track twice, I heard him yell out 'Ouch'!" His bike had fallen down and he picked it up by the almost-red exhaust pipe. Was he hurt badly?"

I said, No."

He said, "I'm just worried about him remembering his plays."

During my last year at ECU, on home games Edie and I would drive down to the Outer Banks of North Carolina about 70 miles and just watch the birds and beach and then drive back for our team meetings. It was relaxing and helped me a lot with a clear head for the games.

My Final Staff

Before leaving this chapter, I want to talk a bit more about my final staff as a head football coach. Every successful coach must have a good cadre of assistant coaches. As I have stated previously, I felt I was blessed by God with the ability to find and hire excellent assistants during all the times I was a head coach. Earlier in this chapter, I discussed my ECU beginning staff. It was an excellent staff but, as is common, it changed during the years. Some will "come"; some will "go." If you have a good assistant on your staff, somebody else may seek him for their head coach or an assistant coach.

My final staff was outstanding. Several of my original staff members were with me all four years. Steve Shankweiler was our offensive line coach and one of the very best. Jeff Fila was the tight end coach and helped Steve with the offensive line. Ken Matous was receiver and slot back coach; he also headed up the special teams and was very good at it. Don Powers was assistant head coach and secondary coach. He was so loyal to me and was a genius at organization and computer use. The only thing about Don: If I asked him a question at a staff meeting, he would stammer a lot and it took him all day to answer. Someone said if you asked Don what time it was, he would tell you how to build a watch. But I'll never forget that when the chancellor and athletic director would not make a decision about extending my contract in the end, Don had a tremendous number of Pirate Club members calling to support an extension of my contract. Several graduate assistants were great for us, too.

Other members of my last year's staff who were with me three years included Clyde Christensen who worked with our running backs; he is a wonderful Christian friend who later coached at several other universities as well as Tampa Bay, Indianapolis, and Miami in the NFL. Ellis Johnson was our linebacker coach; he was about as good as they get. He subsequently coached at several universities including stints as head coach at The Citadel and Southern Mississippi.

Those who were with me my last two years included Kevin Gilbride; he was the offensive coordinator (I was still very much involved on offense, especially the option part). Kevin later coached in the NFL for Houston, Jacksonville, San Diego (head coach), Pittsburgh, Buffalo, and the New York Giants. Donnie Thompson was our defensive line coach my last two years, and he was as good as they come. After stints at North Carolina and Illinois, he returned to ECU as an assistant. Chuck Driesbach was also with me my last two years. He was the defensive ends and outside linebackers coach, and he was an outstanding recruiter. He recruited Robert Jones, an All-American and All-Pro player. Chuck later coached at several universities and with the Buffalo Bills and Cleveland Browns; Robert later played in the NFL for Dallas, St. Louis, Miami, and Washington.

With me my last year was Richard Bell, my defensive coordinator (he had been fired by Steve Spurrier at Duke). I hired him and paid him a portion of my television show monies to come to ECU. He had previously been head coach at South Carolina. And, Henry VanSant, a long-time ECU graduate and coach who had been away from ECU, wanted to come back, and I recommended we bring him back as my football operations coach.

As I said before, this was an outstanding coaching staff. It's really a shame we could not have continued at ECU; we could have been very good!

Others who coached for me at times during my ECU tenure included Andy Friedlander, a former kicker, who did a great job with our kickers; he deserves a lot of credit for developing John Jett, who later kicked in the NFL for Minnesota, Dallas, and Detroit. Others were Mike O'Cain, who later was head coach at N.C. State and Clyde Chastain, an ol' FCA friend, who later coached in the NFL for Tampa Bay, Indianapolis, and Miami. I hired Mark McHale from Appalachian State; he stayed a year and left for Southern Mississippi.

Moving On

Prior to my last season at ECU, I had pains in my upper abdomen and went to a doctor who discovered I had a gall bladder full of stones. This was in August prior to two-a-day practices. He wanted to operate immediately, but I told him I couldn't possibly have surgery that close to practice. He said, "Well, I'll put you on a special diet and just maybe you'll make it till the end of the season, but I doubt it." I nearly starved that season, eating so much chicken and fish that I would have killed for a "Big Mac." But my gall stones did okay and I made it through 11 tough games.

After the season ended, I went the next week into Pitt Memorial Hospital for gall bladder surgery. After I resigned, Dave Hart offered me a job at ECU as assistant athletic director dealing with student athlete development. While I was in the waiting room for my surgery, I called Dave and told him I would not take his job offer but would accept the job offer at USC. I stayed several days in the hospital, and then went home to recuperate. Man, that doctor split me open with an incision 15 to 18 inches long. [This was about six months before they began to take gall bladders out through the belly button.] When they did old gall-bladder surgeries like mine, they had to cut through the stomach muscle which took forever to heal, and at least two to three weeks of rest was recommended.

My surgery was on November 30, and I had agreed to speak to a high school football banquet in Sumter, South Carolina, on December 12. Then being the tightwad I am, I was being paid by ECU through December, and if I reported to work at USC by December 15 I could "double dip" for two weeks. The drive to the football banquet was about two and a-half hours, and I don't remember a more painful ride in my life. Edie drove her small Mazda, and every bump we hit between Greenville and Sumter I would groan, and I'm telling you I hurt all the way to the banquet. After the banquet we drove on to Columbia and the groaning and hurting continued.

King Dixon had arranged a furnished apartment for us, but it was upstairs! When we arrived at the apartment, I felt like I had played a full football game and been tackled on every play by Dick Butkus. We had packed two full suitcases so we could stay a while. Edie could not carry those suitcases; it was 11:30 p.m. and there was no one to help. So I had to lug two big, heavy suitcases up those stairs. I got paid double for two weeks, but my stomach muscles hurt every step I took. I sure wish they had invented the "belly button" procedure six months earlier.

I went back to Greenville a few days after I got all "signed up" at USC and met all my staff at the Gamecock club. I called Bill Lewis from my Greenville home to congratulate him on his appointment as head coach and offered to go over any part of the ECU program. He was nice but declined, which was probably wise on his part. Three years later, the Pirates had a great (11-1) season and Coach Lewis won the National Coach of the Year Award. Edie and I were there when he received the honor and congratulated him.

We left our home in Greenville with the real estate friend who had promised to sell it when we left. He eventually sold it to a relative of George Moore (of Todd and Moore Sporting Goods store in Columbia), who helped me find my first coaching job at McColl High School. We really loved out Greenville home; it helped us many times to entertain prospects who signed with us.

14 AT THE UNIVERSITY OF SOUTH CAROLINA

Although I was not ready to get out of coaching, Edie and I did look forward to moving back to Columbia. After all, I had visited Columbia while growing up in Sumter, Edie had gone to Columbia College there, and we had lived there two years while at Fort Jackson and subsequently six years while at Eau Claire High. In fact, the six years at Eau Claire constituted our longest stay at any one place thus far.

Since all our children were "out of the nest," Edie was able to move to Columbia with me right away. As I mentioned in the last chapter, King Dixon, the USC athletic director, had arranged for us to stay in an apartment and had arranged for basic furnishings. It was nice but was upstairs, which was tough on my recuperation from surgery.

As soon as we sold our house in Greenville, we looked at several nice homes and settled on one that had been on the market some time. It was located in "The Commons," a gated community in northeast Columbia. It was a nice home with a nice deck out back. The one bad thing about the house was that the kitchen was far removed from the den; thus, Edie was often in the kitchen while everyone else was watching TV in the den. The grandsons loved to visit and fish in the "Commons" pond. The "Commons" also had a pool close to our home, which we used a lot. Edie and I began to walk at night, a habit we still enjoy. It was a great place to live.

We rejoined College Place Methodist Church after a 24-year absence and picked up where we left off there.

A Whirlwind Arrival

While I was back in Greenville for a weekend visit, Joe Morrison, the USC head football coach, called me to congratulate me on coming to USC. Moreover, he asked me if I wouldn't like to be his offensive coordinator there rather than associate athletic director (at the same salary). I told him that he already had an offensive coordinator, and he told me to let him worry about that—that he was offering me the job. Not being ready to leave coaching, I was elated about the prospect. South Carolina had enjoyed another great season and was headed for the Liberty Bowl. I told King about the offer. He was not surprised but said he would have to talk to Dr. Holderman, the USC president, about it. King was not really against my going over to the football staff, but when he mentioned it to Dr. Holderman, Dr. Holderman said no, he had hired me as Head of the Gamecock Club.

In early January the NCAA was meeting in San Francisco, and King wanted us to go. We did and Dr. Holderman had a dinner for all of us there the first evening. He pulled me aside and said, "Art, one reason I hired you is that I want you to help me fire Joe Morrison."

I said, "Dr. Holderman, Joe is a fine coach."

He said, "That may be, but I want him fired."

I found that strange coming from the president. I knew I didn't want any part of that.

In early February, the last recruiting weekend, there was a running back/kicker potential recruit from Barnwell, South Carolina, who was visiting and I knew his dad. Joe asked me to have breakfast with them on Sunday morning. I did and while walking out to our cars afterward, Joe told me the signing date was on Tuesday and he wanted me to come over to the stadium Tuesday morning and he wanted a final answer about the job from me then. I was really leaning hard towards taking the job against Dr. Holderman's wishes.

Sunday night Edie and I were talking about taking the job (she knew how badly I wanted to coach) when the phone rang. It was Dick Bestwick calling to tell me Coach Morrison had died at the stadium of a heart attack. Joe was very popular among Gamecock fans.

Dick was the USC athletic director from March 1988 to October 1988, when he resigned because of health reasons, at which time Albert "King" Dixon, Jr. became the athletic director. King and I had been friends since my Presbyterian College days when he lived a few miles away in Laurens, South Carolina. He was a great running back for the Gamecocks back in the 1950s. He and Alex Hawkins, the other halfback, were hard to stop.

There were several memorial services for Joe and much speculation about who would replace him. King and Dr. Holderman asked me to do the "leg work," and King and I began to make a list of top candidates. At the top of our list was Dick Sheridan, a USC graduate serving a very successful tenure at N.C. State, having played in several Bowl games. Our main problem was that this was mid-February and most football coaches were already preparing for spring drills, just having completed recruiting, and none of the very successful coaches wanted to leave their situations to come to USC. Too, neither King nor I had any experience in formulating a coach's financial "package," which was in the process of drastic change across the country. Suddenly, head coaches' salaries went from around $100,000 to multi-hundred-thousand-dollar packages, which included cars for the coaches and their wives, country club memberships, expense accounts, radio/television shows, speaking engagements, equipment contracts, and ample salaries for their staffs.

We worked hard trying to entice Dick to come to USC. He was, and still is, one of my closest friends. A USC alumnus, he was on my staff at Eau Claire High and Furman, where he succeeded me as head coach when I left for The Citadel. Dr. Holderman thought my closeness with Dick would "swing" him to come. Dr. Holderman, King, and I flew to Florida State in Tallahassee where Dick was visiting with Bobby Bowden's staff to try to persuade him to come. Dick called me later and told me he just didn't feel good about coming to USC and leaving N.C. State with spring practice so near, so he turned the job down. We then contacted Fisher DeBerry, who was head coach at the Air Force Academy. He was born in South Carolina, attended Wofford, and had coached football in high schools in South Carolina. He turned us down. We called Don James, the head coach at Washington; he turned us down too. I really thought the USC coaching job was a great opportunity and couldn't understand why Dick and Fisher turned us down.

Then we began to look to the smaller I-AA successful coaches, such as Curley Hallman of Southern Mississippi, Jimmy Satterfield of Furman, and Sparky Woods of Appalachian State. Several outstanding coaches were contacted without any success.

One day we were having a staff meeting with all those involved in the search for a coach. Chip McKenney (assistant to the president), Dr. Holderman, Art Smith (vice president), Terry Parham (USC legal officer), King, and I were present. We were discussing our difficulty in hiring a top coach. Art Smith said, "Why don't we give the job to Art Baker?"

King said he would second that. Others were supportive.

I reveled at the prospect; as I mentioned back in Chapter 7, ever since I had been coaching, I had secretly hoped deep down that someday I could coach at USC.

I didn't revel long, however—no more than a few seconds—as Dr. Holderman said, "No, we hired Art to run the Gamecock Club." He continued by saying he wouldn't feel comfortable hiring a coach with a losing record in his last job and he wouldn't feel comfortable giving him a five-year contract which any coach would need to successfully recruit. Terry said they could give me a five-year contract with a "side letter" stating that after one year I would resign if the president was not pleased with the outcome. I indicated I would agree to that, but Dr. Holderman was firm.

Sid Varney, who had been one of my coaches at Presbyterian College, was now a vice president at USC. I was disappointed that he did not step up and speak for me. I later called him to ask for his support. He said, "When I applied for the chancellor's job at East Carolina, where were you?" I had tried hard to help him get the job, but the committee members had already made up their minds.

Jim Carlen found out that I might have a chance at the job; he insisted that I go to Dr. Holderman and convince him I was the man for the job. I tried to see Dr. Holderman, but he sent word by King Dixon that he was not going to give me the job. That was the end of that.

The committee then zeroed in on Jimmy Satterfield and Sparky Woods, who had previously been "not interested." A member of Dr. Holderman's staff favored Sparky, and Sparky got the job. He had Todd Ellis at quarterback and some other pretty good players, but I felt he "put all of his eggs in one basket" with Todd, and sure enough Todd was injured and South Carolina did not have a backup quarterback. Sparky coached well and recruited well, but losing a quarterback like Todd really hurt him.

The Associate Athletic Director

After the "whirlwind" was over, although disappointed at not getting the rather unexpected possible chances to be an assistant coach or even a head coach again, I settled into my job as associate athletic director and found my hands full. Two of my secretaries were about to physically fight almost every day. All of my working years, I had worked with football coaches and staff, and always had one good secretary. Margaret Seymore at Furman was great for me and helped break me in as a head coach and kept up with the impossible task of all the part-time scholarships and financial aid and was a valuable consultant and friend. Anne Smith at The Citadel also did a good job for me but never quite got as involved with the coaches and players as Margaret. At East Carolina I inherited a secretary who was not really suited for the job. She moved to another job, and fortunately I hired Joyce Pruitt, who was another great football secretary; she loved the players and coaches and was a great friend to me and my family. When I talk about athletics secretaries, however, I have to mention Emily White, the USC athletic director's secretary for eight athletic directors; she was great. I bet she could write a great book.

After having worked mostly with men, I came to USC where I found five women were on my staff. To say this was a cultural shock for me would be an understatement. They were all great ladies, but they about drove me up the wall at times. I wasn't used to staff crying, for example. Two of them in the same office really didn't care for each other. When I dealt with coaches and they had problems, I brought them in and we settled the differences by talking things over. Then and now, that didn't seem to work with women. But I was, on the other hand, fortunate that they knew more about my job than I did, and they were dedicated to trying to make me a good Gamecock Club director.

There were two other associate athletic directors—John Moore, who had been there since Paul Dietzel was coach some 15 years earlier, and Sterling Brown, whom Dick Bestwick had hired just before I was hired by King. "Brownie" was a former coach, so we got along well. Both were good men and good at their jobs.

Having been a football coach all my working days, I soon realized I was in deep water. I had had neither formal training nor experience in the three areas of my primary responsibility—heading up the Gamecock (booster) Club, fund raising, and marketing. I had worked with booster clubs at all schools where I had coached, but I soon realized that running them was another thing. I was missing coaching but determined to do the best job I could. It was actually a real challenge and I've always liked challenges, so I rolled up my sleeves and determined to be as good an associate athletic director as I possibly could. But it was tough; for example, I found most all the Gamecock Club members wanted seats on the 50-yard line. What was I to do?

First, I had to learn how the Gamecock Club operated. Fortunately, the ladies in the office were experienced in the operation, and they filled me in on a daily basis. I concentrated initially on spring meetings just around the corner. I wanted to meet as many local club presidents as I could, so I began to attend business meetings all over South Carolina. These meetings (along with the office ladies) really taught me what the operation was all about. I was technically still recovering from my surgery and was not yet going full speed; my insides hurt!

Tommy Gardner, a former football player, had been the interim Gamecock Club Director when I came on board, and he became my assistant. He stayed on the road a lot. He soon left to work with his dad in the fast-food market in Atlanta.

The NCAA sponsored several seminars on fund raising and marketing—my first experience in these areas. As the football coach at all my previous schools, I had some tangential experiences in these areas, but none as the director. I learned a great deal attending these NCAA meetings and began to formalize a plan for marketing and major gifts. I was allowed to hire an assistant director to replace Tommy, and I had plenty of applicants who wanted the job. I chose Herb Sharpe, a Lexington native who had been the long-time executive director of the Gamecock Club Board. He was retired from the South Carolina Electric and Gas Company. He actually knew more about the Gamecock Club than I did. We got along well, and fortunately some things he liked to do job-wise were things I didn't like. He and I made a good team. One thing I had to attend was the USC Foundation meetings, where all departments at USC sent directors to share ideas on fund raising. They were all a bit jealous of the fact that only the Gamecock Club could offer football tickets as incentives for giving. Herb was a great man and had a great family, and he knew how to deal with all members.

King included us in all athletic meetings and trips; we made some nice trips. Then the spring meetings began. At that time we had some 40 meetings, and I made every one of them. It was a lot of traveling, but at least I was meeting Gamecock Club members and learning more about my job. One night after having attended three or four such meetings in one week, I was driving back to Columbia from Myrtle Beach doing about 65 mph on cruise. I suddenly "woke up" off the side of I-20 and tried to ease the car back onto the highway. Instead, the car spun around and headed back toward Myrtle Beach. By the grace of God, there was no one close behind me, and I had no accident. I thanked the Lord for the angel that woke me up and then drove on to Columbia a bit shakily.

Another amusing incident happened between Columbia and Myrtle Beach, although this time I was headed to the beach. I was leaving Columbia with Edie to speak at the beach. I was wearing shorts, tennis shoes, and a tee-shirt. Sometimes the need to go to the bathroom exceeds the ability to hold it. I was desperate and we were coming about even with Shoney's. I was afraid to say anything; things were so urgent. I whipped the car into Shoney's, parked at the entrance, and ran inside for the men's room. I rushed into a stall "just in the nick of time"!

Then I heard two female voices and realized my wildest fear; I was in the ladies' room! I'm thinking: I'm the head of the Gamecock Club, a church member in good standing, and respected in my work and community. I shuttered to think what would happened if I were "discovered." Soon, there were women's voices everywhere. Several times they tried the door to my stall. Finally, a mother asked her daughter, Mary Jane, to look "down there" and see is anybody was in the stall. Mary Jane said, "Yes, there is mama, but she sure has big feet!"

Finally, when I heard no more female voices, I moved as fast as I ever have out of that ladies' room, jumped into my car, and squealed off, leaving rubber on the parking lot—all the time hoping nobody had recognized me. What a headline that would have made in "The State Paper"! I sweated all the way to Sumter before Edie and I could stop laughing. So much for the transgender thing!

My office manager Kim Stanley decided to resign and help her husband in his insurance business. I decided to make Kim Bailey, who had worked in the ticket office, my office manager. She was a little more assertive than Kim, but both were very good. We were still short at least one secretary. To cut back on some of the overload, I was able to hire graduate assistants who needed to complete their internships. Lance Shealy, whose father Dal was the head football coach at Mars Hill, Carson-Newman, and Richmond and later headed up the national FCA office in Kansas City, was an intern for a year. I also hired several volleyball ladies and Robert Gahagan, who later provided us with Atlanta Braves tickets when he worked for the Braves and subsequently worked for the Clemson network but remained a Gamecock fan. There were several others, including some football players. They all did well. Young people are super—at least most of them.

Probably the most interesting graduate assistant was a young lady from East Carolina who was working on her master's degree at ECU when I was leaving. ECU didn't offer a degree in sports marketing and she asked if she could be an intern at USC. She told me she was married and had a young son, but her parents would keep him. I hired her, as I always liked to help young people trying to move up in their field. I didn't expect her to take the internship, but she did. She was a nice-looking young lady, but always managed to be late or have some other problem. I think one of her main reasons to come to USC was to find a boyfriend (or a husband). She dressed like a college coed and flirted with all good-looking men (that left me out). I had to call her into my office on several occasions. I would fuss at her for being late or whatever, and she would start crying. She wore a lot of makeup and it would run down her face. I've never been good at what to say to crying women. Thankfully, the older secretaries befriended her, especially Annette who took her under her wing. All the secretaries teased me all the time about my "problem child."

We had the "Gamecock Open" sponsored by the Gamecock Club for Gamecock Club members to play golf with the coaches after recruiting season and before spring practice. We usually played at one of the beach golf courses. The first one we had, Annette and the aforementioned intern came along to run the bar for the golfers. Of course, all the golfers liked to have her there. The next year I decided she wouldn't go. We got down to Fripp Island to play golf and "she" was down there, staying with Annette and wearing an outfit so tight I don't see how she got into it. Needless to say, I sent her home.

One day while I was out of town, she came to work with a "see-through blouse." Herb Sharpe had to send her home. The ladies in the office all got a big laugh out of that incident. They got another good laugh some weeks later. I had been on the speaking tour (Gamecock Club meetings) and came into my office early one morning. The secretaries had a blowup dummy in a miniskirt, a wig, and dark glasses sitting in my chair. They were eagerly waiting to see my reaction, and we all had a good laugh. I think we all drew a breath of relief when she finished her internship and headed back to North Carolina. We kept up with her through Annette for a while, but she certainly left her mark with us. She was completely uninhibited but meant well.

One of my toughest assignments was to raise the levels of the Gamecock Club dues after having remained the same for over ten years. This went over like a "lead balloon." You can believe Herb, the secretaries, and I received plenty of nasty letters and phone calls. One friend, Ben Cogburn, who owned one of the most popular restaurants in Columbia for many years, called and really chewed me out. I said, "Ben, I can remember paying $2.50 for a steak sandwich at your restaurant some ten years ago and now you charge $7.95 for the same steak. We have to pay much more for helmets, shoulder pads, and uniforms now."

He said, "Heck, that's a different matter."

We laugh about it now, but he continued to pay the higher dues, and I continued to buy his steak sandwiches, which eventually went up to around $9.75. Like most Gamecocks, the Cogburns are great people; they are now retired.

The toughest and probably most unpopular part of the job was hiring and firing coaches. I have already discussed the problems encountered in hiring Joe Morrison's replacement as head football coach. Later, a big decision was the firing of basketball coach George Feldon, a popular former player for Coach Frank McGuire. George was a good coach, but he made the mistake of celebrating a little too much at several Gamecock Club meetings. King and Dr. Holderman appointed a selection committee of five people, one of whom was a woman, to find a men's head basketball coach. For some reason, the press seemed to know every word that was said in our "closed" meetings.

King and I interviewed some of the "big boys." Larry Brown was interested, but by this time a lot of the leading universities had developed very popular "packages" I have discussed previously. I represented our basketball coach at the SEC basketball coaches' annual meeting. The round-ball coaches enjoyed pecking at an old football coach during the meetings. I knew we would love to have Eddie Fogler and asked him if he would be interested. He was the person who actually told me how to go about developing a package, but for whatever reason, we didn't develop one.

We decided to meet three top coaches in Chicago; among those were George Karl and Donnie Walsh. The entire committee went along.

George was my choice and he was interested but had committed to coach in Europe for the next season. Our female committee member asked him during the interview, "Coach, what are you going to do next season if you're our coach when we play Kentucky in Rupp Arena?"

He said, "Lady, I'm going to try to beat the hell out of them!" I followed up with George later, and he had a timeline of five or six days before he had to leave for Europe. Dr. Holderman was not willing to meet his timeline or salary line, so we missed George.

Rick Barnes, who later coached at Clemson, Texas, and Tennessee, was recommended to us highly. He was at Providence, winning big time. He wanted to keep his interest out of the media, so he asked me to have supper at his home while we talked. It was an enjoyable meeting. He was somewhat interested but was concerned about the lack of an attractive package. His wife is a good cook and they have beautiful children, but we couldn't get him to budge. We talked to Coach John Kresse of the College of Charleston; he had too many years there to leave.

Finally, after talking to several I-AA coaches at Southwest Missouri, New Mexico, and Murray State, we offered the job to Steve Newton, a successful coach at Murray State. This was after searching for 57 frustrating days. He took the job, then after a day wanted to back out. King said no way; we were tired of talking to basketball coaches, so he became our coach and was less than impressive, leaving after two years with some NCAA violations.

During my seven years, I was allowed to hire an assistant to help me with marketing and our television and radio network. I was very fortunate to hire Liz McMillan who is very capable and very good. She now heads up the Gamecocks IMG Sports Marketing. I also requested that we hire Van Newman from Newman, Saylor & Gregory Advertising Firm to assist us in our marketing and fund-raising operations and proposals. Van was a most valuable professional addition to our marketing and fund raising. One of our most successful ventures was to raise over $350,000 for a new basketball practice and office building.

Another successful venture on which I worked very hard was to approach the Midlands Coca Cola Bottling Company to become our major donor in return for signage in our football stadium and basketball arena. The deal was all agreed upon when Dr. Holderman informed King that he had granted concessions to Pepsi Cola in all dormitories. Coke bowed out.

In 1993 King Dixon resigned as athletic director. He did a great job as athletic director. He succeeded in getting the Gamecocks into the Southeastern Conference—the one single fact that "jumped" the Gamecocks up several levels in our sports. [Sparky wasn't that excited, however.] King and I had many fun times working, hunting, and supporting the Gamecocks. He went home to Laurens, South Carolina, where he grew up. He and his beautiful wife, Augusta, live a wonderful, full life there.

King was succeeded as athletic director by Mike McGee. When he arrived to accept the job, I sent word to him that I would like to have five minutes of his time. When he came by my office, I told him that I knew coming in as athletic director, he might want to hire someone else as his Director of the Gamecock Club. He told me I was the first person he wanted to remain on the job. I had known Mike for a number of years. His management style was a lot like his playing days; he was tough, mean, and demanding, but very capable. We got along well.

One of Mike's first chores was to find a new head football coach, as he did not renew Sparky Woods's contract. He asked me to be a committee of one to assist him in hiring a new coach. When he asked me for recommendations, I gave him Kevin Gilbride, offensive coordinator with the Houston Oilers, and Brad Scott, offensive coordinator at Florida State. Kevin was having trouble getting a release from the Oilers, and Mike liked Brad. I had worked with both of them. Kevin was my offensive coordinator at East Carolina. Brad was my offensive line coach at The Citadel and was on the offensive staff at Florida State while I was the offensive coordinator there. Mike chose Brad.

When Mike came to South Carolina, I told him about a proposal from Ed Robinson to build a university club in nearby Blythewood whereby every member had to be a Gamecock Club member to join the club. Mike liked the idea and asked me to follow up and assist Ed. He finally got permission from our Board to proceed, and he built what is now Cobblestone Park. In appreciation, Ed named the entrance building "The Baker Center" and gave me a life-time membership in the Golf Club. Edie and I lived for a while in a cottage that looked out over the golf course. Ed was successful in building the University Club, but new owners who were not Gamecock Club members would fill in lots to begin with. Incidentally, the "Baker Center" does not have my name on it, and most people who live there now call it the "Guard House."

Ed Robinson also bought part of an old railroad track running behind the football stadium and brought in "cockabooses," which were old cabooses remodeled for entertaining and painted Gamecock garnet. They have become very popular through the years and are shown on the SEC network. They are also a sight of great interest to visiting fans.

In another incident Mike asked me to accompany Mark Berson, our soccer coach, to Greenville (South Carolina) with plans for a new soccer stadium. We were going to ask Eugene Stone and his son, Jack, for a donation towards building our stadium. The Stones owned "Umbro," which supplied soccer uniforms worldwide. Going to Greenville, Mark asked me how much I would ask for, and I asked him how much did he think. He said he would be "tickled pink" to get $500,000. Mr. Stone was a USC graduate, and in the drawing of the stadium we had put his name on the press box. After formalities, Jack Stone said, "How can we help you?"

I said, "We want to build a soccer stadium and we need your help."

He said, "How much do you have in mind?"

I blurted out, "One million." Mark almost fell out of his chair.

Jack agreed (and later provided an additional $350,000 to complete it).

When we returned to Columbia, Mark had to go to practice, but Mike was waiting in his office. I walked in and he said, "Come on, tell me what you got."

I said, "Mike, what would you say if your fundraiser came in and said he had a gift of $500,000?"

He replied, "I would kiss his rear end."

I said, "What would you say if he had a million dollars for the soccer stadium?"

He said, "I would kiss his rear end on the Horseshoe."

I never collected on his offer. [For the uninitiated, the first 12 buildings on campus some 200 years ago all faced into a beautiful garden area where students could gather. These buildings formed a U-shape, which is now known as the "Horseshoe."]

During the time we were trying to hire a basketball coach, I had received a call from Presbyterian College about me becoming their head football coach. I loved P.C., it being my alma mater, and I had always dreamed of being the coach there when Cally, my good friend, left. I had been at USC only two years at the time, and I needed three to complete my South Carolina full-retirement need. After deep consideration, I made a very painful decision for me—not to go to P.C. and to remain at USC. About the same time Newberry College asked me to be their head coach for the second time since I had been at USC. My good friend Grady Ray was on the selection committee. I really hated to say no to Newberry also, especially since I was not ready to get out of coaching.

I was poised to retire in 1994. USC was offering a nice "buyout retirement bonus" for people in my age and experience level. I signed up to accept the offer, but the next morning Mike sent for me. When I walked into his office, he tore up my request, telling me I could not retire until I sold 18 new suites at the football stadium. I sold them all in one month.

The Consultant

I did formally retire in 1995. Mike and the athletic department gave Edie and me a trip to Hawaii and cruise to all the islands. It was a wonderful experience, but it was saddening to see the results of Pearl

Harbor and where all those 1177 men still lie entombed on board the sunken Arizona.

Although I retired, Mike made me a "consultant" to Brad Scott (and later Lou Holtz) and that kept me involved with football for ten more years. It was not exactly being a head coach, but I was still keeping up with X's and O's and especially with the football players. I sat in on staff meetings and offensive meetings. John Reeves and Rickey Bustle were the offensive coordinators under Brad, and they allowed me to put in ideas; but they of course ran the Florida State offense like Brad wanted it. Brad had been the offensive coordinator under Bobby Bowden and really wanted to run offensively exactly what they ran at Florida State. He was a hard-working, caring, intelligent, knowledgeable coach, but I always felt he needed to be more of himself. He had kept logs on everything Bobby had done in every situation and tried to emulate Bobby almost too much, in my opinion. I often asked him, "Brad, what do you think, you've got a great mind, you decide." Brad was a great coach and friend, had lots of good stories, and was a super recruiter and coach.

Brad and I had a good relationship during his time at USC. He had some great wins, including USC's first bowl victory. Our families had been together many years though the FCA. He and I had many good times hunting and fishing together. There were some great friends who invited us. Dr. Skeet Burris, from beautiful Cummings, South Carolina, provided us with great duck and quail hunting. He and his sons built themselves a beautiful plantation with six or eight duck ponds; they are leaders in the tree farms of South Carolina. Their beautiful home is a masterpiece of southern homes.

On one such trip, we had Coach John Zernhelt hunting with us, and after shooting ducks we hunted quail. We hunted in pairs, and John and I hunted together. We were hunting along a pond's edge, and the dog we had, a small spaniel, "pointed." It was John's turn to shoot; he missed. We went on several more yards, the small dog pointed again, and "Z", as we called him, missed again. The third time the small dog pointed and as we walked up to shoot, the dog looked around at us. I said, "Z, you know what he's saying?"

He said, "What?"

I said, "Let the little man [me] shoot!"

Another good friend "Z" and Brad and I had was Joe Taylor, a Wofford graduate and owner of "Log Cabins." He was secretary of commerce under Gov. Mark Sanford, and he was responsible for me being honored by receiving the "Order of the Palmetto" by the governor. We had some great dove and quail hunts in Swansea, South Carolina, with great country cooking afterwards.

As a consultant, I did not coach any positions, but did put in my "two cents' worth." Sometimes they listened; sometimes they didn't. I felt my reason to be on Brad's staff was to give him advice as a head coach. My office was next to his. We were good friends and close; he would listen to me or we would talk it out. Mike McGee wanted Brad to fire a coach and was getting a lot of criticism from fans. Brad would not do it. At the same time a lot of fans were opposed to a couple of Brad's offensive coaches' offensive-play selection. This was bad and I tried to help Brad work through it, but he needed to do it himself.

Finally, the last year Brad coached, Mike talked to me often about letting Brad know what he needed to do, but by that time "the die had been cast." Mike decided to let Brad go. In the beginning Brad had negotiated a very good contract, having had an agent who helped him design his "package." They practically bought his home for him, gave him very generous benefits in retirement, annuities, two cars, and staff salaries—especially with some staff being given two-year contracts. I really couldn't understand these kinds of salaries, benefits, etc. My highest salary as a head coach was $65,000 plus my television show, which varied from $5,000 to $8,000. Brad was making $350,000 plus all sorts of benefits. All of Brad's assistants made more than I made at East Carolina. Of course, nowadays, some coaches are making millions of dollars. My conclusion is that I came along too early to get rich in coaching! But, I got to shake hands with many great coaches on the field before and after games!

When Brad was released, Mike really wanted to treat him right by making his "payout" as generous as possible. Brad knew all the "ins and outs" through his agent. Everything was going well until Brad accepted a job at Clemson. Mike felt Brad could have gone anywhere but Clemson, and everything would be okay. [This reminded me of my situation years earlier when I wanted to leave Clemson for South Carolina, and I was told I could go anywhere except South Carolina. The rivalry between these two schools is intense!] He felt Brad had betrayed him. He probably should have known that Tommy Bowden, the Clemson coach, and Brad were good friends through Florida State. Anyway, the move to Clemson made Mike mad. Brad thought he had landed a good job. I was trying to stay out of the way, as both of them were my friends.

Mike and I hunted some. He always liked to ride horses when we hunted in Beaufort, South Carolina, on a beautiful plantation named "Laurel Springs" owned by the Lightseys. Mike liked to tease others, but all knew not to tease him. We were riding horses while hunting in Laurel Springs one day and had to jump a small ditch. Mike was a good horseman, but his horse threw him. There were four of us watching, but there was not one smile or comment. He climbed back on his horse, and nothing was ever mentioned about it that day. Who wanted to "cross hairs" with a first-round NFL draft pick? Not me!

On another hunt at Laurel Springs, it was very cold—20°. When they handed out horses, they gave me a horse named "Blackie." The hunt master said, "Now coach, when she gets around water in the road, you have to watch her; she will sit down in the water—just switch her. Sure enough, a little later in the hunt, we came to a part of the road that had several water puddles, and sure enough Blackie sat right down in the water with me on her, despite the fact that I was switching her. I got soaking wet in freezing water. The next time we were there, when the hunt master gave me Blackie again, we mounted and he said, "Whoa, wait a minute," and he gave me a life jacket. Everybody laughed, including me.

Mike asked my opinion in hiring the next coach but not near as much as he did with the hiring of Brad. Finally, the rumor around was that he would hire Lou Holtz. He called me in one day and asked me what I thought of Lou. I told him I liked Lou. He asked me who I would recommend. I suggested Fisher DeBerry. He was from South Carolina and had taken the Air Force Academy to bowl games around ten years in a row, so he could recruit and coach. He said, "How would you compare him to Lou?"

I replied, "Lou would bring a lot of media coverage, but I like Fisher."

He said he was going to hire Lou.

Fortunately for me, Lou asked me to stay on in my "consultant" role. He did not have an administrative assistant as all coaches do today to handle travel, hotel arrangements, and other administrative duties. Enter me!

When Lou came, I was in my office next door to his and mostly taking calls for him and returning those he wanted me to. I answered one call and it was a young man who said without any opening conversation, "I'm calling from Ohio and I want to commit to Coach Holtz and South Carolina."

I said, "Hold on."

I went to Lou's office and told him he had a call. He kind of frowned and said, "I don't have time to take a call. Get the number."

I said, "It's a young man named Ryan Brewer who says he wants to commit to you."

None of us other than Lou and whoever was recruiting Ryan knew who he was. Lou took the call, and four years later we all knew who Ryan Brewer was. He was a great running back and could even punt. He was the MVP of the 2001 Outback Bowl when UCS defeated Ohio State 24-7. It was a bit ironic that Ryan was "Mr. Football" in Ohio as a high school senior, but was never offered a scholarship by Ohio State.

You talk about a big show! Hiring Lou Holtz was one big show. Lou can play the public and the media like a guitar. He's smart and a great motivator and very knowledgeable about the game. He made his son

"Skip" his offensive coordinator but depended on Skip to do 95% of his administrative duties but would not buy into Skip's "new" offensive philosophy. I sat in on offensive meetings, and Lou would come in and take over the meetings. Skip was really the only coach Lou would trust, but he would let Skip put in about as much offense as he could, then likely change it later in the week. Every day during the offensive staff meetings, Lou would come in and tell Skip to put in the previous day's practice tape, even though the coaches had already seen it and graded the players. He seemed to never find good things—only the bad. He would argue with a coach over a step of six inches and threaten the coach that he would take over his drill at the next practice and did on occasion. It seemed to me, and I might add to the players, that this was demeaning to the coach. During the six years he was at USC, Skip was the only coach allowed to disagree with Lou. Skip, out of respect for his dad, would usually do his criticizing in Lou's office or in private. One Sunday Skip became so upset that he hit a door and broke his hand, requiring pins.

The only coach I remember who challenged Lou was Joker Phillips, the wide receivers coach who later was the head coach at Kentucky. He put it simply one day, "Well, coach, you criticize us every day and expect us to change game plans at a moment's notice; we really don't know where we stand with you." Lou stammered a bit, seeming not to know what to say.

Lou was a master at creating incidents at practice or in meetings. He would arrive at team meetings right on time to the minute. Whenever he arrived, the doors were usually blocked by the strength coaches who admitted no one arriving late. There were usually two habitual offenders who seemed to test Lou about arriving on time or otherwise messing up. If Lou was in a bad mood, they were really blasted; other times not much was said until later. Lou once said about one of them, "He will either play for an NFL team or sweep the floors in an NFL stadium." History proved him a prophet.

Lou's pregame (Friday night) meetings were well orchestrated, much like his pregame talks on television today. He was usually well organized and had his thoughts already planned. Some of the players began to complain that they were hearing the same stories and points after three or four years. We coaches are all guilty of these things. What can I say? I never won a national championship; he did and more.

Through my years of coaching at all levels, kickers are often "flakes," who are constantly worrying about the wind, the turf, the protection, the holder, his steps, etc. The best kickers are the ones who also play a position and don't have time to worry about all the nitpicking things. Lou was very mechanical and technical over the proper steps for the player or kicker to take. I've seen him take over a drill until every player took the seven-inch step he demanded. He had definite ideas about the place kicker's steps, especially where the lead step was to land. Most kickers have already developed these steps and they have a terrible time changing their lead step several inches to meet Lou's demand. So as can be imagined, the kickers stayed in a frenzy trying to put their lead foot where Lou wanted it and making the field goal or extra point. One day Lou was kneeling where he had indicated the mark for the kicker's lead step on the place kick. There was this young kicker who was obviously scared to death of Lou. He missed multiple kicks and was getting worse. Finally, Lou said, "Son, what's wrong with you?"

The boy said, "Coach, I'm scared of you."

Coach said, "Well, if you're scared of me, what will you do when you have 80,000 people watching you kick?"

Seasoned players, line backers, quarterbacks, defensive backs, and so on can understand the strategy of the game. Kickers think they are smart but usually are not football smart. Several incidents point that out. Lou had a couple plays that further explain kickers and how football smart they are, or how we as coaches assume they know. In 2000 USC was preparing to play Ohio State in the Outback Bowl. Lou installed a fake kick-pass where the holder would fake the hold on a field goal, then get up and run to his right and throw a screen pass to his left to a side back. This play, like most "special" plays, was designed to take advantage of a hard rush from that side. When we ran the play in the bowl game, the rush stayed back and played the screen pass. Guess what? We had not told our holder what the alternative was, so we had a busted play.

Again some years later, we scored late against Georgia and Lou decided to call an onside kick. He told our kicker, "If they are in a bunch, pooch the ball over their heads; if they are spread out, kick the onside kick."

They were in a bunch, but the kicker kicked the onside kick and one of their front-line defenders caught the ball on the first bounce and ran it 50 yards untouched for a touchdown. Lou blasted the kicker, who came over to me and said, "Coach, what's a 'bunch'?" Once again, I learned that you have to cover everything, as he did not know what Lou meant by a "bunch." Incidentally, our kicker that day later went on to law school.

There was really not adequate room or a goalpost on the practice area for the kickers, snappers, and holders to practice kickoffs, punts, field goal, and extra points, so Lou usually sent this group to the stadium to have sufficient room to work and to practice kicking from different positions on the field. Lou would occasionally drive his golf cart over there and more often than not, he would find them playing around.

One day I offered to Lou to go to the stadium with this special team. I knew I could not coach them (being a consultant, I wasn't one of the nine coaches); I would simply chart the snaps, kicks, and holds, sometimes filming them. I made sure they did not goof off and got plenty of work.

Over time I think they improved their skills considerably. Edie often cooked a homemade meal and we had the entire kicking team of 10 to 12 kickers, snappers, and holders over to our home. Edie and I got a great kick out of the stories they told on each other.

Later, on January 1, 2002, when we were playing Ohio State the second time in the Outback Bowl, we dominated for the first three quarters, but Ohio State rallied to tie the score at 28-28. With less than a minute left, Demetris Summers made perhaps his most important run to put the ball near the 30-yard line. All during the game, I was trying to keep the kickers in a good frame of mind. Dennis Weaver went in and lined up to kick the all-important field goal that would win the game. The snap was good, the hold was good, and the kick was made. As millions of fans at the game and on television watched, the ball got good height and was headed toward the goalpost but seemed to never get there. As the ball turned end over end, it turned over the bar in its rotation, and the Gamecocks beat Ohio State for the second Outback Bowl game in a row. Now the papers, radio, and TV did not mention it, but there was one guy on the sideline who thought he might have helped that ball turn over the bar. I smiled all the way to the locker room.

I always regretted the way Lou's last season, 2004, ended with the Clemson game. The teams had a very ugly fight—actually a brawl—late in the game. And, South Carolina lost to its rival 29-7.

I was fortunate to work under Lou; he didn't have to keep me as a "consultant" but he did. His coaching prowess is unquestionable; his 1988 Notre Dame team was undefeated and was the consensus national champion. He is a great motivator. ["Motivation is simple. You eliminate those who are not motivated." (Lou Holtz quote)]. And he is funny, as millions of people know from watching him on television, ranging from Johnny Carson's show to his commentary on ESPN. I always enjoyed being around him.

One final "Lou story": One morning Lou came into the athletic office and related what had just happened in the parking lot. As he drove into the lot, a man and his sons had just parked in Lou's personal parking space. A bit miffed, he approached the man and said, "What are you guys doing here?"

"We are moving to Columbia and I just wanted to look around the university," the man replied.

"Where are you moving to in Columbia?" Lou asked.

"We're moving into the governor's mansion."

The man was Mark Sandford, who had just been elected governor of South Carolina. During the football season, Lou, like most football coaches, was so engrossed with his team that he hadn't paid much attention to what was going on in the political area.

Lou recovered quickly and said, "Pleased to meet you, governor. You can park here or anywhere else on campus you want to."

Steve Spurrier succeeded Lou as our head coach. I had known Steve for a number of years and I left him a note telling him what I had done with Brad and Lou. He said that he had never operated with a "consultant" and probably would not need my services. Edie and I had already talked about our situation. We had grandsons Taylor, Wellington, and Austin all playing high school football and we wanted to see them play.

In 2005 Mike McGee retired as athletic director and was replaced by Eric Hyman. I had hired Eric as a graduate assistant when I went to Furman in 1973. He decided he would not keep paid consultants, but he wanted me to stay on as a consultant to him. He did not ask much of me. I mostly seemed to be speaking more for the athletic department or for FCA. I spoke to civic clubs, church men's groups, and the like. I enjoy speaking and make a point to speak about the problems facing our youth and that they (the youth) are America's greatest resource.

In 2008 I had an unusual opportunity to speak to the S.C. Bankers Association, which was meeting at Amelia Island, Florida. The convention was held at the Ritz-Carlton, where they put us up in a $500 suite. We ate our meals at the "Salt" restaurant, a five-star restaurant. I think I made a good talk, even though the president of the association introduced me as "Art Baker, former football player for Syracuse University and the Buffalo Bills." That Art Baker happens to be black; I am white. Edie interrupted the introducer and said, "That's not my husband!"

Shortly thereafter, Edie and I attended an FCA conference at Saint Simons Island, Georgia. We stayed at "Epworth by the Sea," a Methodist camp. The island was established in the 1700s by General Oglethorpe, who established the Georgia colony, and John and Charles Wesley, who established the Methodist Church in America. Several weeks later I was asked to go back to Saint Simons Island to speak to the Glenn County (Brunswick, Georgia) Coaches (about 100) for the FCA. Once again I stayed at "Epworth by the Sea" and made some new friends.

I stayed on in my "consultant" role with an office under the stadium, my code to the coaches' locker room, and my locker there. If I went into Columbia to play tennis and needed to go to a meeting afterwards, I would shower there. I went to my office once or twice a week to check my calls and stopped by the football office to check my mailbox. I sat in the coaches' box during games and occasionally helped with coverage or pass routes.

Time to Really Retire

In 2012 Eric left USC to become athletic director at Texas A&M. He did an outstanding job as athletic director at USC (and subsequently at A&M). Many of the improvements in facilities were due to his planning and fundraising. Soon after he left, I was told my office was needed for another person, I was informed by a secretary that my mail box was discontinued, and the code to the coaches' locker room was changed. Later, I was told by an associate athletic director that Alabama had been using former head coaches in the press box and they had to discontinue the practice; so USC had to comply. I was moved outside the press box. Finally, I had for years had a good friend in the equipment room, Jake, who kept me in the latest coaching shirts, shoes, and jackets. He left to become the head equipment man at Colorado—a much deserved promotion. When he left, I was politely told those things were no longer available.

I was never good in math, but I "put two and two together" and concluded I was "history." Thus, I fully retired for good in 2012 at age 82. I thoroughly enjoyed my time at USC, and they were very good to me. Having been a graduate student there myself, I love the university, as I am sure most everyone who ever attended there does. [I did not get to finish my master's degree at USC before leaving Columbia (Eau Claire) and going to Clemson. My first summer at Clemson, I told Coach Howard I needed only one class (statistics) to complete my degree, so could I go to Columbia to complete my degree. He said sure I could go if I had that much leave time. Of course, he knew as well as I did that I did not have that much leave time. Thus, I never completed that degree.]

Although I quit "working," I didn't quit living. More about that in the next chapter. [I put "working" in quotations because I never really felt I "worked" at a job; I got paid to coach football. In my mind, it doesn't get any better than that. How fortunate I was!]

More Grandsons

As I noted in Chapter 13, our grandsons, Marshall and Taylor Kirkman, were born while we were at East Carolina University. Our third and fourth grandsons, Arthur Wellington Baker III and Robert Austin Baker were born to Artie and Sherri while we were at USC. Wellington was born on June 22, 1989 and Austin, on September 13, 1993.

As I mentioned above when Steve Spurrier succeeded Lou and he said he would not need my services, Edie and I were actually relieved as our grandsons Taylor, Wellington, and Austin were all playing high school football and we wanted to see them play more than we had been.

Austin played on Thursdays and Taylor and Wellington, on Fridays, so Steve's decision helped us and we really got to watch the boys play. Austin and his brother Wellington both played guard. I had always coached quarterbacks and running backs. I never knew how much fun it was to watch a guard play. Their dad, Artie, and I hardly knew where the ball was; we were watching the guards so hard.

15 ANGELS ON MY SHOULDER

In 1999 Edie and I moved from our home in Columbia to a nice cottage we built in the aforementioned university club, Cobblestone Park, in Blythewood near Columbia. It overlooks the golf course. We enjoyed living there immensely. We walked a lot at night in the neighborhood, usually after 11:00 p.m. We have two sideline Gamecock warm-up suits with hoods we wear during the winter. One cold night about 11:30 we were walking with our hoods on, and a neighbor looked out her window, saw two people with hoods on, and called security to report two suspicious-looking characters walking in the neighborhood. The security guard replied, "Oh, that's just the Bakers; they walk late at night."

Travel

We have always loved to "travel." College and the army limited our travel some in the early years. Child bearing and funding limited our travel after the army. We were fortunate, however, to stay at least a week every summer at Ocean Drive Beach in South Carolina even when we were in Texas. It was a plain ol' beach house that survived Hurricane Hazel in 1954. After I retired, our travel possibilities were less inhibited, and we took advantage of that.

Some of our travel I have already mentioned. When we were at Eau Claire High in Columbia, Aunt Bess kept our children for Edie and me to spend a weekend in Boone, North Carolina. When we were at Clemson, we took the two youngest chaps to Washington, DC, where we met Senator Thurmond. At Texas Tech we had several wonderful trips with the family through the southwestern states to California. We also traveled back to South Carolina several times by different routes, so the kids could see as much of our great country as possible. As a head coach attending "Bowl Rousers" in summers, I was fortunate enough to win a couple tennis tournaments and won a seven-day trip to St. Thomas Island and two trips to the Bahamas (remember the thong bathing suit!).

Other travel I believe I have not mentioned includes a nice trip to London, England. I once was in a shopping center in Columbia and filled out a ticket for a drawing for a free trip for two to London. I got home and was taking a nap, and the phone rang. I answered and a lady said, "Are you Art Baker"?

I said, "Yes."

"Well, you have won a trip for two to London."

I went back to sleep and when I woke up, I was a bit "fuzzy." I thought to myself—did I dream that or did it actually happen? So I called back, and the lady asked again if my name was Art Baker. When I said yes, she confirmed that I had won the trip.

We really enjoyed that trip. Our hotel was near so many things we could walk to. And the trip included two side trips—lunch on a Thames River tour boat and a bus trip to the Cotswolds. We were able to mix in "The Phantom of the Opera," John Wesley's home, and some old cathedrals and museums. It was a wonderful trip—and free!

Another great trip was a cruise to Alaska. Alaska is a beautiful country; everywhere you look, you see "scenery."

Edie and I have also taken several trips with YMT, a travel company that knows "how to do it." One such trip was to Hawaii for ten days where we saw all the sights and all the islands. Edie established a reputation on all these tours. As you would guess, all touring companies operate on a tight schedule. Edie's personal habit is somewhat slower than others. The tour guide would say, "Okay, Edie is here; we can go." It didn't please her too much; she knew her own ways.

In 2010 I was asked by a friend who was a missionary in Italy to come over to Italy and conduct a number of football clinics. This was when Italy was beginning to have American football teams. My friend coached one of the teams, which was made up of cooks, pilots, artists, factory workers, etc. I didn't speak Italian, so we had to use interpreters. They had no actual football stadiums, so I had to teach on soccer fields. I did have films I could use. Because the players worked at their jobs, the clinics were at night. This gave us the daytime to sightsee. We lived with the family in Monte Paraiso, a small village 18 miles from Rome. In the mornings, some member of the family would take us into Rome on the "slow train," a passenger train that stopped at every small village. Or, we would drive into Rome. We got to see the Colosseum, the Senate, and the Catacombs, among others. One day we went to Florence and saw David's Sculpture.

Another day they sent their 15-year old son to be our guide. He was given specific directions to get us to Salerno. He got confused and put us on the "rapid train" (100 mph). We were supposed to stop at Monte Paraiso, but we were going so fast I barely recognized the station. I asked our host's son if he could ask the conductor how to get back to our station. I think he was a little frightened about how to get us home. We had gone a number of miles beyond our station and finally stopped at a village. I asked a conductor, who could speak a little English, how we could get back. He told us to get off the rapid train, go underneath the rails, and get on the slow train we could see some 50 to 60 feet away. We did and finally got back home.

On another occasion, we had been invited to a cabin on an orchard to have supper. They had grilled sausage, huge bowls of salad, some pasta, and a huge supply of wine, which the local priest drank the most of. They were good, friendly people, though we mostly didn't know what they were saying, and they didn't know what we were saying.

Another memorable trip was to Israel. It was awesome to walk where Christ walked many years ago. Unfortunately, I had recently had hip surgery and was walking with a cane. I really wanted to get in the Red Sea, but the area getting out to the sea was full of rocks, presenting a problem for someone with a bad hip and a walking cane trying to get out into the water. I hobbled out there and sat down in the sea, and finally we made it back without injury. Another thing I wanted to do, like everybody else who was there, was to be baptized in the Jordan River. But again, my bad hip and cane came into play. To get to the baptismal location required going down a walkway into the water to chest deep. The river was flowing rapidly, and I was afraid I would be knocked over. So I missed the chance. We did, however, bring back about a quart of holy water from the Jordan River, and the minister at College Place Methodist used it to baptize some people.

In addition to traveling, we have maintained an active life in retirement; in fact, we have hardly slowed down. Almost every Wednesday I meet at a restaurant with some 30 to 50 Eau Claire High School guys—mostly my old football players. [Occasionally, an ECHS female will be there; in fact, at our last meeting, my coauthor's sister, Bunny Evett Williams, attended.] This is rather remarkable to me, since it has been over 50 years since I coached at Eau Claire. Recently, one of the attendees asked me how it felt to be meeting with some of my former players who are older than 70 now. My answer? Very good to be here!

Furthermore, Edie and I still attend USC football, basketball, and baseball games. I am kind of on standby in case they need a gofer. Recent hip surgery and moving from our home to another have curtailed my hunting, fishing, and golfing recently.

Angels on My Shoulder

"Angel on My Shoulder" is the title of a 1946 movie, but I think it fits the title of this chapter (actually fits my life). I have led a blessed life, thanks in large part to many "angels" who have, figuratively speaking, been on my shoulders guiding me and helping me through my life. At the risk of unintended omissions, I want to remember them now.

First of all, there is, of course, my family. My parents, grandparents, and great grandparents provided the backbone of rearing me through childhood and beyond. My mother's mother, "Grandmother Holiday," showed us all how to overcome obstacles and to have faith in the Bible. Her minister said at her funeral that she sat every Sunday on the first row in church with her Bible open. And, I can't fail to mention my Aunts Katie, Ruth, and Bess who were all very instrumental in my upbringing. Aunt Katie, especially, taught me the "three Rs" and how to act like a nice boy. Also, Edie's parents, Mr. and Mrs. Edens, were so important during my formative years, and they made the ultimate sacrifice of entrusting their daughter to me.

Beyond family, probably the most influential person in my life was Coach Harvey Kirkland of Newberry College. God sent him as a most important angel exactly when I needed him most. Not only did he teach me a lot of what I ever knew about coaching football, he also taught me how to be a Christian, how to live my life, and how to treat others. Our families vacationed together at the beach some 20 years. He was a giant angel in my life.

I worked as an assistant under four outstanding football coaches— Frank Howard, Jim Carlen, Ed Emory, and Bobby Bowden. I have, of course, described how it was for me while working under them, but suffice it to say they were great to work for and taught me a whole lot about recruiting, coaching football, and treating people. I would also include here Brad Scott and Lou Holtz for whom I worked as a consultant after I formally retired.

And then there were assistant coaches who worked for me. God blessed me with a wonderful talent for finding and hiring great assistants. They were all outstanding men who could coach and recruit. They were loyal to me and without them I would never have achieved what I did as a head coach. I am so proud that 20+ of my assistants later went on to become head college/pro coaches.

There were also many assistant coaches who worked side by side with me while I was an assistant coach. While we often worked together trying to figure out what the head coach wanted and how to win games, we always strove to develop young men to become gentlemen as well as to win football games. I personally learned a lot from all these colleagues, many of whom also went on to become head coaches. Some of them became life-long friends and we still stay in touch.

Then of course there were the players. Without good players, I would have been nothing. I would estimate over 1000 young men played for me in high school, college while I was an assistant coach, and college while I was a head coach. Even though I was the "teacher," I learned a lot from them too. I am proud that many of these players, probably 30+, went on to play professional football. One of the biggest rewards I receive now in my 80s is to hear from them—now successful husbands, fathers, and businessmen or whatever, and for them to say something in our program helped them in their lives.

Some head coaches tend to avoid contact with fans—certainly personal contact. I did not. I enjoyed my contact with fans everywhere. Some became close friends—the Buycks, Rosser Thrash, Jack Kirkpatrick, to name a few out of many.

There were also a number of Methodist ministers who were important in my spiritual life. I hesitate to single one out, but the Rev. Eben Taylor was important to me early in my life. He was the minister at College Place Methodist Church when I was head coach at Eau Claire High in Columbia. He was a wonderful speaker and motivator for my football team as were almost every minister at our stops at Methodist churches.

. Continuing the religious theme, I must mention the Fellowship of Christian Athletes. FCA contributed greatly to my spiritual being, and it was always an inspiration for me to the see the same kind of influence on thousands of athletes. I also had many friends through FCA, including Bobby Richardson (who introduced me to FCA in the first place), Twig Gray, Dal Shealy, David Welsh, to name a few.

Research has shown a correlation between longevity and having close friends. This correlation definitely applies in my case. Throughout my long life, I have accumulated many close, life-long friends. While the majority of them resulted from my career in football (including players, coaches, and others), many of them came from other sources. Again to name a few, Steve Robertson, Dick Weldon, Jack Fligg, Jimmy Satterfield, Dick Sheridan, and Frank Singleton—the latter still living and full of life (and he is older than I am!). These friends and many others helped to mold my life. Sadly, some of them are dying out. We are all mortals. [Very sadly, three of my best friends—Kirby Jackson, Leonard Shealy, and Joe Kirven—suffered long and hard, and eventually died of Alzheimer's disease.]

And then there is Edie. What a wonderful wife and mother she has always been and still is. From the time we married while I was a student at

Presbyterian College until now, we moved to Columbia (Fort Jackson), to McColl, to Newberry, to Columbia (Eau Claire), to Clemson, to Lubbock, to Greenville (SC), to Charleston, to Greenville (NC), to Tallahassee, to Greenville (NC), to Columbia. During most of the moves, I always had to move right away to get started in the new job while Edie stayed behind— sometimes for months on end—to let the kids finish the school year, to sell our house, and to prepare for the move. The nature of my job kept me away from home a lot. Edie always kept the "home fires burning." She is my best friend, counselor, lover, and critic.

From the first time I ever laid eyes on her in a dark movie theater, I was struck that she was the one I wanted for my life. Though there were many obstacles in our dating, I recognized the angel I needed and wanted. We both realized early on that to reach our dreams, we needed an education and we got one. Many angels in our lives helped us along the way— relatives, friends, and people who just wanted to help. There is no way anyone could even guess how she has helped an ol' boy like me, who married way over his head, to reach so many goals in my coaching and my life. I could not tell you all the many ways she has helped me through every problem I ever had. No wonder God had made her my angel long ago. What a mother and light for Christ she has been to everyone who has known her. Ask her children!

Finally, there is God. He has truly blessed me. I have always felt God had a plan for my life. I have striven to conduct my life according to his plan. I have lived a full life where in my mind God has been in control. From early family influences with some tough times, dedicated ministers, and wonderful participation in churches, I wish I could say I have been "lily white" throughout. I haven't, and I regret my "back sliding." But I have often asked for, and I believed received, forgiveness. Edie came along just in time for me in this regard; her influence has been tremendous. I knew I had to walk a "straight and narrow path" if I was to have a chance at that girl. Then I was introduced to FCA, and my love for our young people brought it all into focus.

My Family

Throughout this book I have included considerable discussion of the members of my immediate family as the chronology of my story played out. However, I want to conclude now by updating their statuses. These include: brothers, George and Bobby; children, Artie, Kim, Ryan, and Curtis; grandsons, Marshall, Taylor, Wellington, and Austin; and a surprise.

George

Being only 19 months younger than I, my brother George ("Bubba") and I grew up together. Although we fought a lot—both against each other and against others—we always loved each other as brothers. George went to Warren Wilson Junior College in Swannanoa, North Carolina, where he met his wife, Irene. He finished high school and two years of college there, and then went to Presbyterian College for two years where he joined the Marine Corps ROTC program. After graduating he went into Marine Corps Officer Training as a lieutenant.

He went to Vietnam and when he came back he was put in charge of the White House Marine Guards at Camp David, where he was in charge of preparations when dignitaries came to visit Camp David. Quite often President Johnson took George to shoot skeet. From there he went back to Vietnam and became a major. He was wounded in his second tour there, and when he came back he went to the Naval War College and later taught in the Naval War College.

During the time between his Vietnam tours, he earned his Ph.D. at Duke and got into a "new" field. Community colleges/technical institutes were just being developed, and he and a colleague began preparing people to be teachers and administrators in community colleges/technical institutes. He taught in this endeavor at the University of Texas and later at North Carolina State University, where he received a "Chair."

George is retired now and currently lives in Greer, South Carolina, with his wife Irene. They have two sons, Brad and Derek, and a daughter, Allison. George has received the "Gold P" from Presbyterian College, the highest alumni award that P.C. makes. He plays golf and has authored a text book and memoirs as well as newspaper and magazine articles.

Bobby

Being nine years younger than I, my brother Bobby and I did not exactly grow up together. He was only four when I became a teenager; he was in elementary school while I was in high school. We did, however, develop a close relationship when he as a teenager lived with me and Edie at McColl and Newberry as has been discussed previously.

After graduating from Newberry High School, Bobby attended Gordon Military College in Georgia for a year; however, not liking "the military," he left school and returned to Sumter. Despite not liking the military, he joined the army and went to Germany, where he spent some time playing baseball. While home on furlough, he met Barbara Hill whose sister Sarah was dating his cousin Fred. We had known the Hills all of our lives. Bobby and Barbara were married upon his return from Germany.

Having received some army training in fire prevention, Bobby went to work for the Sumter Fire Department, eventually becoming the assistant fire chief. He was elected in 1994 as the President of the South Carolina

Firemen's Association. He retired some years ago from the fire department and lives in Sumter with his wife Barbara. Even though retired, he has his own business whereby he goes into a company and qualifies them for their fire safety status. He also makes and sells fire extinguishers.

Bobby was always a very good athlete and he still participates in the Senior Olympics each year. He also takes part in Three-on-Three Basketball, which is a national program. He has a drawer full of Senior Olympics gold medals. His sons tease him that he should sell the "gold" (which is of course not gold).

Bobby and Barbara have two sons—Robbie and John. Robbie is, as of this writing, running for coroner in Sumter County. I offered his son John a scholarship while I was coaching at The Citadel; he was a very good defensive end and linebacker. After he visited The Citadel and saw the Spartan life led by the cadets, he said, "Uncle Art, I love you, but I don't think I'll come to The Citadel." He went on to obtain a degree from the University of South Carolina in environmental engineering and spent an outstanding career at a large timber-management company in South Carolina.

Artie

After graduating from high school, Artie went to Mars Hill College, Furman, Greenville Tech, and North Greenville, before deciding to work awhile. He finally graduated from Lander College and found a teaching job in elementary school and a coaching job at his mother's alma mater, Hillcrest High School in Dalzell. [His granddad, Mr. Edens, always said Artie thought Dalzell was next to Heaven.] He eventually became the offensive coordinator, and one year they won the state championship. He married another teacher, Sherri Tickel, and they have two children—Wellington and Austin (see below).

Kim

Kim always liked to earn her own cash money. She went initially to Furman. While there, she and two of her Furman classmates asked me about getting a vehicle for them to drive on a trip to visit all the contiguous states. Edie and I discussed the danger but decided they would do okay. I rented from one of my coaches a pickup truck with an enclosed cover over the back where the girls could stow their sleeping bags and air mattresses (they overnighted at KOAs and state parks). The father of one of the girls called me and criticized me for making these arrangements. I told him I had faith in my daughter and if his daughter didn't want to go, so be it. [She did go.] We had some anxiety, but they did fine. Their only complication was when they had a flat tire, but a truck driver stopped and helped them change the tire. The trip was a great experience for them.

They kept a "log" of their trip and received credit towards a course at Furman. Kim and the other two girls (ladies now, I guess) still get together from time to time. Edie and I thanked the good Lord for watching over them.

Kim transferred to the College of Charleston when I went to The Citadel. She graduated from the College of Charleston and later earned a master's degree from The Citadel. She married Gil Kirkman and they lived in Mt. Pleasant, South Carolina. They have two children—Marshall and Taylor (see below). Kim taught school at Stratford High School but later changed to James Island Charter to avoid the 25-mile trip to Stratford. Kim and Gil later divorced, but they have worked hard to keep up with their sons together. She is now a retired teacher but subs several times a week. She is very involved in her church "Sea Coast" and volunteers quite a bit.

Ryan

Ryan received a two-year degree from Nilson Electronics School in Charleston, finishing on the Deans' list. He worked for a while at "Square D" in Columbia and as a desk clerk at the Clarion Hotel in Columbia. He now lives at Cornell Arms Apartments about three blocks from his work at Republic Parking. Ryan visits Edie and me every week where he always gets popcorn and cake and whatever he wants mom to fix. He sometimes vacuums and cooks for us—I like his spaghetti. Like Kim and me, Ryan likes to read; we often read the same book.

Curtis

Curtis initially enrolled in Presbyterian College where he worked in the sports information office. He is 5 ft, 11 inches and 150 pounds and now laughs about when he reported to P.C. early, they thought he was a football player and "ratted" him. I was pleased that finally one of my children attended my alma mater; however, he transferred to Florida State when I went there to coach and eventually received his degree in criminal justice there.

After working for a lawyer friend in Greenville, he got a job collecting delinquent bills with Wachovia Bank in Beaufort, North Carolina. He later landed a job with the S.C. Probation and Parole Department in the Lexington office. A few years later he was pleased to get a transfer to his beloved Charleston, where he was elevated to supervisor of agents. After making many weekend trips to USC in Columbia, he earned his master's degree there. He teaches evening classes at Trident Tech and Troy University. He is currently retiring and moving to Bluffton, South Carolina, near Hilton Head, where his lady friend, Diane, lives.

Curtis has a condition called cerebellar-atrophy which affects his motor skills. He has a little trouble walking and a slight slurring of speech. He has been examined by some of the top neurosurgeons at Duke University Hospital, Texas-Baylor Hospital in Houston, and Emory University Hospital in Atlanta. All have helped his condition very much but not cured it. Curtis himself has researched this condition on the Internet and has set up his own strength program which has countered some of his problems. He is my greatest inspiration because of the way he is handling and working on his condition. I am very proud of him.

Marshall

Marshall did not play sports in high school, but he developed quite well as a surfer, skier, fisher, and hunter. He received a degree in landscaping from Trident Tech and had his own business in landscaping and yard work. He accepted Jesus Christ as his Savior and became active as a singer and guitar player at Seacoast Church. [All four grandsons accepted Christ at an FCA camp in Black Mountain, North Carolina.] He was the song leader at Sea Coast Satellite.

Marshall now works at the International House of Prayer and sings in their choir. He is an accomplished musician, writes his own songs—most of them spiritual—and has cut several CDs. Just recently, a recording company signed him to a contract to promote his CDs; he is very excited about that. He went on a Seacoast mission trip to Brazil to build a church. He teaches "How to Write a Song" at International House of Prayer College. He loves hunting, fishing (which he is very good at), and hunting Civil War relics and arrow heads.

Taylor

Taylor had a somewhat adventurous childhood and youth. He went to Newberry College to play football, but that didn't work out. He attempted to join the navy, but that didn't work out. He worked for a while in Vail, Colorado, cooking in a restaurant. He lived down slope, so he caught the lift up to work, taking his snowboard along and storing it at work. Then after work, he snowboarded home. [Nice commute to avoid traffic!] For the last four years he has gone to Alaska to fish commercially during the fishing season. Afterwards, for a couple years, he would fly to Hawaii to surf. He attended "Sea Captain School" in Florida last year and received his sea captain's license. He plans to go back to Alaska soon, as of this writing, for one more fishing season.

Taylor has met a great girlfriend Jennifer from Alaska, now in Charleston, with two young daughters.

Wellington

Wellington came up through the "B" team and junior varsity programs and played on the varsity football team in high school. He then received a scholarship to play football at Presbyterian College. He hurt his shoulder as a freshman and subsequently transferred to the Darla Moore School of Business at USC from which he graduated. He works now as a CPA at an accounting firm.

Wellington married Amy Pauly on June 4, 2016. When he and Amy were attending different high schools and did not know each other, three high schools got several football players and cheerleaders together to take a photograph for the cover of a magazine. In the photo, cheerleader Amy was sitting on football player Wellington's shoulders. Who would have ever thought they would be married some years later!

Austin

Austin attended Thomas Sumter Academy in Dalzell. He was sort of a quiet student but excelled in sports, including football (where he was nicknamed "Tank"), basketball, baseball, and track. He played in the (football) Shrine Bowl game. He also excelled in track, winning the state track meet gold medal on his last putt after being in third place. He was All-State in track and field. He is currently a senior at USC majoring in athletic administration and is doing an internship in the USC football strength and conditioning program.

Austin and Wellington along with Marshall and Taylor love hunting and fishing.

The Surprise

While working at the University of South Carolina, I learned that I had another brother! I received a surprising letter one day at work from a man unknown to me named Michael Capers. In the letter, he told me that I might not want to get the letter and that I could tear it up and forget about it if I wished. He went on in the letter to tell me he was my (half) brother, and he would like to get to know me and my (his) other brothers. Needless to say, I was astonished. Here's what had happened.

Way back before I was married, my mother and father separated, and my father was doing some dating. One summer when Edie and I were at the beach and I was working in her sister's Soda Shop, Edie saw my daddy with another lady at the beach. She didn't say anything about it at the time, but much later it was learned from that lady that it was on this trip to the beach that my brother was conceived. She was divorced at the time and had several other children. Without telling anyone else, her brother took her to Duke Hospital under the pretense of having some kind of medical treatment. There she had the baby, and he was adopted by the Capers family who named him Michael.

The Capers family are "Citadel people"; there is a Capers Hall at The Citadel named after one member of the family. They were from Ohio but had relatives in Darlington, South Carolina. They moved to Winston-Salem, North Carolina, where Michael was raised. He went to Wake Forest there.

Later when Michael was an adult, his oldest son, Alan, kept asking him who his biological parents were, so eventually he made a search and found his mother, who told him of the circumstances of his birth. He also learned he had two sisters and a brother on his mother's side and three brothers on his father's side. His mother and her two daughters were big Gamecock fans and through the Gamecock Club they knew who Art Baker was. Thus, Michael learned of me and sent the aforementioned letter to me at my office at the university.

When I got the letter, I called my two brothers and we readily agreed that we wanted to meet Michael, so I contacted him. It just so happened that shortly thereafter USC was playing West Virginia in the Carquest Bowl game in Miami on January 2, 1995 (we won that game 24-21). Michael was living at the time in Tequesta, Florida, a small town on the Atlantic Ocean about 90 miles north of Miami. He and his wife, Leigh Ann, were running a lucrative business there that his wife's father had developed. He had invited his mother and her two daughters to come down to Florida to attend the game (I think I got tickets for them). He suggested that we meet one day before or after the game. Hence, we (Edie and I) met him and his family then at his house for the first time in person. His mother's name was Nellie Deaton, and we got to know her well. We got together a number of times thereafter. She said it was the best day of her life when Michael called her that first time; she had been waiting for that call for 40 years! She lived in Florence, South Carolina, until her death some ten years ago.

Not too long afterwards, Michael was passing through Columbia on a business trip, and we (including my two brothers, George and Bobby) all had dinner together and got to know each other. Michael actually resembles George in looks, size, and personality, and he also favors my father. We brothers (and our families) continue to keep in touch and have gotten together often since then, including visiting him recently at his current home in Fancy Gap, Virginia, where he lives with his third wife, Linda.

In addition to son Alan, Michael has twin sons, Neil and Austin, with his second wife in Florida. Austin went to Florida State for a semester and then went into the army during Desert Storm. During that time he wrote me and asked if I could get Coach Bowden to sign a Florida State flag and send it to him to fly with his outfit. I contacted Bobby and he sent an autographed flag, which went over big over there in Desert Storm. When

Austin completed his Desert Storm tour, he returned to Florida State and graduated. He was the head of a veterans group in the graduating class, and the university president asked him to speak at the commencement representing the military. He is now back in Florida working with his mom in the family business.

Looking Back

Looking back, I am amazed at the great life I have had. I never really worked a day in my adult life. I made a living coaching football. I enjoyed immensely what I did. I got a first-hand look at hundreds of football games, ranging from McColl High School playing Clio High School to Alabama playing Clemson with truly legendary Coaches Bear Bryant and Frank Howard on opposite sidelines. I won many games and I lost many games, but I enjoyed every one of them; I must admit, however, I enjoyed the wins more than the losses.

Except I guess for my first job at McColl High School, I never really sought out another job. People always called me seeking my services. Three head coaches called me "out of the blue" asking me to join them as an assistant coach as did King Dixon call me asking me to become his associate athletic director. I guess things could have turned out differently. I had "shots" at becoming head football coach at a number of universities including South Carolina, Clemson, North Carolina, Wake Forest, Elon, Presbyterian, Newberry, Western Carolina, James Madison, and Mars Hill, as well as several high schools. For one reason or another, none of these came about.

It seems I often inherited programs "in the tank" and rebuilt them— both in high school and college. As a head coach, I hope I left all programs in better shape than when I arrived.

Looking Ahead

As I mentioned above, Edie and I previously lived on a golf course in Blythewood, South Carolina. Recently, we moved to a retirement home in Columbia where we have some meals provided and better (quicker?) access to health care. [In fact, we are still unpacking boxes!] We have enjoyed 64 years of marriage. We both enjoy good health for our ages (86 and 85). [I recently had my yearly physical examination and my doctor said to come back in a year.] We just plan to "keep on keeping on."

And who knows? Maybe Jack and I will write another book!

Thanks, Jack

I want to thank my coauthor. I first met Jack when I went to Eau Claire High as head football coach in 1959. He was a senior my first year there. He did not play football for me as he had little or no athletic ability, but he did film my games that first year. He spent many hours working on this book.

Jack has a large family, which includes a lovely wife Linda, four children (Susan, husband John; Scott, wife Stacey; Sarah, husband Damie; and Sallie, husband Michael), nine grandchildren (Kayla, Ashlee, Carley, Camryn, Abbey, Trevor, Jordan, Tyler, and Emilie), and two step grandchildren (Colson and Julia).

His parents, "Dutch" and Lennie Evett, were good friends of ours and were "pillars of the church" (College Place Methodist). On one occasion, Edie and I were on a cruise ship to Alaska. At a place where two ships were docked, I was amazed to look up and see Dutch and Lennie there. We were on different cruises, and neither of us knew the other was going to Alaska.

Jack's grandparents, Burnie and Annie Goldson and his aunt, Dot Goldson, were good friends and "pillars of the church" too. Mr. Goldson worked many years with my Aunt Bess at the Railway Express Agency in Columbia.

Jack's sister and brother-in-law, Bunny and Doug Williams, were in the Eau Claire High band which performed during halftimes at football games while I was in the locker room with the players. They live on a tract of land "in the country," which has eight or so small buildings on the grounds. Edie and I have enjoyed many "outings" at their place. They are musicians and have performed frequently at our "leisure club" at College Place Methodist Church where they perform every Christmas. We also enjoyed their performance at the Newberry Opera House.

We also enjoyed "outings" at the Lake Murray home of Jack's aunt and uncle, Margaret and George Holladay. For many years they owned and operated the ESSO station in Eau Claire near the high school; it was a community gathering place. Their daughter (Jack's cousin) and son-in-law, Georgie and John DeLoach, also played in the band. John's brother, Bobby "Boomer" DeLoach, played on my football team as a punter.

Jack also has two cousins, Roy Neville and Paul "Buster" Turner, who played on my team. Roy's brother (Jack's cousin), John Neville (now deceased), was the drum major in the band.

The Last Word

I have tried very hard to be accurate in every respect in writing this book. However, having to rely on my memory going back in some cases over 70 years, I may have made some errors in names, spellings, football scores and other statistics, and may have omitted some things or persons I should have included. I apologize in advance for any such errors and omissions.

Mother and Dad—Sarah and George Baker

Aunt Bess, the matriarch of our Family

Aunt Katie, who effectively raised me from 1 to 5

Aunt Ruth, Uncle Ally and Aunt Katie

Mr. and Mrs. Edens

Me, with Cousins Jerry Don and Arthur Ray and their Wives

Cousin Billy Baker, with Son Paul on Left and Wife Carolyn on right

242

Brothers—Arthur, Bobby, Michael, and George

Grandsons—Wellington, Taylor, Marshall and Austin

Edie, Me and Daughter Kim

Brothers—Arthur, George "Bubba" and Bobby

Children—Ryan, Kim, Artie and Curtis

Taylor and Marshall

Edie and Sisters Helen (left) and Alice (right)

Baker Family with Mr. Edens (age 86)

Artie

Ryan with Neighbor Joey Batson

Driving Mr. Edens' Hunting Wagon

With Curtis

With Granddaughter (in-law) Amy and Wellington

Austin, Artie and Wellington

Just Me and Edie!

The Tennis Player

Sgt. Baker, Giving Physical Fitness Training to Army Basic Trainees

Amid Beautiful Flowers Aunt Katie Grew

Sgt. Baker, Changing Diaper

Sunday Go-to-Meeting Clothes beside 1934 Ford

Just Me!

The Speaker

The Hunter

Me the Coach

Was That a Good Play I Just Called? Head Coach at The Citadel

Student or Coach? Head Coach at Eau Claire High

Go for It or Not? The Patrolman Says GO!

1964 South Carolina Shrine Bowl Coach. (We Beat North Carolina 28-14)

Pre-Game Warmups while Working with Coach Lou Holtz at South Carolina

East Carolina Head Coach 1985

Offensive Coordinator and Assistant Head Coach at Florida State

Friends

With my Beloved Roommate and Football Teammate, Cedric Jernigan

With Covington "Poss" Parham, my Best Boy-Hood Friend. He Played Football at Princeton.

While Coaching at ECU, George and Billy, Two Down Syndrome Young Men, Showed up Every Sunday Afternoon Asking for Coach Baker While We Coaches Were Coaching. We Eventually Became Great Friends

With Friend, Fraternity Brother and Football Teammate, Dick Weldon and Bart Cox

With Robert and Dolly Lunsford, Former Students at Newberry High School. He Played Basketball for me.

With my Life-long Friend, NY Yankees All-Star Second Baseman Bobby Richardson

My Furman Staff 1974

Texas Tech Staff 1970-1972.
(Head Coach Jim Carlen at Right End)

Staffs

My First Staff at Eau Claire High 1959

My East Carolina Staff 1986

ARTHUR W. BAKER and JACK B. EVETT

Coaches with Whom I Coached

With Clyde Christensen—at East Carolina

Frank Singleton—at Eau Claire High (Boyhood Friend)

With Head Coach Frank Howard—at Clemson (He Gave Me My First Collegiate Job)

With General Bob Jones and Banks McFadden—at Clemson

Dale Evans—at Texas Tech

Donnie Layton —at Newberry High (My Only Coach there)

Eric Hyman and Wife Pauline—at Furman and South Carolina

Ken Matous and Family— at East Carolina

With Lou Holtz (left) and Mike McGee (right)—at South Carolina

Richard Bell and Family—at East Carolina

Dick Sheridan and Son Bobby— at Eau Claire High and Furman

With Dan Utley (left)—at The Citadel (He Played for Me at Furman)

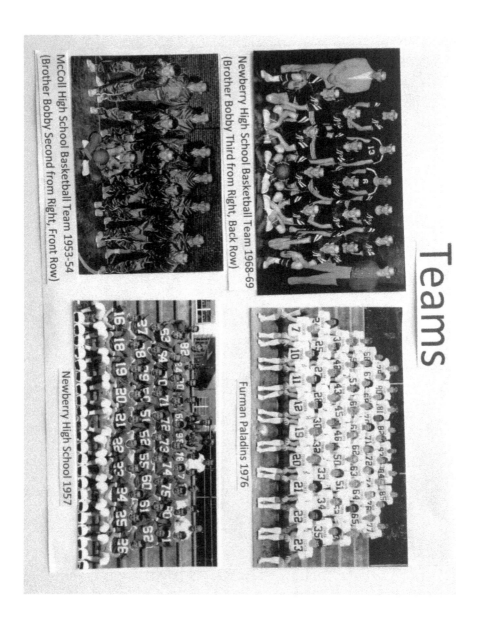

Teams

Newberry High School Basketball Team 1968-69
(Brother Bobby Third from Right, Back Row)

McColl High School Basketball Team 1953-54
(Brother Bobby Second from Right, Front Row)

Furman Paladins 1976

Newberry High School 1957

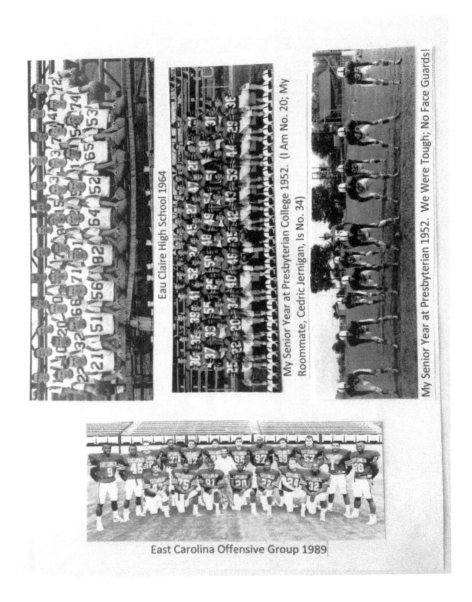

Eau Claire High School 1964

My Senior Year at Presbyterian College 1952. (I Am No. 20; My Roommate, Cedric Jernigan, Is No. 34)

My Senior Year at Presbyterian 1952. We Were Tough; No Face Guards!

East Carolina Offensive Group 1989

Players

John Henry Johnson and Pete Patterson, Eau Claire High (Pete Completed Passes Both Right and Left Handed)

Gerald Toney, The Citadel (Played Both Football and Basketball)

Tommy Vermillin and Mike Moore, Eau Claire High (Track Performers)

Terry Long, East Carolina

Jessie Hester, Florida State

Billy Ware and Family, Clemson

Earnest Byner, East Carolina

Charlie Waters, Clemson

George Rogers, Heisman Trophy Winner, South Carolina

No. 1, Kevin Ingram, Quarterback; No. 44, Ernest Byner, Running Back, East Carolina

Travis Hunter, East Carolina Quarterback

Stump Mitchell, The Citadel

David Whitehurst, Furman

Orion Rust and David Kreber (Left to Right Bottom Row); Paul Gillis and Stump Mitchell, The Citadel

Vince Perone, Furman

Buddy Gore, Clemson

Larry Robinson, Furman

Miscellany

Edmunds High School Coach Bill Clark with Co-Captains Arthur Baker and Bennie Skinner 1946

Edie on Deck; Me Throwing Ball to Curtis; Ryan Blocking 1975

Playing at the "Masters" 1977   With Actress June Lockhart

Clemson Players Who Showed up for My Talk to Greenville Touchdown Club 2014

My Presbyterian College Class of 1953 at 2003 Reunion

Newberry Head Football Coach Harvey Kirkland, a Giant Angel in My Life

Edie Receives a "Church of the Year" Award 1974

My Co-Author Jack and His Wife Linda. Both Are South Carolina Graduates

Friends Bobby Richardson, Bobby John, Clebe McClary and John Graham 2015

An Honor to Have Lunch in the Senate Dining Room with Senator Strom Thurmond, Standing Second from Left

ARTHUR W. BAKER and JACK B. EVETT

ABOUT THE AUTHORS

Arthur W. Baker grew up in Sumter, South Carolina. He earned a bachelor's degree from Presbyterian College and did graduate study at the University of South Carolina. He coached football at six colleges/ universities and was associate athletic director at another university. He has been active in the Fellowship of Christian Athletes and the S.C. Governor's Council on Physical Fitness. He wrote several football articles for annual coaching conventions and an article on injuries for the S.C. Medical Association. He received five coach-of-the-year awards, was inducted into the S.C. Athletic Hall of Fame, and received the Order of the Palmetto, the highest honor for an S.C. citizen. Coach Baker and his wife reside in Columbia, South Carolina.

Jack B. Evett grew up in Columbia, South Carolina and attended the University of South Carolina, earning bachelor's and master's degrees there. He received his Ph.D. degree from Texas A&M University. He is a retired civil engineering professor from The University of North Carolina at Charlotte. He authored/co-authored seven textbooks plus a number of articles published in professional venues. He was a member of five professional societies and five honor societies, and was a professional engineer and land surveyor. Professor Evett and his wife reside in Harrisburg, North Carolina.

CPSIA information can be obtained
at www.ICGtesting.com
Printed in the USA
LVHW051450121218
600207LV00024B/919/P

9 781985 377769